THE UNIVERSAL SOLDIER

THE
UNIVERSAL SOLDIER

Fourteen studies
in campaign life
A.D. 43-1944

◆

EDITED BY

MARTIN AND FREDERICK
WINDROW WILKINSON

COLOUR PLATES BY
GERALD EMBLETON

◆

DOUBLEDAY & COMPANY, INC.,
GARDEN CITY,
NEW YORK.

Other Books in this Series

ENGLISH AND IRISH GLASS (1968)
by Geoffrey Wills
SBN 85112 117 9

ENGLISH POTTERY AND PORCELAIN (1969)
by Geoffrey Wills
SBN 85112 145 4

ANTIQUE FIREARMS (1969)
by Frederick Wilkinson
SBN 85112 164 0

EDGED WEAPONS (1970)
by Frederick Wilkinson
SBN 85112 171 3

BATTLE DRESS (1970)
(A Gallery of Military Style & Ornament)
by Frederick Wilkinson
SBN 85112 172 1

BRITISH GALLANTRY AWARDS (1971)
by P. E. Abbott and J. M. A. Tamplin
SBN 85112 173 X

ENGLISH FURNITURE, 1550–1760 (1971)
by Geoffrey Wills
SBN 85112 174 8

ENGLISH FURNITURE, 1760–1900 (1971)
by Geoffrey Wills
SBN 85112 175 6

Published in Great Britain by
GUINNESS SUPERLATIVES LTD.,
2 CECIL COURT, LONDON ROAD, ENFIELD, MIDDLESEX
Printed in 10pt. Century Series 227
by McCorquodale Printers Limited, London.
Monotone and 4-colour half-tone blocks by Gilchrist Bros. Ltd., Leeds.

Acknowledgements

The editors would like to express their gratitude to the individuals and organisations who gave generous assistance during the production of this book, and particularly to the contributors who gave help and advice on matters not strictly connected with their own chapters.   Our thanks are also due to:

L. Archer
H. Blackmore
W. Bromley
Bella Buckley
David Damper
Michael Dyer
Franz Durst
Paul Forrester
Beatrice Frei
Hargrave Hands
Kenneth Homer
Ingeborg Magor
R. Marrion
G. Mungeam
Harold Peterson
Geoffrey Pleasance

Fred Pryor
T. Ralph
Michael D. Robson
Jack Woodhouse
Kenneth Wynn
Aerofilms Ltd.
British Museum
Historisches Museum, Basle
Imperial War Museum
Library of Congress
Maggs Bros.
Museum of the Confederacy
National Army Museum
Schlossmuseum Grandson
Ft. Ticonderoga Museum
Dean and Chapter of Westminster

All photographs of items from the Tower of London are Crown Copyright, and reproduced by permission of the Department of the Environment.

ADDENDA

Chapter 7, p. 105: '*Siamese knives*'. This description of the equipment issued to French troops is quoted from a contemporary document, but it has proved impossible to find an explanation for this particular item. Louis XIV had exchanged embassies with Siam in the 17th Century, and a certain amount of trade had ensued, but in the 18th Century contact diminished due to the justified suspicions entertained by the Siamese court of European motives. It seems very unlikely that these knives were actually imported Siamese items; the name may refer to some particular style or shape, but no firm identification has been possible.

1: *The Universal Soldier*

I T must be admitted at the outset that there is no such being as the universal soldier, any more than there is a universal man. The soldier is shaped far more by the nature of the society which bears him than by the experience of soldiering itself. In a brutal and unenlightened age, the soldier will be brutal and unenlightened; in a superstitious society, he will be superstitious; in a static and unquestioning century, he will be docile. Nevertheless, the profession of arms is one of those callings which set a man rather emphatically apart from the attitudes of the mass of his contemporaries on certain narrow aspects of life; and for all that he is a creature of his time, he has more in common with soldiers of other ages and nations than his own civilian brothers in his reactions to certain situations.

Any serious examination of the soldier must strongly indicate that he is not a species apart. The great majority of men have it within them to become soldiers, competent and effective soldiers, and to survive the experience without lasting emotional damage. There have always been those whose temperament rebels against violence, just as there have always been those in whom the liberation from normal standards of conduct, which war encourages, has awakened dark and murderous appetites. Even so, it remains a matter of record that the vast mass of men, even men born and raised in enlightened and protective societies, can become killers if the right stimuli are applied; and having killed, can return to civilian life unconscious of permanent change in their personality. Thousands of examples to the contrary can be cited, but it is the millions who conform who make this generalisation permissible. The lesson can only be that there simply is no inherent prohibition against the taking of life built into the human brain. The inhibitions are all external, and in time of war they are carefully removed.

The means by which a ploughboy or a clerk can be turned into a soldier have varied with the mental climate of the centuries. The rationale has sometimes been religious—'Kill, to guard the flame of the Only True Church against the assaults of heresy': sometimes chauvinistic—'Kill, to fulfill the destiny of the fatherland': and more recently, idealistic—'Kill, to liberate the oppressed proletariat', or 'to guard democracy against the abyss of communist barbarism.' These rationalisations do not often survive the experience of actual battle. Except for the few fanatics, men surrounded by the terribly simple realities of combat find them irrelevant. They are replaced by simpler concerns, which seem to have remained constant throughout history because they have brought genuine comfort and a sense of security to men who are often frightened, often cold and wet, often confused, often in pain, and often deadly bored. The soldier does not question his cause, because he is surrounded by friends and countrymen who do not question it. His behaviour is regarded with tolerance, approval or open admiration by his superiors and his compatriots. He feels, perhaps for the first time, the deep satisfaction of comradeship, that comfort which springs from identification with a closely knit group of men, mutually dependent, sharing both misery and triumph. Sometimes he will admit that in the

immediate aftermath of terrifying danger he feels alive and vital on some inner level beyond the reach of reason or received morality. He feels moved, and by association ennobled, by witnessing the acts of sublime courage and self-sacrifice which war can sometimes inspire in perfectly ordinary men. His revulsion at the horrors of battle will usually fade with each new experience. And if he genuinely believes that he is forced to kill and destroy to protect his community and his loved ones, then no subtle reasoning, no outraged moral attitudes in the world will shake him. On that ancient level, there can be no argument and no compromise.

The soldiers described in this book are neither heroes nor monsters, but the faceless men in the ranks. Some are soldiers because they believe that their communities are threatened by some

specific danger—the Swiss cross-bowman who answered the muster when Charles the Bold marched south; the potter of Tours who left a leg at Verdun. Some take their places on imperial frontiers, to guard an order of things which it never occurs to them to question; although separated by eighteen centuries, Caius Largennius and Thomas Ovenden have a great deal in common. Most are soldiers for a number of tangled motives—the desire to escape personal or national stagnation, the simple hunger for loot or excitement, deeply ingrained principles —for in real life men do not often conform to the labels of the sociologists. Whatever their reasons for becoming soldiers, their priorities are often very similar once they have settled in to the new way of life. Generally they are concerned with the problems of finding food, shelter, a dry bed, alcohol and women, and with staying alive until another day has passed. Soldiering brings out many things in a man, but above all it makes him vastly practical.

THE aim of this book, then, is to examine the way of life and death of the ordinary soldier down the ages. The means we have chosen is to invite a group of specialist writers to contribute essays on campaign life spanning nineteen centuries and eight nationalities. How successful this exercise has proved must be for the reader to judge. Within this formula the book has a secondary purpose—to inform the large and growing public who interest themselves in militaria. The emphasis throughout is upon the men themselves, but at the same time we have tried to present for the interest of the specialist reader reliable data

on the clothes they wore, the weapons they wielded, the burdens they carried, the food they ate, and the life they lived.

Each chapter of the book is a self-contained essay devoted to a single soldier. In some chapters the soldier's name is a matter of historical record, but in the majority the man himself is a creation of the author. To mix fact and fiction in this way is a dangerous formula, and it is to allay any understandable suspicion on the part of the reader that the contributors have appended clear notes on this point at the end of each chapter. In the majority of the chapters only the man himself and his immediate family and friends are fictional, and all other named persons— officers, NCOs, comrades, enemies—are known to history and described in their correct context. The units in which the imaginary soldiers served were actual units, the places they fought or marched through are accurately described, and their experiences are as authentic as surviving records and primary research allow.

Even the subject soldiers themselves are not fictional in the true sense, but rather 'composite personalities' whose characters and circumstances have been borrowed from historical sources. All speculative material has been scrupulously avoided. Infallibility is beyond the reach of the historian, but many of the names on the contents page of this book—names internationally respected —are their own guarantee of scholarly standards of research.

On all aspects of the everyday life of the common soldier, there has been a conscious effort by the contributors and editors to present the facts as nearly as possible through contemporary eyes. It was partly to this end that the device of the imaginary soldier was adopted; it provides a discipline, an obstacle to the intrusion of 20th Century judgements which have no relevance. Inevitably the material *has* been affected by subjective standards. It is simply impossible for a 20th Century man to think with the mind of a 15th Century man, to see with his eyes, to feel with his emotions. All we can do is apply scrupulous care, and leave the rest to the reader. This we have done.

A few words on the selection of material: all the men described in this book are common soldiers. Some have attained junior rank, but none are genuine leaders of men. The universal soldier is a follower, and often a bewildered follower. The contributors have been at some pains to exclude material which would be beyond the knowledge of the man in the ranks. Nevertheless, some passages would be meaningless to the reader without a minimum of historical information, and this has been given both in the text and in the footnotes which accompany each chapter. The superior numerals in the body of each chapter refer to these notes. A short list of sources or recommended titles appears at the end of each chapter.

THERE has been no attempt to inject 'drama' into these essays. While some deal with famous battles or harrowing marches, others reflect the boredom and inactivity which make up the great part of the ordinary soldier's experience. Popular fiction notwithstanding, the universal soldier rode in many cavalry charges which petered out in confusion rather than crashing home on the enemy lines. He spent his entire service without hearing a shot fired in anger. He died accidentally, or in some pointless skirmish quite without military significance. He was as likely to come home enfeebled by diarrhoea as heroically bandaged round the brows. For every Heinrich Elsener, saving the banner amid flashing blades and plunging hooves, there were a thousand Louis Ménades, wincing with rheumatism and wondering

where their youth had gone. For every Isham Harrison, bitterly trudging home with the flame of romantic loyalty unquenched by defeat, there were a thousand Dan Abbotts, wondering how they could extract themselves from dangerous situations with a minimum of risk and a maximum of prestige and profit.

Equally, there has been no attempt to drag into these pages descriptions of gratuitous horror. The realities of battle and retreat have not been avoided, but neither have they been selected deliberately for their shock value. To do so would have been to open the door, again, to 20th Century judgements. The soldiers described in these chapters react to the episodes of cruelty and callousness according to their own lights—sometimes with passive acceptance, sometimes with distaste, but never with any great surprise.

It should be borne in mind that even the victims of these horrors were probably not *surprised*.

The chapters which follow are presented in a number of different styles, but as a sequence they provide many insights into the development of military life. The decision to end the sequence at the close of the Second World War was made for a number of reasons and was not an arbitrary choice. In the past twenty-five years two types of warfare, and two types of soldier, have emerged. One is not significantly different from the soldier of 1944; the other—the conscripted son of an affluent society thrust into confusing and harrowing post-colonial campaigns under a barrage of public comment and propaganda—would require a whole book to himself. Whether he will prove to be a short-lived phenomenon, or whether he will mark the beginning of a whole new chapter in our violent history, it is far too early to say.

The soldier of 1944 would be incomprehensible to the soldier of A.D. 43. Caius Largennius signed on for twenty-five years. Throughout that period he carried his own food, weapons and clothing on his back, walked on his own feet halfway across the known world, laid his own roads, built his own barracks, bound his own wounds, and purchased many of his necessities out of his own pay—including his own funeral. Bert Fisher was called up for the duration of the war, yet the government which mobilised him spent more on his training and equipment than he could normally expect to earn in half a working lifetime. In order to free him from any distraction from the rôle he was being trained to play—essentially the same rôle as, say, George Morrison of Wellington's Light Division—the government fed him, clothed him, cared for his health, developed his mental and physical abilities, provided at least a semblance of regular recreation and entertainment, supplied the means and granted the opportunity for fairly frequent home leaves, ensured that his family did not suffer avoidable material hardship during his absence, and finally transported him to the exact spot where he was to fight. It was not regarded as very remarkable that this three-year investment was 'used up' inside a week; if that particular operation had gone as planned, the actual fighting career of this unprecedentedly expensive soldier would have lasted exactly *two days*.

This growing emphasis on the soldier's specialist skills and individual initiative can be traced in several of the chapters in this book. Other themes also emerge, among them the parallel growth of impersonal warfare—the killing of tens of thousands whose faces are never seen—and individual compassion—the acceptance of certain minimum standards of behaviour toward civilian and enemy prisoner. How valid these comparisons may be is for the reader to judge. The soldiers in these chapters will not be found delivering balanced judgements. Soldiers are too busy to judge, and too practical. They do not care for philosophy; it will not keep the rain off. They do not care for the quarrels of princes or statesmen; you cannot toast a claim of sovereignty on the end of a knife on a cold night. They do not care for reasoned debates on the rights or wrongs of their war, or any war; debate will not stop a swinging sword or a flying bullet.

The essentials of the trade have remained unchanged over nineteen centuries, and more. It is a trade followed only by man, for man is a uniquely dangerous form of life. The human race is the only species on the planet which regularly and persistently pursues its aggression to the point of wholesale killing of its own kind. That is the dramatic truth. The truth of the chapters which follow is that this awesome killer is supremely undramatic, supremely ordinary, recognisable and homely. It is reasonable to suggest that at some time in his life everyone who reads this book has known a man who has been a soldier. Potentially, we are all soldiers. This book is about us.

2: *Caius Largennius*

CAIUS LARGENNIUS, optio of the century of Titus Claudius Fatalis in *Legio II Augusta*, leaned back against the timber parapet and studied his tightly sandalled feet stretched out before him.[1] Those feet had carried him many hundreds of miles since the day almost ten years ago when he had joined the army. They had carried him from his home in southern Gaul to this lonely fort on an island at the edge of the world, and only Lord Mars knew where they would have to carry him in the years ahead. He took a last, long look at the green rolling country and the patches of dark woodland which stretched away to the horizon, the familiar setting for the past five years of his life, and at the huddle of native huts by the banks of the river below the fort. A smell of charred wood still hung over the post, drifting from the burnt-out cook-house and barracks. Below him the neat, geometrical roadways between the buildings of the fort were busy with soldiers, hurrying to

A legionary, a standard bearer and a centurion, in the earlier forms of helmet and body armour which began to be replaced in the middle of the 1st Century AD. The legionary wears the ring-mail *lorica hamata*, the other figures, scale armour. The centurion's rank is indicated by his transverse crest and staff; he wears greaves, and displays decorations in the form of *torques,* and *phalerae* mounted on a leather harness.

the shouts of their officers as they prepared for the march. A clumsy legionary dropped an armload of tools, and was rewarded with an irritated swipe from a centurion's staff. One of the auxiliary cavalry *turmae*[2] attached to the garrison was vaulting into the saddle, hampered by a jittery mount which stamped and backed and shouldered the horses on either side. The sounds and smells and sights were as familiar to Caius, and as comforting in their familiarity, as the home in which he had grown up before he joined the army.

When those first gruelling months of physical training were over, he and thirteen other new recruits had been collected by a hard, middle-aged centurion and marched northwards from southern Gaul to Argentorate[3] to join their legion. Though still very much raw recruits, Caius and his companions had rejoiced together that they had made the grade. They had taken the oath of allegiance to the Emperor Caligula—more properly called Caius, like his new soldier[4]—and each had become *miles legionis*, a soldier of the legion, sworn to live and die in the service of Rome. They had stood in the great hall of the *principia*, the legion's headquarters building, and ranged themselves in line before one of the tribunes; on the tribune's left stood the chief centurion, and a little in front and to the right the *aquilifer*, holding the shaft of the beautiful golden eagle with the victory wreath about its upheld wings.[5] The chief centurion had picked the man next to Caius at the right of the line to repeat the oath after him, and then each man had to say in turn, 'The same in my case.' For Caius the golden eagle, symbol of the God Jupiter and of Rome, came to represent the most wonderful thing in his life—it was the embodiment of Roman might and right and the soul of his legion.

For about five years he had lived in the great fortress at Argentorate learning the military arts and becoming proficient in his duties. Gods, how hard that first two years had been . . . Digging ditches, building breastworks and then filling them in again, flattening the earth so that they could begin again the next day—and this, frequently, after a march of twenty-five miles in full marching order. How he had hated that tool kit which had to be carried with all his other gear, and Oh, Lord Mars, that bronze mess dish and cooking pot, which clanged incessantly as you marched along for hours at a time.[6] The tools were now a part of his trade and he used them like a craftsman, treating them with care; for who knows, the continued existence of the legion might one day depend upon them.

Fortifications had become his great joy, especially gates, with their flanking towers and guard chambers. Was not the *porta praetoria* in the east wall of this very fort made under his supervision? It would have been more satisfying if they could have built it in stone, but who could want a permanent post in this forsaken place! It had been so different in Argentorate; there, the large civil settlement outside the walls had boasted wine shops, brothels, and stalls and booths of every kind, where a man might spend the remains of his pay on a rich sword belt, or gamble it away on a cockfight. Here, on this nameless hill, there had been few pleasures; harrying the barbarians was seldom very rewarding. In those early days of his service when deductions for equipment, food and burial club seemed to take almost every *denarius* he earned, a game of knuckle-bones or checkers in the bath-house would quickly wipe out the miserable pittance left in his arm-purse.[7] Fatigues had dominated his life, for he never seemed to be able to save a few coins to bribe his centurion to let him off one or two of these endless chores—guard duty, bath-house fatigue, latrine fatigue, general camp cleaning, *ad infinitum.*

Arms drill, foot drill and battle formations were essential parts of his chosen trade, and he had thrown himself into these with a zest which had delighted the drill-master but annoyed his fellow recruits. Those who had shown less aptitude than Caius had been jealous, and had cold-shouldered him for days afterwards until they too had done well enough to earn a few words of praise.

Caius was the son of a veteran, and he had joined the legions because it was the only way of life he had any inclination to live. He had shared his father's pride in the *II Augusta*, and had carried his father's letter of introduction to his old friend and colleague Marcus Liburnius Fronto, now senior centurion in the second cohort. Caius had been determined to make his father proud—and by the Gods, how his father's face must have shone when he heard of Caius' promotion to optio, and of his decorations, now so carefully packed away in his kitbag lying

Reproduction of legionary armour and equipment, created by the author in the workshops of the Tower of London Armouries, showing the wooden shield with metal rim, boss and strengthening plates. (Michael D. Robson)

there on the rampart walk. He had been a good soldier, of this he was proudly sure. During times of boredom he had had his wild moments, like the fight he had with the auxiliaries at Argentorate when they had tried to fondle his pet serving-wench in the wine shop he frequented. That had cost him a lot of pay and two solid weeks of guard duty, but Gods! it had been worth it . . . He still smiled when he thought back on that line of four battered Thracians facing the camp police across the wreckage of that miserable wine shop. He had never seen his little golden-haired serving girl again, for she was a slave and her owner had sold her, saying that she was more trouble than she was worth. He got paid out, though; one night Caius' friends, resenting their drinking companion's absence on guard, had fired the shop, and put the owner out of business.

WHEN the Emperor Claudius[8] decided to add the island of Britain to the Empire, *Legio II Augusta* were paraded in full dress kit, with their crests on their helmets and everything polished until it shone. Their new *legatus*, Titus Flavius Vespasianus, had recently been appointed to the command of the *II Augusta* by the Emperor, to prepare them for the task ahead. He stood there before his legion and told them of the impending campaign in a strong, clear voice which carried far in the morning air. Caius and his comrades were impressed by their new commander. The word was that he was a man of undistinguished birth, a splendid soldier devoted to his profession. His manner and choice of words were blunt and forceful; under the richly decorated parade helmet his face was weatherbeaten and determined, with a heavy square jaw and a bull-neck rising like a tree from powerful shoulders. He had quickly made his personality felt throughout his command,

and the knowledge that he was to lead them to war gave the legionaries confidence. Although he was a strict commander he was also a just one, and did his best to see that his officers followed his example.[9]

It was under his command that Caius had first received recognition for his ability as a builder of fortifications. When his old century commander retired from the service a new centurion was appointed, and life had taken a turn for the better. This new centurion, Titus Claudius Fatalis, though a strict disciplinarian, was, like his commander, a real soldier who got the best out of his men. He was also ambitious for his century, since if they showed ability he too gained credit; and so it was that he singled out Caius to assist the engineers of the legion to instruct newly arrived recruits in fortification. Caius was then free of those soul-destroying fatigues, and in his new position discovered that he had a natural ability to instruct clearly and also to inspire others to attain the high standard of craftsmanship which he had found so satisfying.

When the legion finally marched to the coast Caius lost the duties of instructor, but he was now established as a senior man in the century and one to whom responsible tasks could be entrusted. Their optio, who served as non-commissioned officer to the century, was an old soldier named Didius. With only three more years of his twenty-five to do, he turned more and more to Caius for assistance, and the centurion accepted this without question. Military service matured a man quickly, and Caius, at twenty-three years of age, was no exception. Responsibility rested squarely on his shoulders, and he slept soundly at night, whether in a tented marching camp or a stone barrack room, a man contented with a good day's work.

The legions and their supporting auxiliaries had gathered on the northern coast of Gaul, where ships and transports of the fleet were also gathering for their expedition to this island on the edge of creation. The *XX Valeria* had come from Novaesium, the *XIV Gemina* from Moguntiacum, and the *IX Hispana*, who accompanied the Commander-in-Chief Aulus Plautius, had marched a thousand miles from Siscia in Pannonia, on the banks of the Danube. The auxiliary units of infantry and cavalry were drawn from many parts of the imperial frontiers, and included Gauls, Thracians, Germans and Batavians.[10] What a camp that had been, with its miles of leather tents and eternally smoking cooking fires; on a still day the columns of greyish smoke rose straight up like a vast forest of tall, ghostly trees.

It was here that stories about the mysterious island began to circulate around the camps, and before long these simple men lost their courage for fear of the terrible destructive seas filled with unknown horrors, and the dark island covered with cold mists and gloomy, impenetrable forests. Varus and his legions had perished in such forests in Germania,[11] and the great Julius Caesar himself had suffered much discomfiture from those awful seas.

And so it was that this great army had refused to move out for embarkation. Messengers rode poste-haste to Rome to tell the Emperor, and eventually, after several weeks' delay, his freedman Narcissus had arrived to investigate the cause of the mutiny—for mutiny it was, on a very large scale. Though the officers were angry they too must have shared some of the general dread, for they made no effort to find ring-leaders. In fact there were none; the men were of one mind, and acted spontaneously. Narcissus persuaded the commander to let him speak to the assembled legions.

He stood on a timber platform with the legates and tribunes, whilst the soldiers crowded round and gazed sullenly at this man the Emperor had dared to send to speak to them. A freed slave to address free-born men! This was an insult no man should be expected to bear. Optio Didius, who had something of a sense of humour, suddenly saw the funny side of the situation and called out, 'It's like Saturnalia!' At the festival of Saturnalia, lasting for seven days each December, slaves were allowed to put on their masters' clothes—and here was Narcissus, speaking for his master. The cry was taken up on all sides, and suddenly they were laughing, their tension broken and their fears slipping away. They

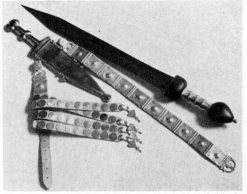

Legionary sword, with bone grip, broad blade and tapered stabbing point: the waist belt, with decorative metal buckle and plates and attached groin protector: and the broad-bladed dagger. (Michael D. Robson)

would go to *alter orbis* as their Emperor commanded, even if they all paid with their lives. Had they not sworn to do so when they joined the Eagles, and had they not renewed that oath to Claudius only a short time ago?

Contrary winds delayed their sailing still further, but eventually they went aboard the hundreds of ships and sailed out on a calm night into the unknown. The fleet was in two main divisions; after a cramped but uneventful night they landed without opposition on their respective sectors of coastline many miles apart. Caius landed with the more westerly division. While cavalry scouts were out, the remainder of the force threw up fortifications and unloaded their supplies. The local natives had not been expecting the Roman landing and in many villages they were completely taken by surprise. They realised that resistance was futile and so saved their homes and families from destruction and death. Further inland, as word of the invasion spread, the tribesmen began to move towards the seat of their king[12]; but by then the Romans were moving inland from their base camps, to meet up at that very spot.

As Caius marched under the burden of his kit in the rear rank of his century, he looked at the new, unfamiliar, and rather motley appearance of his comrades. In the past they had all worn simple bronze helmets with a flat, rounded neck-guard at the back and large cheek-pieces. When fencing together they had frequently aimed blows at each other's neck-guards, to knock the helmet to one side and thrust at the unprotected neck beneath it. Now a new iron helmet was being issued, which came well down on the neck behind and made such tricks of fence a waste of time. These new helmets of bright silvery iron were trimmed with bronze bosses, and the edges were also wrapped in bronze, so that those who wore them, including Caius, felt as if they had been made centurions. The only difference was that when they wore their crests they ran from front to back instead of from side to side in the fashion followed by centurions, who wore theirs at all times for easy recognition.[13]

Caius and others around him in the ranks of *II Augusta* also had new body-armour. The old heavy mail shirts were being replaced by laminated iron cuirasses which were mounted on leather straps. They were lighter, more comfortable and very flexible, and if you had to erect fortifications while wearing them they did not tire you as much as mail. Some men had also been issued with a lighter pattern of sword, but Caius was glad that he had bought his own—with a silvered hilt and scabbard—from a cutler in Argentorate. The maker, Lucius Valerius, was famous for his strong, broad blades and long, efficient stabbing points.

Each man had been issued with seventeen days' rations of wheat, salt and sour wine. As well as these, his tool kit, and a change of clothes, each man carried two *pila muralia*—stakes to be driven into the top of the earthworks when the unit made camp; two heavy throwing spears[14]; and of course his great rectangular shield, slung at his left side on a thong passing through the hand grip. They certainly felt like 'mules of Marius'[15] as they marched north to rendezvous with the other half of the army, but at least every meal reduced their burden of grain and wine.

When the great army joined up again the line of march turned north-west, and as they went deeper into the unknown tribesmen on horseback and chieftains in chariots began to harass the fringes of the column. Syrian archers and Cretan slingers from the auxiliary forces were deployed to deal with these nuisances, but when the army reached a river of some size[16] they saw the opposite bank swarming with howling Britons, painted in bright colours and wearing little more than shoes and trousers. Most of them were armed only with spears and oval shields. Some had swords and axes in reserve, but only the chieftains and kings wore rich bronze helmets and cuirasses or mail shirts. To Caius they looked just like the people of Gaul, and from the defiant yells he could tell that they certainly spoke the same language. Their shield bosses and helmets were decorated with red enamel, and the similarity to the helmets worn by some of his comrades struck Caius—some of their decorative bosses had red enamel centres. What impressed him most was the speed and skill with which the barbarian charioteers turned and raced their little vehicles over the grass on the opposite bank. The chariots, with light, spoked wheels and semi-circular wicker sides, were drawn by two small horses, and skimmed over the grass with the driver braced against the reins; the chieftains who rode in them seldom seemed to hold on to the sides, but balanced skilfully, legs apart, like sailors on a storm-tossed deck.

Some Batavian cavalry were swimming across beside their horses—Caius knew that the Batavians were noted for their skill in the water—and then remounting, to bound up the far bank and force back the front ranks of the enemy. At this point *II Augusta* was ordered upstream to a spot where scouts had located a shallow ford. They waded over in waist-deep water, formed up in battle order, and advanced towards the action. Here, in his first real battle, Caius had learned the value of his years of hard, disciplined training. Standing in close ranks he and his comrades had thrown volleys of spears, following up with short charges, swords drawn and shields held well up to form a wall in front of them. The barbarians fought in loose groups, dying bravely on the licking sword-points, or falling back to regroup and then returning to the attack; they held the legion at bay until the evening, when fighting ceased.

Other war-bands continued to arrive on the scene until the following morning, when the *IX Hispana* under Hosidius Geta crossed the river to join the *Augusta*. Geta, as senior legate, took overall command and led the attack against the assembled tribes. The action lasted about three hours, after which the steadiness of the disciplined legionaries and their supporting cavalry eventually drove the

barbarians back in a rout. At one time Hosidius Geta and his guard were cut off, and for an anxious moment it seemed that he was lost, but an *ala* of cavalry was directed to the rescue and in a few furious minutes the enemy chariots and horsemen surrounding him had been cut to pieces. The auxiliary archers and light infantry concentrated their missiles at the British horses, so that chieftains who ran to escape in their chariots found the teams dead or dying and the drivers fled; thus died many who might otherwise have escaped. Groups of tribesmen were seen fleeing to the north and west. It was at this point in the campaign that the Legate Vespasianus was ordered to lead his legion against the tribes in the south and west of the hostile island.

Two legionary cavalrymen[17] were sent with instructions to the commander of the fleet for supporting transports and warships to sail along the south coast to the harbour in the territory of a British king named Cogidubnus, who had maintained friendly contact with the Romans in northern Gaul for some time past. Much important information about the tribes in the south of Britain had come from this friendly source, and as the men of *II Augusta* marched westwards Caius and his comrades felt relieved to think that somewhere ahead there was at least one part of the country that they did not have to fight for.

I T was in the course of this westerly march that Caius had first met Romanius. He was an auxiliary horseman in the *Ala Noricum*, a unit originally recruited in the town of that name on the Danube, and it was while he was watering his own and three other horses that Caius came down to fetch water for cooking the evening meal of his seven mess-mates and himself. They stood looking at each other by an unnamed river in this quiet green valley, and both seemed to like what they saw, for they smiled and introduced themselves. Friendship between Roman citizens and subject peoples was not common, particularly in the army, but there were no rules against it. For these two, as time would tell, it was to be a great blessing.

As was only natural between soldiers they discussed the campaign so far and exchanged opinions on the fighting qualities of the enemies they had come up against. Caius moved up-stream to fill his cooking pot from a stretch of river undisturbed by the horses, and then returned to Romanius and walked back to camp with him. Romanius was really a Gaul by birth, recruited into the *Ala Noricum* when it was stationed in Germania. His Latin was far from perfect but he was obviously trying hard to become as Roman as he could, and he told Caius that his one great ambition was to become a Roman citizen. This honour could be gained in rare instances as a recognition of bravery in the field, but now, under Claudius, it had become the usual reward for twenty-five years' service in the auxiliaries.

Caius was now a big, broad-chested young man of about six Roman feet,[18] while Romanius was a tall, lithe Gaul whose fair hair made Caius look even darker than he was. Caius' father was an Italian and his mother an Iberian, so he retained the black hair and olive skin common to both races.

When the legion moved into the kingdom of Cogidubnus they stayed in camp for five days while supplies were brought from the fleet, weapons were checked and replaced where necessary, and all other equipment gone over before the start of what promised to be a long, hard struggle. Reports had come in that the

Durotriges, the western neighbours of Cogidubnus, were hurriedly preparing their defences and were determined to hold out or die in the attempt.

Some of Cogidubnus' tribesmen travelled with the legion to act as guides for the first part of the advance. One chieftain, riding a small pony, wore a Roman helmet and a scarlet military cloak which Vespasianus had presented to him. He knew some Latin, and it was said that he was one of the Britons who frequented the headquarters in Roman Gaul. Now he was to act as interpreter if any prisoners were taken and interrogation was necessary.

From the moment they entered the country of the Durotriges the hit-and-run attacks began; not desultory affairs, little worse than nuisances, as many had been in the past, but strong attacks by determined bodies of horsemen and swift-running infantry who used slings with deadly accuracy. The rations were now carried in the baggage train, and the legionaries marched with helmets on and *pila* at the ready. The tribesmen retreated into their fortified hill villages, and these had to be assaulted and taken one at a time. Often these *oppida* were small, but others required periods of 'softening up' with *ballistae*[19] bolts before a rush of legionaries supported by cavalry finally crushed resistance.

After some half-dozen of these villages had been successfully taken the Roman force came to one of enormous size, with ditches and breastworks of timber and stone encircling an oval hill with a flattish top, on which stood a timber and thatch village. Their guides told them that this was the great Mai-dun,[20] the fortress of the Durotrigian king and one of the strongest forts in Britain.

The *onagri*, or stone-throwing catapults, and the small javelin-shooting *carroballistae* of the legion were moved up into position before the main gates at each end of the mile-long fortress, and began to pour a steady hail of death into the defences. Under a cloud of smoke from the cornfields fired by the cavalry, the advance began. The storm of stones, javelins and arrows which rattled on their upheld shields brought Caius and his century, the first unit into the narrow gorge-like approach to the east gate, to a halt. Centurion Fatalis barked the order for *testudo* formation, and instantly the great shields of the inner ranks went up to form a roof, those on the flanks and front completing the walls of this box-like defence. Forward they went again, with the constant hammer of stones and spears on the shields shaking them at every step. Spears hurled down with force sometimes penetrated, narrowly missing the upheld arms of the men beneath, but they struggled steadily on until they reached the gate and the foot of the steep, grassy earthworks.

Other centuries were behind them, but it seemed that they must be trapped in this narrow defile and eventually slaughtered by the incessant rain of weapons from above. Caius saw Centurion Fatalis move at his left in the rear of the column, and realised his intention to rush alone at the steep bank. Someone must be at his side, to set an example so that the rest would follow, for one man had no hope of penetrating such a strongly held position. Caius barged clear and was up the bank past Fatalis, shouting as he went, '*Follow your centurion, comrades, he cannot survive alone!*' With a great cheer the century broke formation behind them, and regardless of the missiles scrambled and clawed up to the crest of the bank, to throw themselves at the barbarians who had dropped into the ditch behind.

Caius had been the first into that fight, with his centurion close behind. They hurled their *pila* into the running mass of Britons, then, drawing their swords with

Maiden Castle, or 'Mai-dun', *the great British hill fortress stormed by the Second Legion. (Aerofilms Ltd.)*

the quick downward jerk on the hilt which sent the sheath up under the arm, they drove into the yelling barbarians with shield-boss and stabbing blade, to thrust and thrust until all was still. By now the rest of the century were around them, and other centuries were pouring in behind. Ditches and banks were no longer a barrier. Their blood was up, and this fortress should go the way of all others which dared to stand in the path of the Second *Augusta*.

Eventually Caius and his comrades found themselves in the central area of the camp, faced by snarling men and women armed with anything from swords and spears to stones and wooden clubs. They could see smoke rising from the western end of the fort, and knew that their forces were now within sight of victory. Centurion Fatalis gave the order to form ranks, and once again they moved forward shoulder to shoulder. Caius, glancing to the right and left, realised that Optio Didius was no longer with them; there were other familiar faces missing from the ranks as well. They had not come through without loss this time, and there was still some hard fighting ahead. They began their advance into the howling, savage mob, but because of the scattered circular huts they could not maintain their unbroken line. As they broke ranks to pass on each side of one of the huts a young woman ran out of it right behind the centurion, and made to thrust a levelled spear into his back. Caius cleft the shaft with a blow from his sword, but in a blind rage the woman sprang on him with the butt end and clawing nails. He crashed the boss of his shield into her stomach and then stabbed swiftly to make an end. Ahead he saw Fatalis on the ground with three Britons hacking and thrusting wildly at him. His shield was up, but his right arm and thigh were running with blood from several gashes, and he must soon be killed under that rain of blows. Again Caius used his shield to charge down the enemy, swiftly stabbing first one and then a second before they could recover. The third shortened his spear and drove the point under Caius' shield, but before it reached him his sword cut deeply into the Briton's red-haired skull.

Caius turned to his centurion, who had now risen to his feet. Seeing him stagger, he sheathed his sword and took the wounded man's arm. It must have been at this moment that the centurion's sword was left lying where he had dropped it. Fatalis

Legionary helmet of the type which Caius Largennius would have worn in the middle years of the 1st Century. (Michael D. Robson)

thanked Caius as they made their way to the edge of the now-burning village, and as the soldier helped his commander to a heap of fallen stones from the parapet he was told that he was now Optio, and should return to his century and take charge.

The fighting was over. The trumpets called them to order, and the remnants of the Britons were rounded up. Two thirds of these were women and children who, with the surviving warriors, most of whom were wounded, were given the task of burying their dead whilst the legion set about the destruction of the defences.

The legion continued on its way, taking other, smaller hill forts as it went; and it was on the site of one of these[21] that a cohort of legionaries commanded by the Centurion Fatalis, and seven *turmae* of auxiliary cavalry—including Romanius' unit of the *Ala Noricum*—commanded by a *praefectus equitum* named Velleius Paterculus, were detailed to build and occupy a fort within the ramparts of the native *oppidum*, to hold down this troublesome tribe of Durotriges. Velleius Paterculus, being of equestrian rank,[22] was to be the new fort's commandant.

Before the rest of the legion marched south to take an island called Vectis off the coast, Vespasianus paraded the army and presented decorations. It was then that Optio Caius Largennius was called from the ranks in the sun of an August afternoon, to receive his rewards for bravery and devotion to duty. For being the first over the ramparts of Mai-dun the Legate placed the *corona aurea* on his head; for saving his centurion's life he received *armillae*, or bracelets, *torques*, or Celtic collars, and a set of nine medallions, *phalerae*, mounted on a leather harness to strap over the front of his cuirass.

The legion passed on, and for several weeks the soldiers toiled to build a typical Roman fort of timber and turf within the native ramparts. From the site they could look out over a beautiful green land of rolling hills relieved by patches of woodland.

Centurion Fatalis was proud of his new optio and grateful to him for the credit he had brought upon the century. However, when they held their first parade in the new fort Caius noticed that the centurion carried a common issue sword instead of the fine ivory-hilted weapon he had always used. After parade he took his own silvered weapon to Fatalis and asked that they might make an exchange. A cohort commander could not let his century down by wearing such a sword, he urged, and now that his pay was 337½ *denarii per annum* he would soon be able to buy himself another good one. The centurion agreed, but with reluctance—he already owed Caius a life, but he could hardly refuse an offer phrased in this way.

THEY were in the fort for five weary years; season followed season monotonously, the tedium only broken by occasional policing expeditions among the barbarians in the surrounding countryside. There were few diversions, apart from the usual gambling. The cavalrymen were better off, and occasionally rode out to hunt wolf or boar in the hills and dark thickets, but time hung heavy on them all. Caius and Romanius became firm friends, and their friendship made life in the isolated post much more bearable; Caius liked to think that their example inspired others among the garrison, for in time the relationship between the legionaries and auxiliaries became better than in many mixed forts.

Within a month of the completion of the fort there was a Durotrigian potter with his family working nearby, and before long he was copying the shapes of the red ware the Romans preferred. Some of the starving women who had lost their men in the fighting came for a time and lived in huts the soldiers helped them to build near the river below the fort. They were usually sullen and showed reluctance to give themselves to their conquerors, but in time it became their way of life, and at least they were fed and sheltered. Some drifted away, others came; there were always at least ten women whom a man could visit when his desire was too much to bear, or when his feelings rebelled against the unremitting company of other men. Caius had been a few times, but a cold woman did not give the satisfaction of a warm, willing one.

At last, on a day in the cohort's fifth year at the fort, orders came from the legate for the force to rejoin the main unit in the west. Their task was done, and the Durotriges thoroughly subdued, so that they could now be released for more urgent work.

Just as the messenger left the fort the cry of '*Fire!*' was heard. Soldiers rushed to where the cookhouse roof was in flames and tried throwing baskets of earth on to the blaze, but the south-west wind was blowing strongly and the dry wood shingles on a legionary barracks and a store house were soon ignited by the flying sparks. The men ran to save their kit; when they had achieved this they were set to work pulling the shingles off adjoining buildings to prevent the fire spreading.

In an hour the fire was out. Three buildings had been destroyed by the flames and several others wrecked in the attempts to make a fire-break, so if they were to stay here any longer some of them would be sleeping under the stars until the barracks could be rebuilt. But there was to be no delay; the Commandant came out of the headquarters and ordered immediate preparations for departure. And on the rampart walk above the compound Optio Caius Largennius, his kit stowed and ready, stood bareheaded in the wind from the sea and watched the orderly bustle.

So they were to move on at last. . . How many miles would those feet carry him this march? What did it matter, anyway? He was going to join that beautiful

Magnificently restored gate and ramparts of the 1st Century Roman fort at The Lunt, Bagington, near Coventry. This is typical of the timber-and-turf frontier posts where Caius would have served, such as Hod Hill in Dorset. (Hargrave Hands)

golden eagle of the Second *Augusta*, which he had not seen for five long years . . . Romanius, sitting his horse below, was waving, and the *cornu*[23] was sounding 'Fall in'. Time to leave at last.

NOTES

Of the persons named in this chapter only Didius is a complete invention, although in certain other cases little more than their names are known. A man named Caius Largennius served in *Legio II Augusta* in the first half of the 1st Century A.D. His officers are actual historical characters, described in their correct context.

1. Each legion was identified by a number, given in sequence, as well as a name; the suffix *Augusta* indicates that this legion, the Second, was originally raised by the Emperor Augustus, who reigned from 27 B.C. to A.D. 14. The composition of a legion varied but in general it mustered some 5,000 men. Ten squads of eight men, known as *contubernia*, formed a century, commanded by a centurion who appointed a subordinate known as an optio. Each group of six centuries constituted a cohort, and ten cohorts formed a legion.

2. *Turma:* a cavalry troop of thirty men, or three *decuriones*. The larger cavalry formation was the *ala* or wing, varying in size between sixteen and twenty-four *turmae*.

3. *Argentorate:* present-day Strasbourg.

4. *Caligula:* the Emperor Caius Caesar, who reigned from A.D. 37 to 41, nick-named Caligula ('Little Boots') supposedly because of his father's practice of taking his family with him on active service and dressing the child in a miniature version of military costume.

5. The legion was commanded by the legate—*legatus legionis*—and next in the chain of command was the senior of a number of *tribunes*. In the absence of both, command passed to the *praefectus castrorum*. The senior of the legion's centurions was known as the

primus pilus, 'first spear'. Standards were the responsibility of the *aquilifer*.

6. Tools such as a saw, hook, and length of rope were carried in a wicker basket; at a later period this was transported in the baggage wagon rather than carried by the individual legionary.

7. Burial club: a small sum stopped from the soldier's pay to defray his funeral expenses. Arm-purse: this was of bronze, fitted with a lid and a hoop which slipped over the upper arm.

8. Tiberius Claudius Drusus Nero Germanicus, Emperor from A.D. 41 to 54.

9. Titus Flavius Vespasianus, later Emperor of Rome from A.D. 70 to 79, was a fine soldier and an efficient and enlightened ruler. A lively word-portrait by Suetonius, and surviving busts, are the bases for this description of his appearance and manner.

10. *Novaesium:* present-day Neves. *Moguntiacum:* present-day Mainz. *Pannonia:* present-day Hungary and north-east Yugoslavia. *Gaul:* roughly, present-day France. *Thrace:* roughly, present-day Bulgaria. The Roman provinces of *Germania* comprised only relatively small areas along the Rhine. *Batavia:* roughly, the present-day Netherlands.

11. Three legions commanded by P. Quinctilius Varus were wiped out in A.D. 9 by a confederation of German barbarian tribes, led by one Arminius, in a disastrous battle in the Teutoberg Forest. The closely wooded terrain prevented the Roman column from deploying to advantage.

12. Canterbury.

13. Exact details of Roman crests are uncertain. Polybius mentions black and purple feathers, but the most common types were apparently black, white or brown and made from horsehair.

14. The Roman throwing spear, or *pilum*, was about seven feet long and consisted of a wood shaft to which was attached, by a socket or splice, a tapering iron shank with a small, hardened pyramidal head approximately two inches long.

15. 'Mules of Marius': the legionaries' rueful name for themselves, referring to their burdens on the march. Gaius Marius (157–86 B.C.), one of the greatest generals of the Republican period, introduced many military reforms.

16. The Medway.

17. Each legion had an attached group of twenty or thirty horsemen for scouting and message carrying.

18. The Roman foot was slightly shorter than its present-day equivalent, and Caius would have been about five feet ten inches tall.

19. *Ballista:* large crossbow device mounted on a carriage and used as light field artillery.

20. Mai-dun: Maiden Castle, a large hill fort near Dorchester, Dorset, completed in the 1st Century B.C. and stormed by the Second Legion in A.D. 44. The earthworks are ninety feet high in some places.

21. Hod Hill, near Blandford, Dorset.

22. Equestrian rank: this refers to the status of his family in the Roman aristocracy rather than to a professional military rank.

23. *Cornu:* large curving horn with a simple bell-shaped mouth.

SELECT BIBLIOGRAPHY

Paul Couissin: *Les Armes Romaines*: Paris, 1926.

National Museum of Wales: *Roman Armour—Exhibition of reconstructions by H. Russell Robinson in honour of the International Congress of Roman Frontier Studies*, 1969.

Sir Ian Richmond, *Hod Hill, Volume Two*, British Museum, 1968.

G. R. Watson, *The Roman Soldier*, London, 1969.

Graham Webster, *The Roman Imperial Army*, London, 1969.

Graham Webster & Donald R. Dudley, *The Roman Conquest of Britain*, London, 1965.

3: Roger de Dinan

IT was dusk outside, and the Hampshire countryside was but dimly lit by the moon, the flickering campfires, and the burning houses of Winchester. Inside the house it was even darker, for here the only light was provided by a small wood fire set in the middle of the rammed earth floor. The smoke wafted and eddied in a thick layer below the roof, its only means of escape a small hole in the centre, but it caused little discomfort to Roger de Dinan; he was well used to it, and smoke was but one of the minor, everyday irritations of life. Roger settled himself to enjoy the feast that awaited him. Succulent pork, roasted over the fire, was a luxury not often enjoyed, and as the grease trickled down his chin into his close-cropped beard Roger reflected that earlier in the day his meal had been running around the pen of some Hampshire villein. He sawed off a slab of coarse rye bread with the knife which he carried constantly at his belt, and swigged down a good draught of wine from the skin. Tonight he was dining as well as any man in England and at far less cost than most, for the entire meal had been provided, unwillingly, by the citizens of Winchester and the surrounding countryside.

It had been a hard day and his sore, aching thighs and arms reminded him that he had spent most of it in the saddle, or fighting on foot; but for all that, it had been a good day, and Roger's hand stroked the fat leather purse suspended from his girdle. It bulged and chinked with silver pence, a gold ring, a necklace and several other pieces of jewellery which he had been lucky enough to acquire after the battle.[1] Of course it was said by many that a true knight should be above such mundane matters as money, but in these troubled days of King Stephen's reign it was as well to look to the future. One never knew when the production of a handful of coins or some golden trifle might mean the difference between life and death, or at least, liberty and captivity. Roger had heard from others that three times this day David, King of the Scots, had been captured, and on two occasions had purchased his release. In any case, a knight's pay of eightpence a day might seem generous to a foot-soldier who received only a penny, but it did not represent real wealth, and a soldier was surely entitled to pick up a little extra.

Pleased as Roger was with the new-found weight of his purse, the coins and trinkets were as nothing compared with the other spoils of today's victory. It was not every day that a knight was able to fit himself out with an almost completely new set of equipment—mail, helmet, sword and horse—but today the countryside around Winchester had been littered with arms and equipment. God's wounds, but it had been a day to remember! Yet as Roger munched on a thick collop of greasy pork, he reflected that war was indeed a chancy business; only a few months past all had seemed lost, when King Stephen had been captured at the battle of Lincoln.[2] Roger had missed that fight as he had been carrying dispatches for his lord, but he had heard from survivors how King Stephen had fought like a lion. Armed with an axe presented to him by the citizens of Lincoln, Stephen had held off his attackers until one hard blow, perhaps jarring on a helmet, had snapped the haft. The king had cast it aside and drawn his sword to fight on; and it was only a chance missile—a stone, some said—which had finally struck him to the ground and allowed his captors to seize him. His imprisonment had meant, for many, the end of his hopes, and all expected that his rival, the Empress Matilda, would now hold the throne of England.[3] Roger de Dinan was little concerned with the niceties of the accession, and the anointing of Stephen had settled the matter for him. He had happily transferred his allegiance to Stephen and had sworn an oath to be his man, and was quite prepared to serve him as well and faithfully as he had served King Henry before him. In any case, after seventeen years of military service any other life seemed impossible to Roger, and the thought of returning to his manor and settling down to a quiet country life held no attraction.

On his father's death in 1117 Roger had leased out his manor in return for a fixed rent; he had realised that this meant some financial loss, but it had released him from the tiresome burden of running his estates personally. The dull round of supervising boon work, listening to some niggling and wordy clerk, holding manor courts, and all the other administration involved in the life of a rural land-holder seemed to Roger intolerably dull.[4] With the income from his holdings and his daily wage of eightpence he had sufficient means to gamble, wench and dine with his peers. Roger often felt that it was from his grandfather that he had inherited his roving and adventurous spirit. Old Bertrand de Dinan had left his lands in Brittany to follow the great Duke William in his bold expedition to seize England. He had survived the desperate battle on Senlac Hill in October 1066, and had bored Roger's father with his endless retelling of that day's happenings; but old Bertrand must have fought well, for the victorious Duke had granted him land and properties in Leicestershire. Grandfather Bertrand had taken to wife one of the Saxon women, but—as Roger's father was quick to point out—she had been a lady of noble birth. Robert de Dinan, Roger's father, had been born three years after the conquest. His grandfather had died some years before Roger was born, but the boy had thrilled to the stories of his doings retold by his father to pass the long winter evenings before they retired, shivering, to their crude beds.

Roger's childhood had been spent on their small manor, and he had received the training and education normal to any Norman youth. Reading and writing were mysteries to him; the priest from the local church had offered to teach him, but Roger had resisted. He saw no need to acquire these priestly skills, and regarded them as no proper concern for a man whose grandsire had faced the axes of Harold Godwinson's housecarls on Senlac. He had devoted every spare hour to learning the martial arts, and had

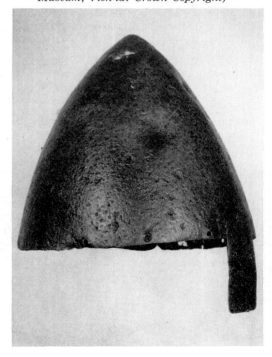

An example of the conical helmet, with nasal, fashioned from a single piece of metal. The holes around the rim were for the fastening of interior padding. Discovered in Moravia, this helmet could date from any period from the 10th to the 13th Century. (Kunsthistorisches Museum, Vienna: Crown Copyright)

sought out and pestered one or two of his father's men who had seen service abroad. One had been on the first Crusade and had lost an eye fighting the Paynims; his tales about the wonders of the East and the Holy Land had been meat and drink to young Roger, who could not really believe all of them, but accepted much that the scarred old man-at-arms had told him as they rested beside the exercise ground after a bout of weapon practice.[5] When his father had received a mortal hurt as the result of being thrown from his horse during a hunt, Roger had decided to leave home and seek adventure. He had travelled to London and offered himself for the King's service, an offer gladly accepted, for good men were hard to come by.[6]

Not all Roger's time was spent in fighting, although he had seen his fill in Normandy, and he had served as a castle guard and travelled the country with the King on his progress to visit his holdings. However, Roger's mind never wandered far from his prime purpose and main interest in life, and he spent much time practising with spear, sword, mace and axe—the tools of his trade. In his youth he had rushed to take part in any tournament he could find; these days he smiled when he remembered his boyish enthusiasm, now somewhat tempered by experience. He vividly recalled those exciting days when the flower of Norman nobility had gathered together to play at war. The tournament could mean death, injury or poverty, for it was common practice for the loser to forfeit arms and weapons to his victor. As a youth Roger had served as a squire to some of those taking part; his job had been to assist his master by rushing into the sprawling, sweating throng to rescue him should he be struck from his horse, and generally to act as body servant and guardian. Tournaments were normally held at set places on open fields, although it was not uncommon for groups of knights to range over the countryside far beyond the lists where the audience gathered. The main event of the tournament was the mêlée, a combat so like real warfare as to be indistinguishable. Some individual combats were arranged and these jousts, commonly fought with normal weapons, were frequently the means of settling disputes and quarrels between members of the court. There was an excitement and exhilaration about tournaments; the noise, the ladies of the court with their bright eyes, the tales of the combatants, the atmosphere, all combined to make them seem more glamorous and less brutal than in fact they were. They served a serious purpose, for they prepared a knight for the business of war; the first time he took part in a battle in earnest he was no stranger to danger and death. Not that there was such great danger for as Roger had learnt, it was the poorly armoured foot-soldier of the militia or fyrd[7] who suffered most; a knight, well armoured and well mounted, seldom met his death in battle.

The thought of battle reminded Roger once more of his great good fortune this day, and with a thrill of pleasure he rose, still munching, and strolled across to the corner of the room where the horses stood patiently. His new horse—he had not yet decided on a name—stood some thirteen hands high, was broad and straight-backed, and gave every indication of being a good destrier.[8] It was during the pursuit across the countryside that Roger had come across the animal caught by its reins in a thicket. With the true caution of an experienced warrior he had circled carefully, fearing that its owner might be lying in wait. However, his fears proved groundless; there was no one in sight, and the blood upon the saddle suggested that the beast's past owner had little or no interest in horses any more. Roger nudged

Left, Great Seal of Henry I, showing hauberk with sleeves to the wrist; the legs have no mail protection below the knee. The helmet appears to be built up of panels set in a framwork, but could possibly be a fluted form. The tailed flag, or gonfannon, flies from the lance. Right, Great Seal of Stephen. The long projection from the back of the helmet may represent some form of fastening, or decorative ribbons. The securing strap of the shield can be seen around the neck.

his puffing mount closer and dismounted, looping the reins over a convenient bush. The trapped animal, white of eyes showing, backed nervously away until halted by its reins. Roger put down his shield and axe and advanced cautiously, speaking gently, fearful that any sudden move might startle the horse into pulling free and escaping. At last he stood by the horse and began to run his practised hand over its legs, checking for broken bones or damaged tendons, but to his delight it was sound in wind and limb. The harness and saddle were of good quality and it was obvious that the animal had belonged to some wealthy knight. Roger rejoiced in his good fortune, and so engrossed was he that he failed to notice the approach of three men who had emerged from the thicket and were creeping towards him. It was the nervous whinny of his own horse that gave him his first warning, and turning he saw the three dishevelled soldiers just as they began their rush towards him. Their long tunics were dirty and torn, and he placed them as some of the foot-soldiers who had formed the central group of the army of the Empress on their withdrawal from Winchester. Certainly the purposeful way in which they handled their swords suggested that they were no simple country youths swept up into the fyrd, but professional soldiers. Roger knew that he was in extreme danger, and gauged the distance to his horse, but decided that it was too great to cover before they reached him; his only solution was to stand and fight. He bent and scooped up his axe, and backed towards a large bush, hoping to gain some protection for his back. Now that the element of surprise was lost the three men had stopped, but they evidently felt that the chance to grab two good horses justified continuing the attack. They spread out and came on slowly as Roger stood, feet slightly astride, with the axe held loosely in both hands.

Suddenly they were on him. He swung the axe up level with his shoulders and down again on the man to his left, who was even then swinging his sword at Roger's unprotected legs. At the instant of swinging the heavy weapon he stepped back, and felt a bone-shaking blow on his right side—the second soldier had also moved into the attack, but Roger's sudden move had spoilt his swing and it was the flat of his blade rather than the edge which struck his mailed body. At the same moment

Roger's axe took the first attacker just below the neck and bit deep into his shoulder, and he felt the familiar stinging sensation of a solid impact shivering through his hands. The luckless man fell headlong to the ground, and it was obvious from the spurting blood and the unnatural angle of his head that he was dead. As he fell the weight of his body pulled the axe from Roger's sweating hands as the momentum of the blow took him staggering forwards. Roger's right hand grabbed for the hilt of his sword, grasped it, and, tilting the scabbard, pulled clear the blade. As he did so his eye registered the third man looming up on his left—obviously he had circled round to come in from behind. With a response which was quite automatic, drummed home by years of war, Roger ducked, pivoted and continued the drawing movement into a slashing cut at his second opponent. The wild swing missed but his sword grated momentarily on his opponent's blade, striking sparks as steel rasped on steel. Off balance, the effort of swinging sent Roger half falling, half rolling forward and in doing so saved his life, for a blade swung down, shaving his helmet and slicing into the grass. As he rolled he tried desperately to locate both his attackers, but saw only the flash of another upraised sword. Instinctively he thrust up his right arm to ward off the blow; his opponent tried to pull back, but too slowly. He gave a gurgling scream, cut short as the point of the sword caught him beneath the chin and his own weight drove him further on to the blade. Roger caught a glimpse of a contorted face, a gaping mouth fringed with dirty stubble; then the weight of the impaled body wrenched the sword from Roger's hand as the writhing man fell, bright blood pouring from the fearful wound. A blow on Roger's back reminded him that he still had one opponent to deal with, but the fate of his companions had unnerved the last of the ragged soldiers, and there was no enthusiasm in his attack; as Roger began to scramble to his feet, reaching for his sword, the man turned and ran.

For a moment Roger knelt, gasping for breath, and then struggled to his feet. There seemed to be no further danger, but there was no point in delay. He picked up his sword and wiped the blade clean with a handful of grass before returning it to its sheath. Despite all the excitement his mind registered the fact that there was a deep nick in the edge, which Ralf would have to hone smooth as soon as possible. Stepping across the bodies without a second glance, Roger retrieved his axe and glanced around warily. An arrow swished past him from the shadow of the thicket; the fields were obviously alive with fleeing men from the Empress's army, and victorious soldiers unparticular about the source of their loot, and Roger delayed no longer. Scooping up his shield, he mounted his destrier and seized the reins of his prize. He put spurs to his horse, and set off back to the house which had been his headquarters during the late siege of Winchester. He did not give a second thought to the two men he left sprawled in the blood-flecked grass. They were of no consequence; after all, they were not even knights.

IN the corner of the smoky room the horse, not yet quite at home with his new owner, fidgeted and shifted his feet as Roger patted him and spoke softly, gentling him. On the ground lay the saddle, with its high pommel and cantle and padded seat. From its sides hung the stirrups which Roger had adjusted so that he could almost stand stiff-legged in them, to give him the greatest leverage and power in his sword arm. As the horse now stood it was worth a considerable sum of money, and Roger was well satisfied to know that many a knight would gladly have sent to Flanders to acquire such a fine beast. A burst of laughter from the other side of the room recalled Roger from his mood of self-satisfaction. Walter, Ralf and Leofric, his three men, were happily recounting their adventures of the day; knowing the craft and skill which they had displayed in the past, their master was sure that they too had enjoyed a profitable day. From outside could be heard an occasional shout of drunken laughter followed by a scream, but this was only to be expected; the victor was entitled to his pleasures, and the day had seen a great victory for Stephen's army. In the past Roger had taken his full share of the bawdy pleasures of rape, but by the time a man reached forty he often preferred warmth and food to the fleeting joys of lust. As a true knight he was, of course, supposed to honour and protect

'David and Goliath', from a manuscript of 1148, showing the mail of the period, with chausses, hauberk and coif. The helmet is of spangenhelm *form, with plates set in a framework.*

women, and he would gladly extend this courtesy to a lady of noble birth; but serfs and villeins could hardly be considered in the same light. They were part of a man's property, not to be treated too harshly—after all, they were responsible for working his estate—but they certainly did not warrant the knightly courtesy being preached by the latest travellers from France.[9] Still, it could not be denied that many of the peasant women were attractive, and despite a mixing of the stock most still retained the blue eyes and fair hair of their Saxon ancestors, although the number of dark-haired children seemed to increase daily. Roger himself betrayed his Breton ancestry with his dark hair and brown eyes.

Women were strange creatures, sometimes gentle and melting, sometimes manlike in their determination and courage. Stephen's wife, Matilda, had shown herself a woman of true breeding when her husband had been captured at Lincoln.[10] Supported by William of Ypres, the faithful leader of her mercenaries, she had rallied support and demonstrated by her raids that although the Empress might claim to rule the country, her power was very limited. Encouraged by the Queen's defiance, London had risen against the Empress and forced her to leave her capital and return to her old headquarters at Oxford. News had reached her there that Henry of Blois, the Bishop of Winchester and Stephen's brother, was wavering in his support for her cause, and had met with her sister-in-law the Queen and pledged himself to Stephen. Furious at his desertion and his subsequent siege of the castle at Winchester, with its garrison of her men, the Empress Matilda determined to teach him a sharp lesson. Late in July 1141 her army, led by the Earls of Gloucester, Hereford and Warwick and David King of Scots,[11] set out for Winchester. According to some reports that Roger had heard, her arrival on the 31st July had been so unexpected that as her troops entered by one gate the Bishop fled through another. Quickly the Empress raised the siege of her castle and set up her head-quarters there, preparing to drive out the garrisons left by Bishop Henry in his castle and palace. On 2nd August the Bishop's men apparently fired most of the town to deny shelter to Matilda's troops.

It was at this point that Roger de Dinan had first become involved in the battle of Winchester; he had previously been serving with the Queen's troops in Essex. Slowly the armies converged on Winchester, their progress across the country marked by smashed hedges, an occasional burnt field and heaps of filth where troops camped at night. Arriving at the city the Queen's troops soon raised the siege of the bishop's castle of Wolvesey, at the south-east corner of the city walls; but the garrison in the centre of the town were still besieged by the army of the Empress, who were now besieged in their turn by the Royalist forces.

Roger both loathed and relished sieges. At least life was simple and static, and this was a relief from the jogging discomfort of riding around the country in search of an elusive foe. Most of the fighting and engineering work was undertaken by the infantry, and the knights spent much of their time gambling, drinking, racing or organising jousts and tourneys. Against this was the sordid discomfort of the camp, soon assailed by stenches so strong that even Roger noticed them; a large permanent camp brought its own inevitable trials—in hot weather, dust and flies, and in winter, mud and misery.[12] There were occasional bursts of activity when the besieged made a sortie from the castle or the besiegers made an attempt to storm the walls, but most of the time was spent in maintaining a strict watch to prevent food or reinforcements from reaching the garrison. The blockade was not always successful; at the siege of Exeter Castle a few years before Judhael of Totnes, one of Baldwin's men, had succeeded by the simplest of subterfuges. After sending a message to the defenders to be ready, Judhael and his men had mingled quite happily with the King's soldiers outside the castle. At a given signal a sudden sortie from the castle had created confusion, and in that moment Judhael and his men had slipped through the gates.

Sieges could last for months and yet end indecisively. Stephen had besieged Hereford Castle for four or five weeks in 1137, and although the garrison sur-rendered they were permitted to go free. History had nearly repeated itself a few years later when Miles of Gloucester had seized the town, but the castle, gar-risoned by Stephen's men, had held out. Normally the church's property was respected, but military contingency sometimes forced action which was likely to evoke a religious reproach; during the siege at Hereford trenches had been dug through the churchyard of the Minster and some bodies had been disinterred. Not only had sacrilege been committed on holy ground, but to gain further ad-vantage the besiegers had placed their catapults on the bell tower of the Minster itself. Roger de Dinan heard Mass regularly and considered himself a true Christian, but he recognised that there were times when military necessity over-rode all other rules. When he felt a superstitious fear of vengeance from above he usually managed to quell his misgivings by an extra donation to the church funds or by having a few masses said.

Throughout the month of August 1141 Queen Matilda's army blockaded Win-chester, while inside the city life for the Empress and her troops became more and more difficult as the net grew tighter. Both the Angevin troops and the citizens began to suffer as supplies of food ran out. For the besiegers, with the resources of

London and the countryside at their disposal, life was quite tolerable; every day the lanes were filled with pack horses and wagons fetching food to the camp. By the end of September the situation in the city had become so serious that the be-sieged commanders held a council of war at which it was decided that the only alternative to slow starvation and surrender was an attempt to break out.

To the north of the city was a small river, the Test, and it was decided that if a small but strongly defended position could be established on the banks of the river convoys of food could be escorted into the city. With this plan in mind a force of some 300 knights, well-mounted and armed and led by John the Marshale and Robert fitz Edith, were selected to make the attempt. Preparations for the foray did not go unnoticed in the Queen's camp, and Roger de Dinan welcomed the opportunity for some action; even he, experienced and cynical soldier that he was, had found the long months of inactivity tedious. As trumpets and messengers called the commanders together Roger began to prepare for battle. A yell brought Walter from his game of dice to Roger's side, and with a few terse words he was instructed to prepare the equipment. Roger donned a pair of loose-fitting trousers, or braies, cross-gartered to the knee, and a thick, sturdy tunic of linen. Walter called Ralf to help him carry over the hauberk from where it hung against the wall on a pole pushed through the arms. The hauberk was one of Roger's prize posses-sions, for it had been expensive when new, although he recognised that it was be-ginning to show signs of wear; one or two of the links had worn thin and there was even a slight split in the mail beneath one arm. Walter and Ralf held the hauberk open at the bottom and, stretching his arms above his head, Roger slid into the coat of mail. A few wriggles settled the hauberk comfortably in place, with the weight distributed evenly across his thickset shoulders. Walter quickly laced up the slit which ran from neck to chest while Ralf fastened the laces at the wrist, securing the long sleeves of mail to his arms. At the back hung the attached hood of mail, the coif, but Roger was in no hurry to put this on—it always made him feel hot and sweaty, and there was time enough for that when action was imminent.[13] At his feet Walter knelt, carefully lacing and tying in position the small prick-spurs. Around his waist Ralf passed the sword belt to which was laced the scabbard, fashioned of wood covered with leather, with the tip strengthened by a small metal cap, the chape. Roger flexed his shoulders to check that the belt was not too tight for it was important that his movements should not be hindered by the hauberk being held too firmly at the waist. Some knights overcame the problem by wearing the swordbelt beneath the hauberk with the hilt of the sword passing through a slit in the mail. Ralf fetched over the tall, flat-topped, kite-shaped shield and checked that the straps were securely in position on the back.[14]

Roger drew from its sheath his fine sword, a possession in which he delighted. The yard-long, parallel, double-edged blade, with its narrow central fuller and carefully-honed edges and tapering point, glinted in the daylight. Roger's hand rested securely against the straight quillons and held the grip of leather which showed polished patches, the signs of hard wear. At the end of the grip was the roughly semi-circular pommel, which helped counter-balance the weight of the blade and made for easier handling. Satisfied that all was well Roger returned the sword to its sheath and strolled across to where Leofric was saddling his horse; like the experienced soldier he was, Roger made a point of checking girth, saddle, head-band and snaffle-bit to satisfy himself that some slipshod fastening would not break

Left, *another seal of Stephen, showing clearly the two attachments at the back of the helmet. The shield differs from earlier representations in having a central boss—also found in other illustrations of the period—and the conical prick-spurs are well defined.* Right, *a seal of 1165 illustrates the guige. The accuracy of these illustrations is always open to speculation, but this example seems to show some form of covering on the back of the shield.*

and bring about a dire emergency in battle.[15] From the pommel of his saddle hung an axe with a three-foot haft, fitted with a good, solid, sturdy head; the tales passed down from Roger's grandfather had made much of the terrible effects of the Danish axes wielded by the Saxons at Hastings, and he knew from his own experience that it was indeed a fearsome weapon. Ralf stood by, holding the lance, a stout twelve-foot shaft of smooth, polished ash fitted with a lozenge-shaped head.[16] Satisfied that all was ready, Roger swung himself up and settled as comfortably as possible into the simple saddle. Ralf handed up his shield and Roger looped the long strap over his shoulder so that the shield hung at his left side. Ralf had meanwhile taken the conical helmet from its leather carrying bag, and this too was handed up and hooked over the pommel.[17] Grasping the lance in his right hand and the reins in his left, Roger touched spurs to the horse and set it trotting towards the muster point.

The camp was now a scene of feverish activity as knights made their way to their rallying-points with their commanders. Gradually the milling masses of horsemen formed themselves into some semblance of order, and soon they were ready to move off. Seeing that action was imminent Roger leaned his spear against the horse's neck and eased on the coif, securing the aventail, the flap of mail which hung down at one side, across his mouth and cheeks and, with fingers made clumsy by haste, fastened the strap and buckle at the side of his head. Removing the helmet from the saddle-bow he placed it on his head and settled it as comfortably as possible, making sure that the nasal was central and did not obscure his vision. As always in these last few minutes before battle, he felt that strange mixture of excitement, anticipation and fear, as well as a certain weary feeling that he had been through this so many times before. The troop of knights clattered their way along the path until, topping a slight rise, Roger could look down towards the city.

From the west gate of Winchester streamed a group of two or three hundred knights, making their way north towards the river. At the sight of the enemy there was a perceptible quickening of pace, and the trained destriers, scenting battle in the air, grew slightly restive. The leader of the mercenaries, William of Ypres, gave a signal, and the whole troop moved forward. In an incredibly short time, or so it seemed to Roger, the two groups met. Roger couched his lance securely under his arm, and felt once again the cold sweat which he had not out-grown even after nearly twenty years of battle. Touching spurs to horse he galloped forward, and in a few minutes was in the middle of a whirling, hacking mêlée of knights. The action was brief and bloody, and Roger's impressions were confused, but he felt sure that his lance had certainly struck home. He had felt the thud of a blow on his shield at the side, but was too concerned with what was happening at the front to give it much thought. One of the Angevin knights struck out at the spear with which Roger was attempting to impale him, and his sword snapped the ashen shaft off short. Dropping the now useless weapon Roger snatched the axe from his saddle, urged his horse forward, and delivered an arm-jarring blow; it struck the Angevin just below the base of his neck, tearing through the mail, driving iron fragments deep into the flesh, and inflicting a mortal wound. The knight lurched from his saddle and disappeared beneath a flurry of hooves. Soon afterwards—Roger had no means of assessing the time—it was over; the scattered enemy were fleeing over the fields in all directions. William of Ypres was too good a commander to allow his men to follow in useless pursuit, and his hoarsely shouted commands restrained the hot-heads among the younger knights. Roger felt no disappointment, only a sense of relief that once again he had sur-vived. On the ground lay a few crumpled mail-clad bodies but, as with most of these engagements, casualties among the knights were surprisingly few. Well satisfied with the outcome, Roger returned to camp.

Some survivors of the column returned to Winchester to report the disastrous re-sult of the sortie. Robert of Gloucester decided that the only hope now lay in a fighting break-out by the entire army. In a remarkably short time the army was drawn up in formation, with an advance guard commanded by Earl Reginald and Brian fitzCount escorting the Empress Matilda. Their instructions were to take her safely to a friendly town at all costs. Next came a number of carts loaded with the usual impedimenta of an army, surrounded by the bulk of the Empress's forces; these were followed by a rearguard of some 200 knights commanded by the Earl Robert himself. The west gate was opened once again and the advance guard cautiously emerged; but on this fourteenth day of September, the feast of the Exhaltation of the Holy Cross, the Queen's army was ready and waiting. The entire force of the besieging army, encouraged by the earlier victory, fell upon Matilda's column. In a remarkably short time the Angevin host turned from a carefully formed group into a confused mass of struggling men. Brian fitzCount, realising that this presaged a defeat, urged his Empress and friends to put spur to horse, and it was only by good luck that they broke through to safety.[18] Soon the army was scattering, and only the rearguard appeared to retain any coherence as Robert of Gloucester held control with a firm hand. Fighting skilfully, this group finally reached the river Test and the crossing of Stockbridge. Here it was forced to stand and fight, and Robert, seeing that they were surrounded and outnumbered, accepted defeat and surrendered.[19]

Roger de Dinan took no part in this action, for once equipped and mounted he had been heavily engaged in the attack on the advance guard. He had fought with axe and sword, for he had not yet replaced his broken lance. Twice during the combat his life had been saved by expert use of the shield with which he had de-flected first a lance-point and then a sword cut. Carried away by excitement he had hacked and slashed with his sword and axe, and, judging by the ache in his arms, some of the blows had struck home. Half blinded with sweat and dust he had seen the first signs of victory, as Angevin knights failed to press home their attacks with quite the old vigour, and soon the first waverers began to leave the field. Panic was infectious, and Roger and his group were soon in pursuit of a broken and defeated host.

It was during this chase that he had come across his new mount. So complete had been the ruin of Matilda's army that many of her knights had seen fit to divest themselves of all means of identification to ease their escape. To the west and north of Winchester the countryside was dotted with discarded equipment and treasures, and so many of the pursuers stopped to gather loot that most of the defeated were able to make good their escape. Roger was no exception and, in addition to his new destrier, he had picked up an extremely fine hauberk which he felt sure would fit him. His delight was even greater when he found a pair of mail leggings; he had never been wealthy enough to buy himself these extra defences. As dusk was falling and there seemed little point in continuing the pursuit, Roger had returned leading his new mount with the mail hauberk and leggings, a helmet, a couple of swords and some cloaks lashed to its saddle. Some of his finds would serve his men, the rest could no doubt be sold.

When he finally reached the camp he heard from Winchester the sounds familiar to every medieval soldier—the shouts and screams which marked the plundering of a city by the victors. Reaction came suddenly; feeling empty and shaky, he laboriously stripped off helmet and mail. Needless to say none of his men was to hand, and Roger guessed that they were busy enjoying the fruits of victory. His sweating body ached, and he gratefully swilled his face with cool water.

Later, when his men returned satiated with plunder and wine, they had, somewhat unwillingly, prepared a meal. As the last traces of exhilaration left him, a sudden weariness took possession of Roger's tired and aching body, and he made his way over to the bundle of straw which had served him as a bed for so long. Tired though he was, he carefully piled his new treasures by his side; it was not unknown for plunderers and looters to make no distinction between victors and vanquished. Roger had no intention of losing his new wealth. Wrapping himself in his warm cloak, he soon slipped into a deep slumber with an ease born of years of campaigning. Tomorrow was another day, perhaps another battle, but tonight Roger de Dinan slept, a happy man.

NOTES

Roger, his father, and his men-at-arms are fictional. All other named persons are accurately described. A Breton knight named Bertrand de Dinan fought in William of Normandy's army at Hastings.

1. Although pounds and shillings were used in monetary calculations the only physical unit of money was the silver penny, which was cut to make half-pence and farthings.

2. The Battle of Lincoln was fought in February 1141; Stephen was imprisoned in Bristol Castle but accorded the respect due to a king.

3. Henry I had two legitimate children: Matilda, and William, who was drowned when the "White Ship" bringing him from France sank in 1120. Despite a second marriage Henry had no further children and, foreseeing trouble over the succession, persuaded his barons to swear allegiance to Matilda as future monarch. In 1114 she had married the Emperor Henry V, who

died in 1125, and shortly afterwards she married Geoffrey of Anjou. The unpopularity of the Angevin with the Anglo-Norman aristocracy made her claim to the throne of England unacceptable to many. On Henry's death in 1135 the barons accepted Duke Theobald IV of Blois as future king; he was the grandson of the Conqueror, the son of William's daughter Adela. However, his brother Stephen forestalled him by crossing the Channel and virtually seizing the throne; he was anointed king by the Archbishop of Canterbury on 22nd December 1135. Matilda appealed to the Pope but he rejected her claim and confirmed Stephen as the legitimate King of England. Matilda maintained her claim and was supported by many barons, some because they still considered their oath to Henry binding, and some from hopes of personal reward.

4. The basis of English rural life was the unit known as a manor, and these varied widely in size and custom. Landholding was the basis on which the *servitium debitum*—the liability to provide knights for the king's service—was calculated, but the exact formula is shrouded in uncertainty.

5. The First Crusade was proclaimed in 1096, and was one of the most successful. Jerusalem was captured, and as a result of this conflict many new ideas found their way to Europe from the East.

6. Mercenaries were employed by most rulers of the day, for they were in many ways more convenient to handle than the feudal knights. Many came from Flanders and Brabant. William of Ypres, one of Stephen's most able and constant commanders, was a mercenary.

7. The fyrd was composed of common men liable for military service, and was essentially an infantry force.

8. Most knights owned at least two horses: the expensive destrier was trained as a fighting horse and only ridden in war or tournament, and for everyday riding a rounsey was used. During service with the army the equipment was usually carried on a pack horse.

9. The code of Chivalry, the courteous, loyal and gallant conduct required of a knight, was primarily a French concept, although William II of England had laid emphasis on a man being bound by his word. During the early Middle Ages the concept of knighthood was far less gracious and fanciful than it later became.

10. The confused events of this period are not simplified by the fact that both female contenders were named Matilda. To avoid confusion Henry's daughter Matilda is here referred to as the Empress, and Stephen's wife, Matilda of Boulogne, as the Queen.

11. David I, King of the Scots, refused to forswear his oath to the Empress and continued to support her claim. In 1138 he led an invasion of England but was decisively defeated at the Battle of the

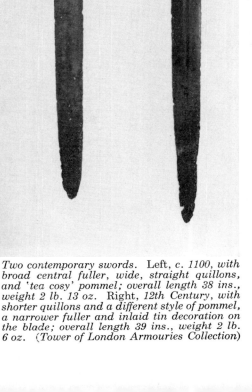

Two contemporary swords. Left, c. 1100, with broad central fuller, wide, straight quillons, and 'tea cosy' pommel; overall length 38 ins., weight 2 lb. 13 oz. Right, 12th Century, with shorter quillons and a different style of pommel, a narrower fuller and inlaid tin decoration on the blade; overall length 39 ins., weight 2 lb. 6 oz. (Tower of London Armouries Collection)

Standard on 22nd August. The *Gesta Stephani* state that at the Battle of Winchester he was captured three times and twice purchased his freedom; the third time he was released, as his captor was a relative.

12. During this period many of the older motte and bailey castles, consisting of mounds fortified with wooden palisades, were being replaced by stronger stone castles with rectangular central towers. Few castles were taken by storm, and starvation was the most potent weapon. A form of catapult known as a mangonel was used to hurl stones at the walls, while other methods of attack included mining, assault by scaling ladders, and the erection of siege towers. Most of these engines of war were built *in situ* by carpenters attached to the army.

13. Mail, a form of defence comprising interlocking metal rings, was used from the earliest times right up to the 17th Century. Our knowledge of 12th Century mail is largely based on carvings and manuscripts, for there are virtually no surviving examples. It seems likely that the mail coat, the hauberk, was lined with some material to prevent chafing; it was slit at front and rear to allow the wearer to sit comfortably in the saddle. Most of the weight was carried on the shoulders and not distributed over the body as with the later plate armour.

14. The shield, of wood and metal, was fitted with a long strap—the guige—for slinging over the shoulder, and two smaller sets of straps—the enarmes—through which the arm was thrust, allowing the shield to be manoeuvred with ease.

15. The bridle of the horse was fairly simple, usually comprising nose, cheek and head bands and a throat lash. Two types of bit, the snaffle and bridoon, were common; the curb bit does not seem to have appeared until the 14th Century. Mail defences for horses, used by the Romans, had been discarded, and did not reappear until the latter part of the 12th Century.

16. The contemporary term was "spear"; "lance" was not used until much later.

17. Helmet design was changing during this century but the commonest type was still the conical form depicted in the Bayeux tapestry. It was either fashioned from a single piece of metal, or built up with plates of metal or horn on a metal framework. A central bar, the nasal, projected down to guard the face from slashes. At about this time flat-topped and rounded forms of helmet were being developed. It is reasonable to assume that helmets were padded and sometimes secured to the head by lacing.

18. The Empress Matilda escaped to Devizes in Wiltshire, and travelled on to Gloucester, arriving in a state of exhaustion.

19. Robert, Earl of Gloucester, illegitimate son of Henry I, also known as Robert of Caen, seems to have taken little part in the succession quarrel until 1138, when he formally renounced his fealty to Stephen. His capture provided the opportunity to bargain for Stephen's release, and an exchange was made in November 1141.

SELECT BIBLIOGRAPHY

F. Barlow, *The Feudal Kingdom of England*, Longmans Green, London, 1966.

J. Beeler, *Warfare in England 1066–1189*, Cornell University, New York, 1966.

C. Blair, *European and American Arms*, Batsford, London, 1962.

C. Blair, *European Armour*, Batsford, London, 1958.

C. and P. Cunnington, *Handbook of English Medieval Costume*, Faber and Faber, London, 1952.

R. H. C. Davis, *King Stephen*, Longmans Green, London, 1967.

H. A. Grove, *The Reign of Stephen 1135–1154*, Wiedenfeld and Nicolson, London, 1970.

K. R. Potter, *Deeds of Stephen*, Nelson, London, 1957.

J. H. Round, *Feudal England*, Allen and Unwin, London, 1964.

4: William Petybon

IF Thomas Petybon had not had important business in Oxford he would never have made the long journey of some thirty miles from his small village of Waterperry; when he offered to take along his younger son William, the lad jumped at the opportunity. When they reached the city after their long ride his father went to visit the merchant with whom he had business and William was left free to explore. He gazed open-mouthed at the wonders of this bustling town, with its great university halls; he listened, uncomprehending, to the learned talk of the students as they strolled past. He marvelled at the size of the streets, and at Carfax he watched the passing of horsemen, trains of pack-horses and hurrying pedestrians.[1] It was while he was standing there that he first heard mention of war. He listened as two students heatedly argued the justice of England's cause and the virtues of King Henry's claims to the throne of France.[2] He could not grasp all the details, but he felt a surge of excitement when he heard that the King, in this month of May in the Year of Our Lord 1415, was recruiting men for the forthcoming campaign.

When father and son returned to Waterperry a few days later William could hardly wait to make his excuses before he rushed off to find Robert Welling. They had been friends as long as he could remember, and it was natural that he should discuss his great plan with Robert. Life in the village was pleasant enough; although his father was not a rich man they lived in simple comfort and ate well. William's main complaint was the lack of anything to do apart from work—like most youths of eighteen he hungered for adventure and excitement. His elder brother Edward would inherit the farm when father—God preserve him—finally died; and the prospect of marriage to some sturdy lass and a settled, comfortable, but dull and subordinate life held little appeal for William. The talk of war seemed to provide the answer. He was a good archer and enjoyed the pastime, spending long hours at the butts; good archers were always welcome in the army.[3] With or without his father's approval William was determined to enlist as soon as possible, and as he had hoped, Robert vowed to join him.

Some of William's enthusiasm left him when he returned to the cottage for the evening meal; the warmth and familiarity reminded him of all the joy and love he had known there, and he wondered why he should want to leave it now. The family sat on stools round the long wooden table while his mother served the meal; when they had finished the steaming bowls of bean pottage she carved the bread and placed great slices before them, on which were served the portions of meat. When the meal was over, and washed down with draughts of good English ale, William felt even less sure that he was doing the right thing. However, as he listened to his father and brother discussing the repetitive business of running the farm he knew that he could not resist the chance to cross the seas, to find adventure, perhaps even fortune as a soldier. When a convenient moment offered, he blurted out to his father what he hoped to do. It was obvious that old Thomas was rather proud, if a little upset; his mother, of course, wept and tried to dissuade him. With some support from his father she was eventually persuaded that if the lad still felt the

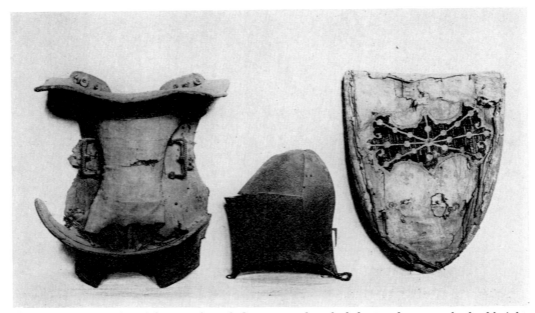

It was common practice, right up to the 17th Century, to place the helmet and armour of a dead knight over his tomb. These three items are from the tomb of Henry V at Westminster Abbey. On the left is the saddle with its high cantle and pommel, centre is his great helm, traditionally worn at Agincourt, and on the right is his shield. (By courtesy of the Dean and Chapter of Westminster.)

same in two weeks' time he might go to Oxford and seek enlistment. William's delight was increased by learning next day that Robert would indeed be joining him.

When the day of departure arrived William was grateful that his father restrained his mother from some of her wilder fancies, but had done his best to see that the boy was sensibly equipped for his adventure. Over his shirt went his new doublet of brown broadcloth laced up the front, tight fitting to the waist and then flared and reaching to mid-thigh. Over his doublet he wore a good thick gown with long sleeves.[4] His legs were covered with thick kersey hose secured to the bottom of the doublet by laces and eyelets; the fitting of these laces—'trussing the points'—was rather a nuisance, and on many occasions William wore the hose rolled half down. Father had pointed out that he was going to do a great deal of walking, and his short buskin boots of thick cowhide would no doubt last him many a long mile. Mother insisted that he took a hood, despite his reluctance; but as old Thomas pointed out, they made fine scarves when pushed back from the head, and the long tail, the liripipe, offered a good hiding place for money—one could knot coins securely in the tip. At the moment his money was safe in a leather purse fastened to his waist-belt, which also supported a dagger such as every man carried. His spare clothing and one or two little personal treasures, such as his rosary and his archer's equipment, were wrapped in his huke, tied in a bundle and slung on his shoulder.[5] Just before they left his father took him aside and pressed into his hand four gold nobles; with these, and the silver pennies, the groat and the two farthings in his purse, William was richer than he had ever been in his life before.[6]

After enduring tearful goodbyes from the womenfolk and much sage advice from their fathers the two lads set out; the weather was fine and the journey to Oxford passed happily. When they reached the town it took them some time to find anyone who could direct them to the Earl of Oxford's representative, but eventually they found their way through the narrow cobbled streets, thronged with carts and horsemen, to the tavern yard they sought. They approached the grizzled old trooper diffidently, and asked if it were indeed true that the Earl was seeking soldiers. The veteran decided after a quick glance that they were good material; both were sturdy, with the broad shoulders and deep chest that an archer needed, their eyes were clear, their skins fresh, and they both stood around five feet six inches tall. Their clothing showed that they were not shiftless vagabonds like those who sometimes tried to wheedle an advance on wages and then disappeared. A few questions satisfied him that they were free men able to volunteer—although this nicety did not greatly concern him—and he pronounced himself glad to add two such likely lads to the muster roll. He questioned them as to their ability with the bow, and listened to their protests of skill with an impassive air. He invited them to demonstrate, and despite their excitement each made a creditable shot at the mark. In due course they were accepted as members of the retinue of the Earl of Oxford, and the old soldier was vastly impressed by William's ability to write his own name; Thomas Petybon, as a man of some standing in his village, had insisted that his children should learn to read and write.

The two boys were informed that their wage would be sixpence a day, but it was pointed out that they would doubtless increase this with the enormous booty that they were certain to find in all the towns they captured; and, who knew, they might even make prisoner the King of France himself, and so share in his huge ransom.[7] For several days they remained in Oxford, quartered in a stable with the other archers; they soon made firm friends among their comrades, who unselfishly introduced them to the joys of drinking and wenching until their purses were somewhat leaner. Eventually the quota of forty lances and 100 archers was filled, and the group was instructed to make their way to the rendezvous at Southampton.[8] The New Forest, the villages and the countryside behind the ports of Southampton and Portsmouth were crowded with thousands of men, horses and wagons, and everywhere there was activity.[9] While they awaited their orders many of the archers were issued with their bowstaves; large numbers had been ordered by the King and collected for delivery at the muster points.[10]

The captain called William over and invited him to take his pick. Most were about six feet long, with a diameter at the centre of about two inches, evenly tapering towards the tips. Some were better finished than others, but appearance was not William's main criterion; he was far more interested in the springiness of the stave. Choosing one that seemed to be well-grained and made of yew, best of woods for the English longbow,[11] William took a waxed thread bowstring and carefully placed one looped end into the notch cut at one end of the stave. Bracing the end across one instep and behind his leg, and using his full strength, he gently bent the bow until he was able to loop the other end of the string in position, He listened closely—no sound of cracking—then ran his fingers lightly over the surface; he could detect no sign of splintering. Next he tested its pull, grasping it just below the centre with his left hand and pulling back the string with the first three fingers of the right hand. He gradually increased the pull, then let the string ride over his fingers; he did not attempt to take the full pull, for to have a string cutting into unprotected fingers with a pressure of eighty pounds was most unpleasant.[12]

He repeated the procedure with several staves, and finally made his selection; this was to be his weapon for the next—who could know how long? William also received two strings which he carefully waxed, using some of the beeswax from the small horn he carried at his belt. This waxing served a double purpose, preserving the string against damp and ensuring that the arrow would part from the string with a quick, clean break when loosed.

Both lads had spent some of their remaining wealth—they had learnt quickly in the Oxford taverns and stews how many people were anxious to relieve them of this burden—on sturdy leather jerkins strengthened with metal plates; these, and the simple helmets of reinforced leather which were issued to them, gave a feeling of security.[13] Some luck with the dice-cup enabled William to purchase a short sword, which he sharpened lovingly and slung in its sheath on his belt; he wore it every where, carefully practising a proper soldierly swagger.

While they waited to embark William and Robert wandered about the camp, devouring all the exciting sights. They became friendly with a man-at-arms, Tom Balinburgh, who pointed out to them some of the notable people to be seen around the huge encampment. There was Albright, the King's armourer, and Nicholas Brampton, the 'stuffer of bascinets', who were kept busy carrying out repairs and advising on equipment. One group which intrigued William greatly were the gunners—until now the Oxfordshire lad had only heard vague and wonderful stories about gunpowder. The older soldiers explained to him how this wonderful black powder, if touched with a burning match, flared into life with a roar and a flash worthy of the Devil himself—indeed, some thought it was an invention from hell. If it were placed in a tube it could expel a ball of stone or metal with incredible force, to strike down a wall or a knight even if they were a long way off. The King's four chief gunners were everywhere, fussing over their precious guns as they were dragged along on carriages, and cursing clumsy soldiers in barbarous English and strange foreign languages.[14] William had never seen so many people in his life before as crowded the camps by the coast; Tom Balinburgh told him that there were 9,000 men gathered there, including 2,000 men-at-arms and 6,000 archers, all of good solid English yeoman stock.[15]

Off shore the sea was alive with ships, for this was no mere raid, and the army and its horses would require about 1,500 vessels to ferry them across the Channel. On Wednesday 7th August the King himself arrived; for the first time William saw his sovereign, and felt an almost religious joy that he should be so privileged. For the next three days the army were busy embarking, and on the Saturday King Henry boarded his own ship, the *Trinity Royal*, and gave the signal to prepare for sailing. On 11th August, to the accompaniment of ringing cheers, the fleet set sail. Although he would never have dreamt of admitting it William was frightened; he had never seen the sea before, and now he had to risk his life in one of these small, unsafe-looking tubs. They looked so clumsy, with their single masts sticking up in the middle and the square sail which the seamen pulled up to catch the wind. His unease had not been stilled by the unfortunate incident when one ship caught fire and the flames leapt across to two others close by in the crowded harbour. They had watched helplessly as men and horses died in the blaze, and many took this as a very bad omen for the expedition.

For three days the fleet sailed across the Channel; fortunately the weather was kind, the wind strong but not rough. Even so, the unusual pitch and toss of the

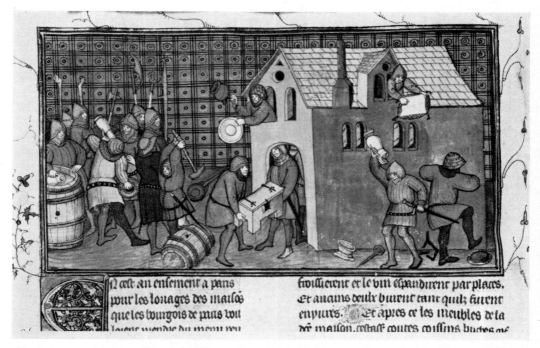

English troops looting a French building. Some hold drinking vessels, another breaks open a barrel whilst others throw down or carry out the valuables. (British Museum. Royal M.S. 20 C VII.)

ship upset William, and he spent the first day lying miserably across the fo'castle rail rueing the day he had left his village. On the second day life was just bearable, and by the third he felt that he might possibly live to see land again. Late on the Tuesday afternoon the fleet dropped anchor in the wide mouth of the River Seine, to great excitement and cheering from the soldiers packed on the decks.

Early on the 14th they began to disembark. Confusion reigned as horses and men slipped and kicked their way through the shallows, stores were dropped and lost, and voices were raised in curses as ship after ship edged as close to shore as they dared, to unload. It was with gratitude that William set foot on firm ground again, and he was also thankful that their landing was not contested by the French. Three days later, before the army moved off, a proclamation was read out which set down the King's rules for the conduct of the war. Church property was to be respected, and there were so many strict orders about so many things that some of the older soldiers grumbled that war was getting to be so regulated that soon there would be no profit in it. Others, more cynical, thought the Ordnances to be so much nonsense, intended only to win over the French and to be forgotten without scruple if things went badly.[16] When they did, at last, begin their march to the west William soon got his first sight of a French town—Harfleur. The English took up position on high ground to the west of the town, and even to his inexperienced eye it seemed a formidable obstacle. In addition to the high walls which surrounded it there were defensive positions known as bulwarks, strengthened with tree trunks, while to the north the ground was flooded and marshy. Soon the English army had encircled the town, and the siege was on.

Although these archers are from the Royal Manuscripts 14 EIV folio 252 of c. 1480, they are essentially the same as those at Agincourt. On the left the archer wears a bascinet with aventail but the others wear sallets with visors. The dots on the jacket of the archer on the right suggests that he is wearing a jacket with reinforcing metal plates.

Instead of taking part in exciting clashes between armoured knights, William and Robert found themselves digging trenches and mines. Probing attacks suggested that it would be a long siege. Life in camp was dull, uncomfortable and sordid, and the lads wondered sourly why they had gone to such trouble to break their backs digging French earth rather than that of Oxfordshire. After a week or so William began to hear talk of the bloody-flux; in reply to his questions old campaigners warned him that he was likely to find out for himself in the near future, and added many crude and earthy descriptions. A few days later Robert began to complain of fatigue and stomach pains, which got progressively worse. Soon his bowels seemed to be on fire, and each of the thirty or forty occasions a day on which he was driven to empty them left him weaker and in greater pain. William feared for his friend's life, but God, luck and a strong young body pulled him through. Others were less fortunate, and as the disease raged through the camp many died or were invalided home—some 2,000 in all, including twenty of the archers from William's company.[17]

After a month of this depressing siege the King decided that the town had to be taken before his army simply rotted away. Preparations were made for an all-out assault, but after a long preparatory bombardment the defenders began negotiations for terms of surrender. It was finally decided that if no French help reached the city by 22nd September it would be surrendered to King Henry. Help did not arrive, and the town opened its gates to the English, the news of surrender being greeted with grim satisfaction by the surviving soldiers. William was much impressed by King Henry's declaration that the victory was not theirs alone, but was God's will. To show his humility Henry entered the town barefoot to attend service at the main church.

The capture of Harfleur revived William's anticipation of his share of loot, but his expectations were soon dashed by the King's decree that all citizens who swore allegiance to the crown would be permitted to retain their goods. Some refused and had to pay ransom, so that some booty did reach the troops, but by the time the captains and other privileged persons had taken their share the amount was small.

William did not have long to enjoy the fruits of victory, although there were enough French maidens impressed by his Anglo-Saxon looks to give him little time for rest. News trickled down to the archers that the King had sent a challenge of personal combat to the Dauphin, but that as this had been ignored they were all going home.[18] Indeed, quite a number had already smuggled themselves back to

England against orders. This was a short-lived hope, for, against advice, the King decided to make a march through Normandy to Calais, a plan which encouraged many to prophesy doom for all of them.

Extra baggage, wounded, sick and wagons were all left at Harfleur, and necessities only were loaded on to the horses. Early in October the depleted army, now only some 6,000 strong, set out. To William's surprise and secret delight they saw little of the French, apart from two very minor brushes. Although William had known hardship in the English camp he was amazed at the wretchedness of the French peasants in whose cottages he sometimes sheltered. Their food was scarcely better than that fed to pigs in England; few had ever tasted bread made of wheat—something which to William was normal everyday food—and they made do with barley cake supplemented with oats. Their main meal consisted of a handful of wheat, barley, peas and beans flavoured with some vegetable oil extracted from walnuts or rosehips, washed down with thin, sour wine.

The march started well enough, with most of the men in reasonable health after a spell of rest and warmth in Harfleur; but many had been weakened by the flux, and this weakness began to show as the strain of physical effort increased. William was in better shape than most, but Robert's condition still worried him, and he gladly carried his friend's bundle as well as his own. The straggling column struck north-east to Fécamp on the coast, and then turned east, reaching the region of Dieppe on 11th October. The castle of Arques opened a very desultory fire on them, and a royal message to the effect that if this did not cease at once the town would feel the weight of English revenge not only silenced the guns but produced a welcome ration of bread and wine. Still marching parallel to the coast, the army reached the town of Eu. As they neared the town shots were fired and a group of mounted knights charged the column. For the first time William loosed an arrow against a fellow man; he was unsure of the result, as the mêlée made it difficult to mark his target, and a counter-charge by English knights drove the French back again. William did derive one benefit from his encounter, however; he gained himself a helmet. One of the French knights, an old man to William's eyes, had charged towards the English until four arrows had dropped both him and his horse dead almost at William's feet. His helmet had wrenched free as the armoured body crashed to the ground; it was a splendid one, with a mail curtain and a pivotted visor.[19] The other archers had joked about William's new acquisition, pointing out with the air of experts that it was a bit ancient, but he prized it, and hooked it carefully to his pack.

Again King Henry threatened the destruction of the town, and again the French submitted and sent out food and drink. Next day the march continued as the English made for a ford over the River Somme, but within six miles of this objective they received an unpleasant shock. A prisoner warned the King that the ford was blocked and heavily guarded. For two hours the King and his commanders debated, finally deciding that their best hope lay in finding another ford further east along the Somme. The spirits of the soldiers dropped when they realised that they were marching further to the east, away from Calais; and many a hardened sinner offered up a fervent prayer to St. Jude when French troops were seen on the opposite bank of the river.

THEY had now been marching for six days, and despite the welcome additions to their rations the food was running short, whilst every weary step took them further from Calais. A few incidents stood out from the monotonous misery of the march. On Thursday 17th October William and Robert were horrified to witness an example of the King's justice; they watched an archer, his hands tied behind his back, hoisted kicking and struggling into the air to gasp out his last breaths at the end of a rope thrown over a tree branch. The word was passed through the army that the same fate awaited anybody else who disregarded the King's orders on stealing. On another occasion the column was halted in wooded country and thick branches were cut and sharpened at both ends to serve as simple but effective anti-cavalry fences.[20]

Faced with this extra burden some of the soldiers began abandoning their belongings, and the wake of the column was dotted with pathetic bundles cast down by the roadside. Many were suffering from a return of the bloody-flux; some staggered along on the arms of stronger comrades, whilst others clung wretchedly to the stirrup leather of a sympathetic rider. Their clothing was fouled and often in shreds although few discarded their rags, for the nights were cold. The army bore no resemblance to that which had left Southampton well fed, well shod and confident; the food had gone, and most of the soldiers were easing their hunger with what berries and nuts they could find near the road. Every house and field that they passed had been stripped bare of anything which might help or feed the hated foreigners; in a vengeful rage, the English put them to the torch.

On the 19th spirits were somewhat restored, for they managed to find a ford across the Somme at last; despite his hunger and misery William was cheered by the thought that they were now on their way to Calais. The following day, Sunday 20th October, the English camp was roused from its miserable apathy by the arrival of three heralds from the French.[21] News of their mission soon circulated among the soldiers, and their promise that the French would certainly wipe out the English before they reached Calais was known to all—and believed by many. Warnings were given that the enemy might attack at any time and that every care was to be taken. To everybody's surprise the next few days passed without any sign of the promised onslaught.

The march dragged on for another four days; dumb and wretched, William mechanically lifted one weary foot after the other. Chilled and draggled by the incessant rain, racked by the flux, their stomachs twisted and their senses dazed by the gnawing pains of hunger, the English shuffled along the endless roads like a procession of feeble beggars.

It was almost with relief that William and Robert heard that the main French army had been reported massing in their path. There was every sign that the battle they had been expecting ever since the march began would be fought on the morrow, Friday 25th October. That night, the eve of the feast of Saint Crispin and Crispinian,[22] William lay wrapped in the sodden rags of his once-splendid huke, shivering with a numb, damp misery. Half asleep, his mind turned towards the warmth and safety of his home, and he felt a great sadness and nostalgia for Waterperry. When cold and hunger wrenched his mind back to the present he offered up prayers for his safety on the morrow. All around him the camp lay wrapped in its own wretchedness and silence, for the King had ordered that all should rest as well as they might. From across the fields William could hear the noises of a bustling, confident French camp. Silhouetted against their camp-fires were the gorgeous pavilions which many of their nobles had erected. Bursts of

song, shouts and gusts of laughter carried through the damp air—well, they had every reason to celebrate, for tomorrow they would win a victory that would be recalled with pride for years to come. Tomorrow—William wondered if he would see tomorrow's sunset. A terrible loneliness and fear gripped him, and a strangled sob died in his throat before the sleep of exahustion took him.

Early on the morning of the 25th the English camp began to stir as the captains went around bringing back to reality men who had for a few brief hours escaped into oblivion. Priests moved amongst them hearing last confessions and giving absolution, and in this dire moment there were few who did not feel the need for spiritual consolation. Breakfast, for those who had any, was very makeshift; many ate all the scraps of food they had managed to hoard, for they feared that they would get no other chance in this life to enjoy a meal. Though miserable and depressed they intended to give a good account of themselves this day. William uncovered his bowstave—he had kept it dry by wrapping it in rags; from inside his doublet he drew the bowstrings, and gave them a quick wipe over with wax. One he placed on the bow, and the other he returned to the inside of his doublet. He had already collected his stock of arrows and checked feathering and straightness, twirling them between his fingers with practised ease.[23] The bodkin-like points, designed to deliver the full penetrating force to the smallest area, were scrutinised to make sure they were firmly in place. Robert had taken up his stand next to his good friend and they periodically exchanged encouraging, if somewhat wan smiles and even managed a few feeble attempts at humour. On William's left wrist was his strong leather bracer, to protect his forearm against the slap of the bowstring, and on the fingers of his right hand he wore finger-guards, for the string could cut into unprotected flesh like a knife into bread. After checking that his stake and sword were ready to hand, he had time to glance around him.

The knights were busy with their far more complicated preparations, for they had to don their full fighting harness. The lucky ones changed into dry hose and shirts, and over these went a padded arming doublet with reinforcing gussets of mail at the vulnerable points such as elbows and armpits. With fingers usually nimble and sure but now made clumsy by cold and damp, squires helped put on the harness, starting at the feet; next came the leg-pieces, hinged at the side and clipping into place, then the thigh-pieces secured to a belt by cords carefully adjusted to ensure easy movement. Next a skirt of mail or hooped plates was attached to the bottom of the breast and back plate, followed by the arm-pieces, secured by laces and cunningly contrived pins. Last to be put on were the metal-covered leather gloves and the helmet; often these were left off until battle was imminent, but in the present circumstances most of the knights were wearing their full harness, with sword and dagger in place at their waist. Many of them were observing all the niceties and had their personal banners flying on poles, or were wearing their jupons embroidered with their arms.[24]

King Henry was everywhere on his grey horse, encouraging, bullying, cursing, nagging and jollying a little spirit into his dejected army. Slowly the force of some five and a half thousand were manoeuvred into the planned formation. The centre group of dismounted men-at-arms was commanded by the King himself, splendid in armour, heraldically embroidered jupon and jewelled helmet. On each side of this group were blocks of archers in a triangular formation, the point towards the French. Each of these archer groups was flanked by more men-at-arms, those on

the left of centre commanded by Lord Camoys and those on the right by the Duke
of York, whilst the extreme flanks were guarded by more companies of archers.
William and Robert and their Oxfordshire comrades were in the group on the left
of the centre.   To the left of the army was the small village of Agincourt, on the
right, Tramecourt; to their rear was Maisoncelles, where many had passed the
night before battle.[25]

Dawn was now well advanced and the English could see, about twelve hundred
yards ahead, the mighty French host.   William thought that they looked magnificent with their gay banners and their armour sparkling in the growing sunlight.
They were forming up in three lines, but so great was the host and so crowded
were they that the effect was more like a solid block of men.[26]   William, prepared
for the worst, stood tense and waiting, expecting every moment to see the mass of
steel-clad men begin their inexorable advance; but to his surprise, nothing
happened.   For hour after hour the two armies confronted one another, and
neither seemed prepared to begin combat.   There was a flurry of excitement when
three French knights left the host, but they only rode up to speak to the King, and
then returned to their own lines.[27]

It was now about eleven of the clock in the morning, and King Henry decided
that if the French would not make the first move, then the English would.   His
orders, passed by word of mouth from captain to captain, were that the entire line
was to advance.   Realising that this was the certain prelude to battle William and
Robert, together with all their comrades, knelt in prayer, and placed a small piece
of earth in their mouths.[28]   Standing again, they heard the order ' *Banners Advance!* ', and the entire army, struggling to maintain formation, moved slowly
forward.   The move was interpreted by many of the French as the beginning of a
general attack, but the English advance was well controlled and stopped when
they came within bowshot range.   Here the archers hammered their pointed stakes
into the ground to form a barrier against horses.   The men-at-arms stood ready,
armoured and with swords, lances, axes and maces in their hands, ready to strike.
William and his comrades pushed their arrows, points first, into the ground at their
feet, conveniently to hand where they could be snatched up and nocked.   William's
mouth felt dry and his breathing was a little faster than usual, but now that the
moment was really here he felt less frightened than he had expected.   The captains
stood ready; and when every man was in position, they gave the order to loose
arrows.

THOUSANDS of hands reached down, seized arrows, nocked them to the strings.
pulled back, and, at full stretch, released the yard-long shafts.   Aiming was
instinctive, for the pull of these bows was around eighty pounds, a force which
meant that few men could stand with the bows spanned.   The thousands of arrows
sang through the air in a lethal shower which struck down horse and man.   For
those killed the end was swift and painless, but for those wounded the agony of an
arrow which punched through armour or mail and then embedded itself in flesh or
bone was intense—no less for horse than man, and maddened animals kicked and
plunged and reared, scattering the ranks of French soldiers.

William and Robert scarcely had time to observe the results of the volleys;
caught up in the excitement of the moment, they leaned into their bows and loosed

arrow after arrow at the French in a deadly rhythm. Young boys were kept busy scurrying between the ranks to bring up the fresh sheaves of arrows, so essential to maintain the barrage. Suddenly the bowmen's concentration was broken, for from each side of the English line came groups of French knights, charging as best they could through the muddy field. Some archers turned their attention to these, and emptied several saddles, and the others were held back by the line of sharpened stakes. One or two were thrown over the fences by their terrified mounts, to be swiftly dealt with by archers or men-at-arms who rushed forward and applied the *coup-de-grâce* through the armpit or opened visor. Some, less skilful or less merciful, hammered at the fallen foe with pole-axes, driving the point repeatedly through breast or back plate. The impetus of the French charge was lost, and the survivors turned back dispirited, only to find that the main body of the army was on the move. As the mass of armoured men advanced the woods on either side of the field had a funnelling effect, pushing the French lines together and cramming them ever closer.

To the archers it was like shooting at the butts for there were few missiles coming back from the French lines apart from a few crossbow bolts and one or two gun-shots.[29] William sent arrow after arrow into the struggling mass, but still they came plodding through the mud with a determination that could not but earn the admiration of the English. Every so often wounded and riderless horses scattered the ranks in their frenzy to escape the tormenting hail of arrows, but always they closed up. William's arms, shoulders and fingers were aching, but so great was the madness which held him that he ignored the discomfort, and continued to loose arrow after arrow as fast as he could nock and pull. There was no respite; still the French pressed forward, and William saw that they were even increasing their speed, while bunching into three columns. The line of attack was towards the centre, where King Henry has positioned himself. More and more Frenchmen fell, but still they came on, slipping and sliding in the mud, and William felt a welling fear that nothing mortal could stop them. All that he could see were shining sword blades, axe heads and maces. With a shout the head of the French column hit the English centre, and to William's horror the line began to give. Bowmen from the wings continued to pour arrows into the flanks of the French but at the centre it was a heaving, whirling mêlée of English swords and axes, while the unfortunate French were packed so close that many were virtually helpless, unable to move, let alone use their weapons. So fierce was the English resistance that the French began to fall back—but those behind them continued to advance, pressing them

Detail based on a Royal Manuscript 20 C VII folio 136 showing men-at-arms in close combat. Most are shown wearing visored bascinets and use swords or axes. The surcoats are represented as quilted.

helplessly on to the English blades. Confusion was complete; many fallen were trampled into the mud to suffocate miserably.[30]

The archers in the centre were now deprived of their supply of arrows, and many dropped their bows, seized swords—their own, or one of the many now littering the field—and hurled themselves into the hacking, struggling mass. William and Robert were among those seized by this battle-frenzy. At first William used his short sword, but finding that it was often ineffective against his armoured enemies he threw it aside and grabbed up a knightly sword lying half covered by a corpse. A joyous savagery took over, and gasping and sobbing for breath he hacked and jabbed with abandon. He was no swordsman, but many of his blows struck home at such close quarters. He yelled incoherently as he fought, but there was no real hate in his mind until, pausing to catch his wind, he saw Robert kneeling on a pile of corpses and gazing stupidly at what he held in his hand. With incredulous horror William realised that it was a severed arm, and at the same instant he saw his friend's blood gushing from the stump. Even as he started to move towards him a struggling Frenchman swung a sword, and Robert's head became a grotesque caricature as his lifeless body fell forward.

Crazed by this appalling spectacle, William shrieked and cursed as he swung blindly, viciously at the knight. His arm-jarring swing knocked his opponent off balance, and William leapt on him, jabbing with the sword at any point where there was the slightest gap in his armour. Most of his stabs grated uselessly on mail, but some found their target; soon the point was reddened, and the Frenchman had stopped his unintelligible shouting. Possessed now with a killing fury the young Englishman hammered and slashed at the mounting heaps of bodies. All around others were similarly engaged, and imperceptibly the French lines began to retreat. Suddenly William found himself without a target, and leaned on the chipped and blunted sword, breath rasping in his throat. All around him lay great heaps of dead and wounded men, in some places piled higher than his head. Somewhere under the layers of French corpses Robert's body had disappeared. Men-at-arms were already busily engaged in searching the bodies of the fallen, stripping them of armour and valuables; wounded were claimed as prisoners, or killed on the spot.

William sank to his knees, numbed and shocked by his exertions and by the sights he had seen, but there was no respite yet. The captains were screaming at their men, and when the words finally penetrated his dazed mind William realised that they had been ordered to kill all prisoners. Many soldiers grumbled and refused to obey—not through pity, but simply because it meant a loss of revenue. The choice was taken from them by a squad of archers under the command of an Esquire, who moved through the lines dispatching all Frenchmen. Hardened by horrors, William scarcely registered what was happening as the executioners went about their grim task. Some were skilled and merciful, bringing rest by a quick upward thrust of a dagger or a knife slit across the throat; others, vicious or inexperienced, hacked at their victims with swords or clubs.[31]

Quite soon it was over, and orders came to stop the murder; the attacks had ceased, and the French were no longer pressing towards the English lines. An incredible victory was England's—a victory gained by luck, bravery, skill and French incompetence. Drained of all feeling, William could comprehend only one thing; in his mind's eye he still saw Robert gazing in horror at his arm, and his features dissolving into red chaos. Summoning his strength he staggered to his feet and began a frantic search for his friend, heaving bodies aside until he found him at last, pinned under three still-living Frenchmen. William paid no attention to their groans. As he rolled Robert over it was at once obvious that there was no hope—the shattered head alone was enough. For a while he cradled the body in silence, then pulled it clear and staggered back to the rear of the English position. Others, less concerned with personal grief, were busy searching the piles of dead for booty, and there was plenty to be had. Fine armour, weapons, furs, clothing and jewellery were there for the picking up, and English soldiers were happily throwing aside pieces worth more than they earned in a year. One or two urged William to join them, and one, more generous than his comrades, pressed some coins into his hand. Prisoners worthy of ransom were collected and taken to the camp, while the bodies of the English dead were piled up in a large barn which stood nearby. William carried Robert's

English soldiers on board a ship of the 15th Century showing its single mast and wooden castles fore and aft. The standard bears the leopards of England. (British Museum. Royal M.S. 14E IV.)

body himself, and placed him tenderly on the pile. When all had been collected the building was fired, to provide a fitting pyre for the dead. The French corpses, now mostly naked, sprawled across the field like pallid slugs, still and grotesque in death, while many of the wounded still writhed where they had fallen, or struggled to drag themselves from the battlefield.[32]

THAT night the English slept in the village of Maisoncelles, and the following day the army continued its march to the coast, its numbers swollen by prisoners and hundreds of extra horses laden with booty. William's fine helmet had lain forgotten on the ground during the battle and after it, but now he wore finer clothes than he had ever owned in his life, for several of his friends had pressed some of their loot on him. He had a fine armour and one or two weapons which he had picked up from the great pile in the camp, as well as a horse of reasonable breeding.

The march back to Calais passed uneventfully. When the troops arrived the townspeople welcomed them not as victors, but merely as chickens ripe for the plucking. Food prices rose, as did the cost of a passage to England, and the huge amount of booty for sale caused prices to plummet. Archers were glad to get half the value of an article, and many traded their prisoners for a fraction of their ransom just to obtain some ready money. William and his group waited at Calais for some days, but eventually, on 16th November, they sailed for England with the fleet carrying the King and his most important prisoners. They landed at Dover on Sunday 17th November, and with the King and his retinue made their way to

London by way of Canterbury. The capital was in festive mood, and the ceremonies organised to welcome the victorious King were elaborate and fanciful. William found that the horror of the battle and Robert's death was fading; he began to respond to the heady excitement of the cheering crowds and festive decorations, and on several occasions over the next few days, his tongue well oiled with liquor in the taverns of Cheapside by admiring townsfolk, he retold the story of Agincourt fight with certain frills and elaborations which perhaps over-emphasised the part he had personally played.

Released in due course from the Earl's service, he made his way home through the winter countryside, on his horse sprung from some French stable. He made good time and on 30th November he saw, for the first time in five months, the thatched roofs of Waterperry. Never had they looked so good. As his mount trotted down the road to the village William realised that he had left it as a wide-eyed, naive boy; now, a few short months later, he was returning as a man, who had suffered and seen suffering. Adventure . . . yes, he had had his fill; but for him the military life was one which memory mellowed. Many times in later life William would recall his service in France with pride and satisfaction—but, just as often, the ghost of Robert Welling would appear to remind him of the realities of war.

NOTES

Personal names used in this chapter are extracted from contemporary lists of those who fought at Agincourt, but with the exception of prominent commanders the rôles played by individuals are fictitious.

1. Carfax: the meeting place of four main roads near the centre of medieval Oxford: the name was derived from *Quadrifurcus*.
2. Henry V's claims were complex, but he based his case on the Treaty of Bretigny made by Edward III in 1360, and on his descent through his great-great-grand-mother Isabella, the daughter of Philip IV, who died in 1314.
3. From the time of Edward I the longbow played an increasingly important part in English battles, and helped win many victories. The practice of archery was encouraged by the setting up of butts, and later, when archery began to lose its prime position, laws were enacted making practice obligatory.
4. The over-jacket or *houppelande* was popular at this period, and was produced in many styles and materials.
5. For outdoor wear cloaks were being replaced by a form of tabard which was passed over the head to hang down front and back in large oblong panels—this was the huke.
6. Silver pence were still in use but in 1280 round half-pence and farthings were adopted. Groats appeared in 1279 and the noble was first minted in 1314.
7. Prisoners of knightly rank were usually held until an agreed sum of money was paid in ransom. The amount, depending on the prisoner's rank, was normally shared between the captor and his leader. Usually the King claimed certain prisoners as his own, no matter by whom they were taken.
8. By the early 15th Century most troops were raised by the quota system whereby a leader undertook to provide a number of men for a certain period of time. The agreement specified wages, terms of service and partition of booty. (See Nicolas, op. cit., Appendix, p. 8.)
9. Since most members of the expedition were allowed several horses each—six for a knight—the total number must have been enormous. If there were 2,000 men-at-arms then there were probably a minimum of 13,000 horses, and since a number of mounted archers also took part in the expedition the total could well have reached twenty thousand.
10. Bowstaves were normally ordered by the sheriff of a county and sent in bulk to a central depot—often the Tower of London. The subject of supply of weapons is well covered in Hewitt, op. cit.
11. It was generally accepted that yew was the best wood for the longbow although elm, pine and beech were also used.

12. The bowstring was held with the first three fingers of the right hand, the first finger above the arrow. At maximum stretch the fingers were straightened, allowing the string to ride off easily. Some form of guard was worn on the right hand to protect the fingers.

13. Armour was expensive, and consequently most archers and ordinary soldiers made do with a simple helmet. Cheaper forms of defence were made by fitting overlapping metal plates on to a stout tunic; these 'jacks' were probably fairly common amongst the English army.

14. The first use of gunpowder in Europe is recorded early in the 14th Century; by the time of Agincourt it was in general use for artillery and, to a lesser degree, for hand firearms. Contemporary accounts make several references to the use of firearms, although they were not a major factor in the fighting. The King's master gunners were Gerard van Willighen, Hans Joye, Walter Stotmaker and Drovanskell Coykyn.

15. A 'lance' used in this context did not mean a single knight, but included his retinue, probably numbering at least three people. Men-at-arms was the term commonly applied to those who fought in armour.

16. The list of 'Statutes and Ordenances made by the Right Noble Kinge Henry' is given in Nicolas, op. cit., Appendix, p. 31.

17. Bloody-flux: contemporary term for amoebic dysentry, which was prevalent at the siege.

18. A translation of the King's challenge is given in Nicolas, op. cit., Appendix, p. 29.

19. Helmet design was changing early in the 15th Century, and the older form of bascinet with pointed visor and mail curtain was being replaced by other forms with plate defences for the neck. In Italy the armet was being developed. Many knights fought in armour which was many years old, and a variety of styles would be found in every group of soldiers.

20. It seems that Henry ordered his archers to provide themselves with six foot long sharpened stakes after the attack at Corbie on 17th October. It was at this time that the archer was hanged for robbing a church.

21. Heralds were still relatively important and maintained a line of communication between opposing leaders. They were accorded safe conduct at all times.

22. Saints Crispin and Crispinian, the patron saints of shoemakers, are supposed to have been brothers executed in the third century.

23. Arrows are often described as being an ell in length; this is usually taken as meaning one yard, although thirty inches is probably more correct. They were usually of birch, with the three sets of feathers—the fletchings—secured

Brass of Sir John Fitzwaryn from the church at Wantage, Berkshire. It was made in 1414 and depicts Sir John in full plate armour complete with bascinet and plate gorget and besagews to guard the armpits. His sword is supported from a decorative belt which often supported a dagger as well.

by binding with thread and/or some type of gum. The feathers, from goose, turkey or peacock, were placed around the shaft so that when the nock—the groove cut in the end of the shaft—was on the string one feather stood out at right angles to the bow on the side furthest from the stave, and the other two were angled at 120° and 240°, in a position which allowed them to ride easily over the stave when loosed. The point, or pile, was variously shaped depending upon its function, but those for war arrows of the period were usually fairly solid with compact heads to give maximum penetration.

24. By this period full plate armour had been developed, although mail was still much used as a secondary defence. A man fully armed was now almost completely covered with metal plates. On his feet were sabatons; then came the greaves, with poleyns at the knee. On the thighs were the cuisses, largely covered by the fauld, a skirt of plates attached to the breast and back plates. On the arms were the vambraces and rerebraces with couters at the elbow, and plates called besagues guarded the armpits. The helmet was a bascinet, probably with plate neck defences.

25. While the precise topography of the battlefield of Agincourt is uncertain it is possible, by combining the meagre information in contemporary accounts, to build up an acceptable idea of the area. The main fighting took place on a fairly flat field running roughly S.S.W. and N.N.E., with woods on either side. The English lines extended across the width of the southern end. At the outset the French were far more extended, for their end of the field was more lightly wooded, but as the lines advanced the flanks found their way barred by the woods on either side and were pushed towards the centre of the already overcrowded lines, which became further constricted and congested in consequence.

26. The French force probably numbered around 25,000 men.

27. This episode is mentioned in contemporary accounts, which state that one of the French knights was very discourteous to the King.

28. This ritual probably signified willingness to return to the earth—i.e. to die.

29. Whilst more powerful, the crossbow had a slower rate of fire than the longbow and required mechanical aids in its loading.

30. The limitations of wearing armour are usually grossly exaggerated, and a fallen knight was not prevented from rising by the weight of his armour. It is a matter of record that some knights suffocated at Agincourt, but this was the result of being held down by the weight of bodies, not armour. An armoured man can perform almost any ordinary movement with minimal difficulty.

31. The order to kill the prisoners was given by King Henry because he feared another French attack, and the large number of prisoners presented a serious potential danger.

32. Casualty figures are always very difficult to assess for any medieval battle, and Agincourt is no exception; contemporary accounts give widely differing figures. Taking a roughly median figure the totals would seem to have been about 9,000 French killed and 1,500 captured, with total English casualties of about 250.

SELECT BIBLIOGRAPHY

C. Blair, *European Armour*, Batsford, London, 1958.

F. R. H. Du Boulay, *An Age of Ambition*, Nelson, London, 1970.

A. H. Burne, *The Agincourt War*, Eyre and Spottiswoode, London, 1956.

C. and P. Cunnington, *Handbook of English Medieval Costume*, Faber and Faber, London, 1952.

H. J. Hewitt, *The Organisation of War under Edward III*, Manchester University Press, Manchester, 1966.

C. Hibbert, *Agincourt*, Batsford, London, 1964.

E. F. Jacob, *The Fifteenth Century*, Oxford University Press, 1961.

Sir Harris Nicolas, *The History of the Battle of Agincourt*, London, 1833, reprinted by Frederick Muller, 1971.

E. Perroy, *The Hundred Years War*, Eyre and Spottiswoode, London, 1965.

5: Heinrich Elsener

ON 18th February 1476 the Diet of Lucerne decided that five days later, on the 23rd, the troops of the canton would be mobilised to go to the aid of hard-pressed Berne. Charles the Bold, Duke of Burgundy, to whom Berne had sent a declaration of war on 24th October 1474, had been advancing since the beginning of this February, and on the day following the decision of the Diet of Lucerne pitched his camp above Grandson and immediately laid siege to the little town.[1] On 21st February his heavy siege guns reduced the town walls, and the Bernese garrison withdrew to the Castle of Grandson, which rose from the slopes above the lake, a short distance from the town. The garrison, numbering nearly 500 determined men, settled down to defend the strategically important castle against the 30,000 Burgundians until a relief force from Berne could raise the siege. At first the Burgundian artillery,[2] which bombarded the fortress from close range day and night, caused only insignificant damage to the sturdy structure, but a series of misfortunes among the defenders soon led to a critical situation. The Bernese master-gunner's head was torn off by a Burgundian shot: the castellan, Georg vom Stein, fell seriously ill and had to be removed from his post: and several barrels of gunpowder exploded, damaging some of the garrison's handguns.

Meanwhile the mobilisation of Lucerne got under way. Early on the morning of 23rd February the troops rallied at their allotted district assembly points. Equipped for a major campaign, they marched in squads through a heavy snowfall to the Allmend outside the town; and among them marched Heinrich Elsener, a tall and well-built young man of twenty-four who, like most of his particular squad, was a member of the carpenters' guild. Heinrich was a skilled crossbowman, and he spent every Sunday morning on the practice range with his friends; he frequently won prizes for his shooting—indeed, the hose he was wearing on that cold dawn were made from a bolt of cloth he had been given the previous year as a prize by the canton authorities.

The bowmen and hand-gunners had separated themselves from the rest of the men at the beginning of the mobilisation, and now hurried towards their particular flag, faintly visible in the flickering light of the campfire which burned on the Allmend. The captain, Rudi Zoger, the ensign, Jost Bramberg, and the lieutenant, Peter Frankhauser, greeted the men as they arrived.[3] Most of their comrades had already arrived and were busy packing their gear on to the baggage train. The Allmend looked eerie; nearly 1,800 armed men had gathered in the light of the fire and the guttering torches. In the centre were the tents of the council of war. The ensign, Jost Bramberg, was usually game for any joke, but now he glanced around at the busy scene with a grave face; the latest messenger from Grandson had brought news which boded ill.

After the arrival of the last squads the captain divided the troops into vanguard and rearguard. Heinrich was appointed to the vanguard, a group of about 100 men, which formed the point when the force was on the march. As many crossbows as hand-guns could be seen in the ranks of the vanguard, for until only a few years previously the gunners had been in a tiny minority. Although the authorities

Schloss Grandson on the Neuenburgersee, as it is today.
(Photo A. Deriaz)

frequently offered more tempting prizes to the winners of gun-shooting matches, Heinrich had no intention of forsaking his crossbow; for one thing, guns were too inaccurate and noisy for deer hunting.[4]

Jost Bramberg gathered the soldiers for inspection, and checked the condition of their weapons first of all. Negligence in the care of weapons and equipment was punished with severe penalties, in blatant cases with sentences of imprisonment. No punishments were necessary on this occasion, however; the presence of the Burgundian army was warning enough, and every man had made sure he arrived with armour polished and sword sharpened. In their bags they carried spare shoes and clothing and other small necessities. Their provisions, of which they made sure there would be no shortage, consisted of oatmeal, cheese and bread.

At dawn they had made such good progress with their preparations that the ensign was able to begin organising the order of marching. Above all it was important to arrange the troops in such a way that they could change from marching column to battle array at any time. It was an icy cold morning, and the sky was lowering and grey. Every necessary movement was welcomed, to warm up limbs stiff with cold; but the long wait was more irksome than the weather, and the younger men in particular could hardly restrain themselves.

Heinrich, stamping and blowing his hands, was placed next to his friend Hans Bogner, whose father kept a large armourer's shop in the town of Lucerne. Proudly he showed Heinrich his new hand-gun, which his father had obtained for him from Nürnberg. It was smaller than most Heinrich had seen, with a well-cast bronze barrel, and it even had Bogner's coat-of-arms painted on the stock. Hans wore an excellent armour which he had himself helped to beat in his father's workshop when he was a journeyman. Heinrich himself made an imposing figure in his Milanese half-armour, which he had got the year before from a Milanese merchant at the Lucerne market. His elegant crossbow, with a painted horn bow, was the product of a Vorarlberg workshop. On his left hip he wore a long Swiss sword with a fine Passau blade, recognisable by the famous wolf mark. The brown leather scabbard also contained a *Beimesser*[5] and an awl. On his right side the wooden quiver for his crossbow bolts, covered with unshaven pigskin, was slung from his belt. Hans carried as side-arms only a dagger and an axe, the latter as useful for fighting as for work on fortifications. Not all the gunners and crossbow-men were equipped with armour; apart from the financial considerations, many of their comrades preferred a lighter breast plate or a shirt of ring-mail. Most of the company wore either small visored sallet helmets, or iron war-hats.

The captain returned to the assembly point after a fairly long absence in the command tent, and mounted his horse. The boys in charge of the baggage were setting up the various wagons and carts ready for departures. At the head of the column stood the heavily loaded pack-mules; at the rear of the train were the carts of the tradesmen, merchants and camp-followers, who never missed any opportunity of plying their profession on the march. Heinrich recognised one of them, a hearty wench named Margaretha, from an earlier muster. Her uncle, a grocer, was doing a roaring trade selling liquor to the freezing soldiers; a beaker of wine and a few jokes lifted their morale as they stood around the freezing camp-ground.

The ensign appeared, swung himself into the saddle, and cantered along the column to check the loading and arrangement of the wagons. The cook and his helpers were getting the day-meal ready, and vast cauldrons of oat-based soup were bubbling cheerfully. As soon as the men had eaten the election of the chief leaders and the swearing-in of the soldiers took place. Each man had a voice in choosing his leader. Again, as for more than ten years past, the old village major Heinrich Hasfurter was chosen to lead the men of Lucerne. With bared heads the soldiers gathered around the banner and the captains, and swore aloud to obey their orders loyally and never to retreat from their enemies. With the aid of the Almighty and the Virgin they pledged themselves to defend their land, their wives and their children from the misfortunes of war.

Heinrich stood up again, and the soldiers impatiently awaited the drum-beat which would signal departure. Led by the captain, ensign and sergeant on horseback, two drummers and a fifteen-year-old piper, they swung into the march. At last, they were off! Many of the townsfolk had gathered to wave goodbye to the long column of soldiers, and many a tear was shed by the women and children left behind. Heinrich was not married, and had no worries in that respect; indeed, he was looking forward to the adventures ahead. It was common knowledge that the Duke of Burgundy had not only brought a strong army for his campaign against the Swiss Confederation, but also large numbers of women . . .

On 26th February, after tiring day-long marches over roads choked with snow and treacherous with ice, the men of Lucerne marched singing into the town of Berne. The hungry and thirsty soldiers received a joyful reception from the townsfolk, who were obviously relieved to see the first contingent from central Switzerland marching through their streets. The Grandson garrison was in desperate difficulties, and only a swift relief column could save them from the worst; and after a short rest, Bramberg ordered his gunners and crossbowmen to take the road for Neuchâtel. The latest news indicated that Charles the Bold intended to advance on Berne by way of Neuchâtel, and the Bernese council of war therefore ordered their contingent which had assembled at Murten to make for the same place.

Again the men of Lucerne marched off singing down the endless country roads, to the beat of the great wooden war-drums. Marching all day and lodging in farm-houses by night, Heinrich and his comrades reached Neuchâtel on 28th February, led by their ensign. The captain and sergeant with new orders, had gone ahead and awaited the arrival of their men in the market square in front of the town hall; their instructions that the soldiers should take a half-hour rest were most welcome. There was much coming and going in front of the town hall and in the alleys leading off the square. Neuchâtel, which had been chosen as the assembly point for all the federal forces, swarmed with activity, and everywhere officers, messengers, envoys and local people hurried to and fro. Grocers had put up their stalls, in many places blocking the busy streets, and the town guards sweated to clear the inquisitive citizens out of the way. In the next three days 20,000 men were expected in Neuchâtel, and for this reason the first contingents to arrive were immediately led through the town and on to outlying villages where they were quartered. The Lucerne contingent was directed to Boudry, a village near the lake and about an hour and a half's march from the town.

Heinrich's company was responsible for the security of the camp, and again took up quarters in the farm buildings; after their arrival the main body of the troops from Lucerne pitched their tents just outside the village. After the evening meal Heinrich went to the village square, which was illuminated by torches on tripods. A sergeant-major pointed out the direction of the enemy, and warned them all to special caution. He reminded them that any guard found asleep on duty would suffer the death penalty. Heinrich was appointed to the first watch, and stood sentry-go with his friend Franz von Sins, a hand-gunner. Franz was an excellent shot, when sober, who was always accompanied by an enormous dog which he led around on a heavy chain attached to its spiked iron collar. Franz had christened this vast beast 'Bary the Bold'; the previous year, scouting ahead of the first march to Waadt, the dog had got on the trail of two Burgundian spies hiding in a bush. The Burgundians, although men of most imposing stature, had gone pale with terror at the sound of Bary's thunderous barking on their heels, and had not dared try to escape.

Boudry was surrounded to the north and west by a long ridge, and from these heights the still-growing camps of the soldiers from Lucerne could be surveyed with ease. More than a hundred fires lit up the many tents, wagons, carts, and mule-lines. It was almost midnight when the last of the rearguard and baggage train arrived; and shortly after the church clock struck twelve the relieving guard arrived. Heinrich and Franz proceeded to the village square to make their report, and then returned to their quarters.

THE next day, 1st March, was spent in the same camp; the arrival of the rest of the army was causing delay, and the troops already assembled seethed with impatience. Charles the Bold sneered at these rugged soldiers as barbarians because they knew no social hierarchy, and because in the fields they bolted their cheese complete with rind, and ate meat almost raw. Rough as their manners were, they were civilised enough to resent waiting around in the freezing cold. Duke Charles had come across the Swiss for the first time as a youth, when he heard mercenaries singing their strange and melancholy songs around the camp-fires of his father's army. He had been impressed with their air of massive strength, and moved by their singing, which sounded more like a chorus of humming

Crossbow of composite horn construction; Austrian, about 1460. (Author's collection)

accompanying a clear, high, bell-like solo ringing from a powerful throat some-where in the flickering shadows. 'Do not trust them, my lord,' the inexperienced Charles had been warned. 'They may bring tears of emotion to your eyes with their barbarous songs, but they kill quicker and better than all others . . .' As he sat in his pavilion in the camp above Grandson that night, the Duke of Burgundy may have reflected on these youthful impressions. He wished to destroy these barbarians, swiftly and completely.

The Swiss were sitting around their fires that evening—the Bernese had also arrived and were encamped just above Boudry—when messengers arrived with terrible news. A few hours earlier the Burgundians had succeeded in forcing the garrison out of Grandson; and in an attempt to intimidate his enemies, the duke had ordered all 412 survivors to be hanged or drowned. The tale of this bloody murder struck the Swiss camp like a thunder-clap. Captains and sergeants struggled to keep their men under control as the news spread from contingent to contingent, and a raving mob took up the furious chant—'*Grandson! Grandson! Grandson!*'

The council of war assembled in Boudry to consider the news. Word had also come that the castle of Vaumarcus, an advanced outpost of Neuchâtel's troops, had fallen to the Burgundians and had been occupied by a group of noblemen backed by more than a hundred mounted archers from the duke's guard. It was decided that the Swiss forces would move towards Vaumarcus the next day in order to entice Charles the Bold out of his fortified camp.

Heinrich slept little that night.

At three o'clock in the morning of 2nd March 1476 the drums of the camps round Boudry beat reveille. In haste, the troops arranged themselves in their order of march by the light of the fires. Their captains took great pains to see that the

Crossbow bolt from Grandson, late 15th Century. The heavy iron head is pyramidal in section and the flights are of wood. At a range of 100 yards these bolts could penetrate plate armour with ease. (Author's collection) Opposite, detail from the Diebold Schilling chronicle of 1483: the Confederates kneel in prayer, and the Burgundian cavalry advance.

soldiers had a hot breakfast—they knew by experience that their prowess seemed to be greatly improved by a well-filled stomach. After the baggage train had been drawn up along the road the sergeant led Heinrich's company to Mass, which was being heard on the main camp site outside the village. Heinrich was not the only one who hardly listened to the priest. Suddenly he caught sight of the Contingent of Schwyz, about a thousand strong, moving as fast as they could along the road to Vaumarcus; singing wildly and beating their drums, they chased past the kneeling ranks of Lucerne. Behind them came 200 men from St. Gallen, dressed all in red.

Not waiting for the end of the Mass the fifteen-year-old piper, Hans Hirt, jumped to his feet and ran off after the passing soldiers, shouting with joy. His example was soon followed. The captains and the angry priest could not prevent a hundred or so eager soldiers from scrambling up and dashing off in pursuit; among them, laughing with sheer excitement, went Heinrich Elsener. As he panted up to the last squad of the red-clad men of St. Gallen he saw 'Bary the Bold' bounding after him, dragging his staggering master on the road of duty—for Franz von Sins had evidently overindulged in the excellent wine of Neuchâtel the evening before.

They marched along the lake, arrived at St. Aubin and left the main road, taking the steep path which they hoped would enable them to outflank the Castle of Vaumarcus. Near the village of Fresens the men of Schwyz, St. Gallen and Lucerne took up a waiting position. The Contingent of Berne were camped just below the village, and now began to join the advance, but there was much more snow here than at Boudry and it was only with difficulty that the artillery and baggage train of the Bernese force were able to follow. The darkness of the pre-dawn hours made the march even more difficult.

Heinrich joined a scouting party about a hundred strong, and by the time dawn rose they were across the bridge over the Combe de Ruaux gorge. Shortly afterwards they almost ran into a Burgundian picket stationed on a wooded mound, but after a short fight the enemy archers retreated to the Castle of Vaumarcus, which could now be seen in the distance in the growing light. Stirred up by this first contact with the enemy the Swiss force marched on without awaiting orders, along the narrowing road to the slope above the Carthusian monastery of La Lance. This audacious party was greatly surprised to find that Burgundian soldiers were erecting tents on the hill behind the monastery; A hurried conference sent a couple of dozen Swiss off down the slope under cover of the trees, to harass the Burgundians with crossbow and gun-fire. This pastime ceased to be so amusing when the enemy reacted with great energy, and Heinrich was forced to scurry back to the road pursued by a large party of Burgundian archers. The

pursuers were badly mauled by the Confederates who had remained on the road,
however, and soon fled back to their camp
site, leaving many dead in the trampled
snow. These unfortunates were cheerfully plundered of weapons and gear by
the Swiss soldiers.

In the meantime the ensigns from Berne
and Schwyz, alarmed by the noise of
fighting, had arrived on the scene with
their men, and the whole force continued
to advance together. After a short time the Swiss troops, now numbering some
9,000 men, reached the edge of the forest, and came upon the unexpected sight of
the whole Burgundian vanguard drawn up near the village of Concise. The captains, conscious now of their imprudence in pushing ahead, ordered the column to
halt so that they could await, and warn, the other Confederation troops. Their en-
raged soldiers, however, had no wish to wait for reinforcements, and once more
took up the chant of 'Grandson! Grandson!' Some bold men from Berne shouted
to their captain that if he did not have the courage then he could stay where he was,
and that they could smash the tyrant's head without his help. After a short consultation the senior officers gave the ensigns the order to arrange their companies.
They dismounted, took the standards from their bearers, and hurried towards the
flatter ground ahead, followed by their soldiers.

Groups of gunners and crossbowmen from various contingents formed the vanguard, which Heinrich estimated to be about 300 strong. Behind them the men-at-
arms formed up in a solid phalanx[6] with a front of nearly a hundred men, under the
direction of the Bernese *Oberfeldhauptmann* Niklaus von Scharlachthal. The
men armed with halberds, boar spears and other short-hafted weapons were surrounded on three sides by eight rows of pikemen, many of them in full armour. At
the sides of the phalanx the Bernese artillery was drawn up.

The Burgundians, who had advanced threateningly to close range, burst into
laughter and jeers when they saw the Confederates kneel down to pray, as was
their invariable custom before battle. They thought that the Swiss were begging
for mercy. Their prayers completed, the Swiss rose to their feet and stood in silent
ranks—until a hundred drums crashed out the signal to advance, more than thirty
standards and banners fluttered and cracked in the *Bise*,[7] and from a thousand
throats came the shout of vengeance—'Grandson! Grandson! Grandson!' His
heart pounding, Heinrich marched forward, his crossbow spanned and loaded with
a bolt.

In front of the Swiss vanguard stood the well-armed Burgundian infantry; their
right wing was made up of cavalrymen in thick metal-studded jacks, who were
fighting dismounted. On each side of the infantry the heavy cavalry sat their
armoured stallions. Heinrich admitted to himself that they made a formidable
picture, with the early sun glinting on polished armour and closed vizors, and their
plumes tossing in the wind. In front of the enemy infantry were positioned large
numbers of field guns, many of them breech-loading.

At about ten o'clock Charles the Bold opened the battle with a volley of cannon-
fire; the shot howled close over the heads of the vanguard and plunged into the

tight-pressed phalanx, raising screams of pain. The men of Berne, Schwyz, St. Gallen and Lucerne walked towards the Burgundian cannon to the rhythm of drums and pipes. The Bernese field guns retaliated effectively. At that moment the right wing of Burgundian cavalry came thundering at the Swiss vanguard at full gallop. The gunners and crossbowmen loosed off a hot fire at the approaching mass of riders, bringing men and horses crashing down in the snow; two chargers bolted, throwing their riders. The meeting of the two sides was terrible. Crowded together, the enemy infantry pushed the retreating Swiss vanguard back towards the phalanx, where they found some shelter under the long pikes. The clash of weapons, the reports of guns and the screams of men were deafening. The pikemen did not break.

The cavalry milled around for a moment, then turned and rode off to reform. Then they charged again, now in a wedge-shaped formation, the front rank consisting of only seven riders. The Swiss gunners and crossbowmen had largely drawn off to each side of the phalanx to impede any flank attacks, but some were mixed in with the spearmen. Heinrich had survived the first attack without injury. After the second charge had been warded off successfully the first few rows of the phalanx presented a dreadful picture. The snow had been churned into a dirty slush by the hooves of the Burgundian cavalry, and in many places was stained red with blood. Everywhere the dead lay heaped, and among them wounded men bucked and writhed in their agony. Broken weapons and trampled pieces of armour testified to the force with which the two armies had clashed.

After some hesitation the left wing of Burgundian infantry began to move. Heinrich could see mounted men-at-arms trotting along the foot of the Jura with their squires and the *coutilliers*, who were armed with short javelins. They were obviously going to try to outflank the soldiers of the Confederation and make a rear attack, but they were foiled in this intention by the intelligent placing of the Swiss phalanx, which was drawn up close enough to the vine-covered slope to prevent their flank being turned. The enemy cavalry therefore turned to the south and burst against the right face of the phalanx with spears couched. Kneeling under the protruding hedge of pikes, Heinrich and his comrades shot bolt after bolt and bullet after bullet into the packed cavalrymen. Heinrich found his hands were shaking with tension, making him fumble over hooking the cranequin to his bowstring. It seemed to take an age to wind back the string and slip a new bolt into the notch, and always he kept glancing up to see if he was still covered by the unshakeable pikes. The powerful crossbow thrummed as he pressed the trigger, sending the stubby, wooden-fletched bolts smashing through steel and flesh with appalling force. Armoured men were hurled from their saddles with great rents torn clean through their bodies: horses crashed down in the fouled snow, their skulls split, pitching their riders into the merciless hedge of pikes and tripping those who followed. One rider leapt his horse straight over Heinrich's head and managed to keep his saddle as he landed amidst the pikemen; other men-at-arms tried to take advantage of the disorder this caused in the Swiss ranks, and urged their mounts forward into the gap. Heinrich, his quiver empty, jumped to his feet among the lurching horses and struggling men, and drew his sword. He struck at a knight who was trying to push past him, and reached up to grab the rider's sword-belt with his left hand in an attempt to drag him out of the saddle; but his feet slipped on a tangle of broken pikes, his elbow-armour became caught up in the

An illustration from the Chronicle showing the victorious Swiss soldiers plundering the Burgundian camp. The group on the right seem to have located the wine.

Burgundian's stirrup-leather, and he was pulled helplessly along as the horse kicked and reared its way deeper into the mass of soldiers.

From his perilous position Heinrich was horrified to see that the rider of the horse was snatching the staff of the Banner of Schwyz, which was jerking and swaying nearby in the struggling ranks. In the middle of the confusion a mighty blow from a halberd dropped the horse, and Heinrich was able to reach over and tear the spear on which the brown, blue and white banner fluttered out of the Burgundian's hand. At this moment a Bernese drove a spear into the knight's body with such desperate force that the point went clean through breastplate and torso and reappeared through his backplate. Only now did the Confederates realise that they had slain the Burgundian cavalry leader Ludwig von Châlon Chateau-Guyon.

In the pause which followed Heinrich crouched among the fallen and refilled his quiver with bolts from the belt of a dead comrade. For more than two hours attack followed attack at regular intervals; as soon as the Burgundian cavalry drew off to reform the artillery took the offensive once more. Then a strange lull fell over the battlefield. Quite suddenly, the infantry and the artillery in the enemy centre began to give ground, as if to invite an advance by the Confederates. The cavalry on both wings stood still. Exhausted and bathed in sweat, Heinrich and his comrades observed this manoeuvre warily; the outcome of the battle seemed uncertain. The captains hurried along the front on horseback, ordering ranks and shouting instructions to the pikemen.

This flagging of the spirits of both sides came to a sudden end at about three o'clock in the afternoon. To the roaring of the great *Harsthörner* of Lucerne and Uri the Confederates who had been encamped outside Vaumarcus, and who had been alerted too late to take part in the battle, now arrived on the field, in great distress that they had not been able to help their comrades sooner and determined to make up for it straight away. Bellowing the battle-cry *'Grandson! Grandson!'*

the newcomers hurled themselves at the enemy without waiting to form up properly: the tormented phalanx took heart once more, and the battle was won. In despair Charles the Bold tried to check the flight of his army, but the call of the great horns had chilled their hearts. In the midst of an escort of his most faithful companions, the Duke of Burgundy was the last to leave the battlefield.

I N the dying hours of the afternoon Heinrich and his comrades moved through the Burgundian camp above Grandson, overwhelmed by the sights that met their eyes. Never had they dreamed that such booty would fall into their hands. The tented camp looked like a great town, and many hundreds of baggage wagons and carts of ammunition were drawn up in laager. The tents of the princes and nobles were lavishly embroidered, and the abandoned pavilions were filled with gold coins, precious silver table-wares, jewelled ornaments, beautiful and ostentatious weapons and armour, and treasures of every imaginable kind. More than 200 cannon of the most modern type awaited the victors, and many of the bronze barrels bore the ducal arms of Burgundy. It was an incredible scene.

Although awed by their good fortune, Heinrich and his comrades determined to extract the maximum enjoyment from the situation. Laughing and singing, they strolled through the camp, celebrating reunions with their friends with draught upon draught of Burgundian wine. In their excitement they seized up the loading-chambers of Burgundian *Feldschlangen*, plugged the touch-holes, and used them as make-shift tankards. The soldiers of the Confederation moved into the tents which the enemy had left standing ready for them. Franz von Sins hobbled up, tethered, as usual, to the enormous shaggy bulk of 'Bary the Bold'. Franz had suffered a deep cut in the leg during the battle, but this did not lessen his enthusiasm for immediately searching out the lodgings of the camp-girls. A sutler told the crossbowmen, wonderingly, that there were over a thousand of them! He added the opinion that the oriental girls would prove to be especially intriguing.

With some difficulty Heinrich and his friends found their way to the crowded women's quarter; the Burgundian wine had had its effect on their sense of direction. At last, stumbling between the tents, they were brought up short. Standing in front of them, eyeing the Swiss soldiers roguishly and apparently unconcerned by the sudden change in their circumstances, were a large group of brightly-clothed girls. The delights revealed by their low-cut gowns caused many a worthy Confederate to goggle with excitement and forget his stern principles.[8] Franz von Sins enquired hoarsely how much their services might cost. They obviously did not understand German, but equally obviously understood the sense of the question, answering with rolling eyes and giggles. Then a Bernese came to the rescue of his German-speaking companions, and asked laughingly in French, 'Qu'avez-vous à offrir, mes dames?' To the delight of the soldiers one of the girls promptly flipped her skirt up over her shapely hips.

'*Grandson! Grandson!* . . .' murmured Heinrich, fumbling for his purse.

Charming illustration from the Schilling chronicle depicting the aftermath of the battle of Grandson.
'Qu'avez-vous à offrir, mes dames?'

NOTES

Of the persons named in this chapter, only Hans Bogner, Franz von Sins and Margaretha are fictional. A Lucerne armourer named Peter Bogner was of an age to have a son such as Hans at the time of the battle. A dog—whose name is not known—did indeed capture two spies in the manner described here; the incident has been brought forward in time, as it actually occurred in the *Schwabenkrieg* of 1499. Heinrich Elsener is known to have prevented the capture of the banner of Schwyz by Ludwig von Châlon Chateau-Guyon, exactly as described here.

1. Strategically placed in the centre of a troubled Europe, the eight old *Orte* or cantons of Zurich, Berne, Lucerne, Uri, Schwyz, Obwalden and Nidwalden, Glarus and Zug formed a loose confederation which only submerged their individual interests in the face of the most dangerous exterior threats. Generally on good terms with neighbouring powers, they made war on Burgundy, with the encouragement of the King of France and the Emperor, in the hope of checking the Duke's expansionist ambitions. Tyrolean counties impoverished by reparations after Swiss victories in 1468 had come into his power, posing a threat to the northern cantons which was enhanced by Charles' stated plans for a power bloc extending from Brussels to Milan.

2. The Burgundian artillery was considered to be the most modern of its time. The heavy bombards—the *Legstücke* and *Steinbüchsen*—were mainly used for siege work, and fired stone projectiles. The lighter and more mobile field artillery was composed of several types of gun, usually mounted on wheeled carriages. The calibre of the long field pieces, or *Feldschlangen*, ranged from about three centimetres to about fifteen centimetres; both breech- and muzzle-loading pieces were used. The *karthaune* or *cartoume* might be described as a very heavy field piece; the smallest-calibre pieces were termed *tarras* or *coulevrine*.

3. The following terms have been used in translation of the contemporary ranks: captain (*Hauptmann*), ensign (*Venner*), lieutenant (*Vorvenner*—senior to the *Venner*, who, it should be noted, only carried the banner when actually in battle), sergeant-major (*Wachtmeister*), sergeant (*Weibel*). The *Oberfeldhauptmann* was the overall commander of a force.

4. While the most powerful developments of the crossbow would not appear until spring steel came into general use, the horn bows of Heinrich and his comrades were terrible weapons, accurate and deadly at 200 yards range. At half that distance—and the bowmen would hold their fire until the enemy was within 100

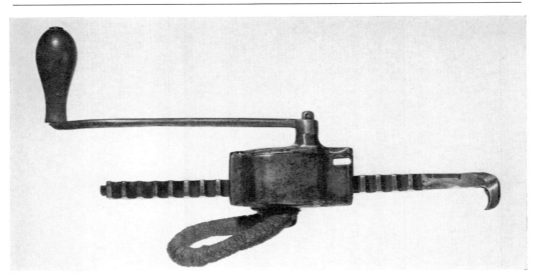

Above, a cranequin or crossbow winder, from the author's collection. Left and below, booty from the field of Grandson – a painted Burgundian shield and a bronze cannon with the ducal arms. (Schlossmuseum Grandson: Historisches Museum, Basle)

yards whenever possible—the short bolts could penetrate with ease any breastplate of the period. The contemporary handguns were by no means as accurate as the crossbow, and eighty to 100 yards was the maximum range at which they could be fired with any reasonable hope of hitting a man-sized target. The crossbow could be fired roughly twice in a minute, despite the fact that a mechanical device was necessary to wind back the string; the handgun's rate of fire was rather slower.

5. *Beimesser*: a small knife carried in an integral sheath on the front face of the sword scabbard.

6. Phalanx: for the sake of clarity this term has been used in translation of the original *Gevierthaufen*, for which there is no exact equivalent. The formation was a solid square block of men.

7. *Bise*: the local term for a cutting wind.

8. The victor's spoils after the battle of Grandson in fact included some 2,000 camp girls, many of them of oriental origin. The distribution of these unusual prizes caused some embarrassment. It seems that of all the confederated cantons only the men of Valais decided to take a number of the girls home with them, and these settled down in the French-speaking areas of the valley. Even today some Valais girls are born with a slightly oriental cast of feature, particularly about the eyes, testifying to the good fortune of their male ancestors four centuries ago.

SELECT BIBLIOGRAPHY

M. De Barante, *Histoire des Ducs de Bourgogne de la maison de Valois, 1364–1477*, Paris, 1826.

Carl von Elgger, *Kriegswesen und Kriegskunst der schweizerischen Eidgenossen im XIV, XV und XVI Jahrhundert*, Lucerne, 1873.

Eugen Frauenholz, *Das Heerwesen der Schweizer Eidgenossenschaft in der Zeit des freien Söldnertums*, Munich, 1936.

Johannes Häne, *Militärisches aus dem alten Zürichkrieg*, Zurich, 1928.

C. F. Landry, *Le Téméraire, dernier duc de Bourgogne*, Lausanne, 1966.

E. von Roth, *Die Feldzüge Karls des Kühnen, Herzogs von Burgund und seiner Erben*, Schaffhausen, 1843.

Diebold Schilling, *Chronik der Burgunderkriege*, Official Chronicle of Berne, 1483.

The Swiss Historical Research Book, Vol. 2.

Captured Burgundian material and works of art from the Burgundian court, Exhibition catalogue, Berne Historical Museum, 1969.

The author and publishers also wish to acknowledge their gratitude to Miss Beatrice Frei for translating this chapter from the original German.

6: Daniel Abbott

L ED by the hand of his seventeen-year-old daughter Jane, Daniel Abbott walked into the hall.

'Where is his certificate?' asked old Sir Thomas Lee, in his quiet, businesslike way; and the girl handed it to him across the long polished oak table. Sir Thomas opened the paper and began to read:

'*The humble petition of Daniel Abbott, of Great Missenden, humbly sheweth that in the beginning of the late warre he was a trooper in the service of the late Earle of Essex in a Regim[t] of Horse under Colonell Arthur Goodwin and continued in the same service for the space of three yeares and upwards and yr poore peticon[r] was in ye first fight at Worcester; at Kyneton where his horse was slayne under him and afterward he was made Corporall; at ye siege att Reading, ye fight in Chalgrove Feilde, after w[ch] yo[r] peticon[r] was made a cornett; ye releefe of Gloucester and ye fight at Newbery (1643) where he did receive a great cutt in the wrist with a sword. He was in Cornwall (1644) where he was wounded by a pistoll so that he hath almost lost the sight of his eyes, he was taken prisoner and lay languishing for the space of 10 or 12 weekes, whereby he is made unfitt for any bodily Laber and so unable to worke to gayne a livelihood for himselfe and two children, his wyfe being dead longe since of ye morbus campestris.*'[1]

'Arthur Goodwin . . .' mused a self-important looking man of middle age and florid complexion. 'He was not for the King, if memory serves me.'

'Your memory serves you better than you served your King,' cut in a dark-faced bearded gallant with a long white scar from eye to lip.

'Sir, y'are discourteous . . .'

'An' if I am?'

'This is nothing to the purpose,' interposed the Chairman quietly. 'Shall he have his pension?'

Edgehill, 1642

C APTAIN WALTER TYLER's troop was drawn up in the front line of Sir James Ramsey's wing—the left of the Parliamentary Army. The day was cold, and scarcely one man in a dozen had so much as a morsel of bread and cheese in his knapsack. Abbott, on his unruly charger 'Petard', was in the front rank on the right of Cornet Bland, who carried the orange-tawny standard of the troop. Ramsey's men were in position long before the Cavaliers came down the steep hill, and Daniel found the wait a trial. He and his fellows recollected only too clearly the way they had fled loose rein and bloody spur before Prince Rupert's men the last time they had been in action, at Powick Bridge exactly a month earlier. Perhaps, thought Daniel, these were the very troops forming up some 800 yards ahead of them now. (As a matter of fact, they were.) Daniel didn't like it, and his horse liked it even less—Petard kept dancing first to the right and then to the left. When he went left, as often as not he cannoned into Cornet Bland and was cursed for not controlling his mount. Daniel thought this very unreasonable, for at least half the horses in the troop were fidgeting about in the same way. When at last Daniel thought he had got control, Petard started walking backwards into the second rank, and Trooper Clarke, who was covering him, had something to say about that.

The great guns began to fire, and cannon-balls winged their way between the two armies. The Royalist guns were on the slope of the hill and their roundshot for the most part ploughed harmlessly into the earth; but there was a Parliamentarian cannon in the hedge not a hundred yards to the left of Tyler's troop.[2] Every three or four minutes it managed to send a six-pound bullet in the direction of Prince Charles' Regiment of Horse, and every time it did so Daniel's equestrian problem was renewed. It was the big bangs Petard didn't care for. When Royalist dragoons began pressing forward down some hedges on their left, and a sustained popping of carbines broke out, the unruly horse did not seem to care.[3] He was standing still when a Royalist gunner on the forward slope of Bullet Hill took aim at Cornet Bland's standard. The gun was a demi-culverin, a nine-pounder, and its crew, two of them sailors from the *Providence*,[4] had loaded it skilfully and laid it with care. The gunner laid his linstock to the touch-hole and the ball sped on its way, wandering only about a yard to the left on its journey towards 'Wat' Tyler's troop.[4] It hissed past the captain as he paced steadily up and down before his men; with admirable *sang froid* he ignored it—it was not his first time under fire. The ball sped a few yards further and with a ghastly thump smashed full into Petard's right shoulder, killing him stone dead. Daniel was hurled to the ground, by no means certain whether he was dead, wounded or gelded. The voice of Quartermaster Wood restored his senses.

'Get up, man! Look to your horse!'

Daniel stumbled to his feet: 'The horse is dead, Sir!'

'Well, take up your saddle, then; that's not dead, and it belongs to the State.'

Daniel stripped his horse of its saddlery and pistols, and looked in a bewildered way at the Quartermaster.

'Make your way to the rear, lad,' said Wood, and Daniel started off with his saddle on his shoulder. But he had not gone fifty yards when he began to dislike the tactical situation in which he found himself. Every now and then a cannon-ball from the Royalist Army rushed past him, but what really troubled him was the sight of Ramsey's second line some 200 yards ahead. *What happens to me if they charge?* he thought. Casting his eyes about him he perceived a hedge to the left flank of Tyler's troop; this, he thought, might prove the best place in which to spend the next quarter of an hour. It was not a bad appreciation.

He circled round behind the cavalrymen and reached the hedge, which was manned by musketeers of Ballard's Regiment.[5] He stuck his saddle in the hedge and began to peer about, trying to make out what was going on. To the left the firing was coming nearer, and this seemed to cause a certain amount of apprehension among the musketeers. Still, the gun now only about fifty yards off to his left was still banging away, and that was a good sign.

To the right Ramsey's cavalry, formed in solid squadrons, made an impressive sight to his inexperienced eye. When a single horseman spurred forward from one of these groups, Daniel could not imagine what it meant. Surely one man could not be so mad as to charge an army? He was not to know that Lieutenant Jon van der Gerish was deserting.

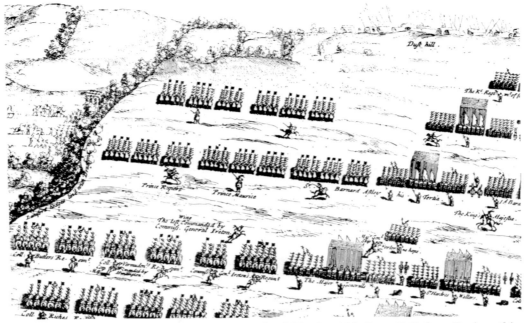

Detail from a map of the dispositions at the Battle of Naseby, 14th June 1645: from Rushworth's Historical Collections. *On the left are 'Hedges lin'd with Dragoons', with horse-holders at the extreme left. The relative positions of regiments of horse, musketeers and pikemen are interesting. (Mungeam Collection)*

Half a mile away the Royalist squadrons stood steady in the ranks, only the senior officers spurring to and fro, evidently giving their orders. Suddenly three of the Royalists' big guns went off together. Daniel saw the smoke, but the shots came nowhere near him. Almost instantly the trumpets began to sound, and Daniel, young soldier though he was, knew that they were about to be charged. The Royalists were walking towards them, the autumn sun glinting here and there on pot, breast and sword.[6] Daniel looked about him. The musketeers seemed resolute enough, and to his right he could see Ramsey's troopers making ready with their carbines. The gun to his left banged off again and he thought he saw a flurry in a Royalist troop a little to his right front. A hit? The popping on his left seemed to increase in volume. A sergeant came up, halbert in hand:

'Make ready . . . Hold your fire! . . . And who are you?'

'Trooper, Captain Tyler's troop—my horse was killed.'

'Make use of your carbine, then.'

'Who's on our left, Sergeant?' said a plaintive voice.

'You, watch your front, Cobb,' said the sergeant.

Daniel didn't think the musketeers were much encouraged by this contribution. Looking through the hedge he saw that the Cavaliers were coming forward in a knot. It seemed that Ramsey meant to receive them with a volley, for his men were sitting their horses carbine in hand. But no! Suddenly a whole troop advanced towards the enemy. A counter attack? That seemed good sense—but why not advance as a body? The single troop pushed on, the gap narrowing between it and the advancing Cavaliers. Daniel had been in one charge, at Powick, but he found it fascinating to watch one as a spectator. But just at the moment when he expected the two sides to set spurs to their chargers, the Parliamentarian troop began to act very oddly; the men began casting aside their orange-tawny scarves, and shooting their pistols into the ground.[7] What could it mean? Before Daniel could fathom Sir Faithfull Fortescue's treachery, the Royalists had broken into a canter and began to bear down on him at full speed. They were in looser order now, but they were still coming on. Daniel lay in the hedge, pushed his carbine forward, and took aim. A Cavalier came careering towards him on a fiery horse, long sword in hand, lengths ahead of his men. He was sitting down in his saddle, apparently ignoring the musketeers in the hedge with supreme contempt. Daniel could not have said whether it was this officer's arrogance or his menace which made him present his carbine at him. Desire outran performance, for though he took steady aim the ball wandered past the Cavalier and dug itself into the soil of Warwickshire. As Daniel rolled on to his back to reload he discovered that he was quite alone. The Musketeers had vanished. At that moment a ragged volley crashed out on his right—obviously Ramsey's front line had fired. To Daniel's disgust their salvo seemed to have had very little effect. He was not alone in this view, for instantly the approaching Royalists flourished their swords and set up an exultant cry. Without more ado Ramsey's men drew rein and took off in the direction of Kineton. Daniel Abbott was alone in his hedge—quite alone, and death seemed very near.

He crawled as far as he could into the hedge and sprawled face downwards; a few seconds later some rider on a wild horse cleared the hedge right above his head, and thundered off after Ramsey and his runaways. In the next few minutes dozens of Cavaliers followed this first dashing huntsman, but none spared a glance for a lone corpse in the hedge. As soon as the thudding landings ceased Daniel raised his head from his forearms and saw that the field ahead was empty save for a few corpses, human and equine. About a thousand yards away were big guns, now silent, and a troop of horse, evidently the staff of the Royalist right wing, if not the King himself. Away to his right he could see Royalist infantry—bluecoats— marching steadily forward not far short of the original Parliamentarian front line. It was a depressing scene, and Daniel could not at once see how he was to extract his valuable person from this embarrassing position. *What happens to rebels who got captured?*, he wondered. Death or capture seemed certain, and indeed might have proved so, had it not been for an old black horse galloping, riderless, in the wake of the Duke of York's Troop. His rider had been struck by a cannon-ball 800 yards from Daniel's hedge, and the horse had merely set off with the rest of the troop. Most of them took the hedge, but the old horse knew better. He had galloped half a mile and he reckoned he had done enough; he pulled up and began to nibble the grass about twenty yards from Trooper Abbott.

Daniel was not slow to take advantage of his opportunity. He stood up, took off his orange-tawny scarf, pushed through the hedge and walked slowly towards the horse, holding out his hand as if to offer it some delicacy. The old horse took no notice, and went on cropping the grass. Rather to his surprise Daniel was able to take hold of its bridle without any trouble at all. It had belonged to a Quartermaster, and had a good saddle; the pistols were still in the holsters, so Daniel was content to leave his in the hedge, but his carbine and portmanteau were more precious.[8] It took him a few apprehensive minutes to attach them to his new charger's saddlery. By the time he had mounted he was aware of enemy dragoons working up the hedge on his left, a few troops of Royalist cavalry rallying to his rear, and, for good measure, an infantry fight going on behind him and to the right. It did not occur to him to charge straight ahead, and left flank and rear seemed altogether too hazardous. He solved his immediate problem by riding away to his right. The bluecoats were far too occupied to pay him any attention. Free of his identifying sash he rode down behind them at a sharp trot, and whenever anyone looked at him he shouted 'God for King Charles!' and rode on. He was relieved to find that his new mount was a good deal better schooled than his last. Behind the centre brigade of the Royalist Foot a little silver-haired old gentleman in a group of mounted officers called out to him 'Hold hard, Sir!', as if he took him for some sort of messenger[9]; Daniel clapped spurs into his horse's flanks and it broke into a gallop, and fortunately the Cavalier officers had much else to attend to and let him go in peace. After half a mile his mount decided to take a breather and slowed to a trot, and Daniel could see that he seemed to have got clear of the King's army, except for scattered groups of horse and foot. He began to veer to his right, making for Kineton, the little town which had been Essex's headquarters the previous night. He trotted on, glancing around him and trying to weigh up the situation. To his right, amidst clouds of musket smoke, the infantry of the two armies were still locked together at push of pike. He could see little groups of wounded limping away to the rear, but nobody paid him much attention until rather suddenly he ran into a disordered body of some 300 horse. A senior officer, gorgeously apparelled, was raging up and down trying to marshal them. This gallant wore a rose-coloured scarf about his waist, and with a sinking heart Daniel realised that these were Royalists. In any case, their commander's language was so frightful that he could not possibly have been a Puritan.

'Where the black pox are *you* going?' cried the officer in an arrogant voice. 'Damn you, rally to your colours, Sir!'

Daniel took one look at the hawk-like countenance, avoided a fierce slash from the gentleman's long sword, and wheeled round to the rear of the nearest squadron. He pulled up behind the rear rank, and a rather calmer officer rode up to him.

'You're not one of ours. What's your regiment?'

'Prince Rupert's,' replied Daniel, who didn't know the names of any others.

'But they're on the right.'

'Well I know it, but this old fellow don't care for cannon-fire.' Daniel slapped his horse on the shoulder.

'Ran away with you, did he?' the officer laughed. 'Well, at least he didn't carry you off to the Cropheads!'

At that moment trumpets sounded. 'Here goes,' said Daniel's new acquaintance. 'Sir Charles is in fine voice, ain't he?'

'Sir Charles?'

'Lucas. He won't be content 'til he's routed the whole damned Roundhead army. I'll answer for you if you'll do as much for me.'

Daniel didn't quite understand this last remark, but he nodded and answered 'That I will.' The officer gave him a friendly smile.

'*Draw swords!*' shouted Lucas in a voice like a trumpet, and the line began to walk. Daniel could make out very little of what was going on, for three ranks of Cavaliers obscured his view to the front. At another sharp command the whole body broke into a smart trot; a hundred yards later the trumpets sounded the *Charge*, and the horsemen bounded into a canter. Soon the horses began to race one another and the squadrons began to break up into little groups. They were among foot now, broken foot, Roundhead foot, who were running towards Kineton. Daniel saw a group of three or four Cavaliers set upon a young ensign with a colour. In an instant the man was down, and a horseman was waving the trophy about his head. Daniel and his new friend sped past, neck and neck. The Cavaliers had spread out so much that he could see what was going on. To his right front the foot of the two armies, immersed in their own powder smoke, were still pushing away at each other, though there seemed to be a big gap near the middle of the line. Daniel began to pull at his horse's mouth, trying to get him into a trot.

'He's tiring,' he said to his eager friend's enquiring glance. A little knot of horsemen, obviously Roundheads, came up escorting a man on foot carrying a red colour.

'*Captain Smith, Captain Smith*,' cried a foot-boy, '*They are taking away the Standard!*' It was the King's great Banner Royal.

'If they do they shall have me with it!' cried Daniel's companion, and shooting Daniel a glance which clearly said *I expect your support*, he rode at the horsemen.

Daniel wheeled to his left and rode for Kineton, without waiting to see how Captain Smith might fare.[10] He was among Roundhead foot now; they were

A simple and crudely-fashioned trooper's 'pot', unlike the conventional English type in that it lacks provision for cheek pieces and has only a single face-bar. This helmet weighs 2 lbs. and is made from two pieces of metal with false lames scribed on the neck guard. (Mungeam Collection)

running as if the Devil himself were at their heels, and most had thrown away their arms. Daniel caught up with a young ensign who still had his colours.[11]

'What regiment are you?', he asked.

'Sir William Fairfax's—what's left of us,' the young man panted. 'Here, take this for me, I can go no farther.' He held up the colour so quickly that Daniel's horse shied, pitching him out of the saddle.

'Damn you for a fool!'

'I'm sorry,' said the wretched boy, giving Daniel his hand.

'Well, no bones broke,' conceded the trooper as he struggled to his feet. His mind was working fast. 'Give me your sash as well—I've lost mine, and if the Cavaliers see you with that on they'll slit your throat for sure.' He gave a horrid laugh, and without more ado the ensign unknotted his sash and gave it to Daniel, who had noticed that it was a silken one, much better than his own had been.

'Better give me your purse as well—they're sure to strip you if you're caught.' The purse was a heavy one. *This lad's a bit simple*, thought Daniel.

'My name's Otter, Ned Otter,' said his benefactor. 'Ask for me, if you get through safe.'

'That I will. Now hold my nag's head, while I mount.' He swung into the saddle and rode off, but this time he did not make for Kineton, but struck off for the west avoiding the floods of fleeing Roundheads and returning Royalist horse. He had a narrow escape once, when a broken troop of Cavaliers gave chase, but their horses were more blown than his, and dusk found him safe back at the farm near Kineton which had been Captain Tyler's quarters the night before. It was getting dark as he rode into the yard, where Tyler and Wood were examining a wounded horse. They looked up and peered at him.

'Who's that?' said the Quartermaster.

'Abbott, Sir!'

'I'd given you up for lost . . . His horse was shot, before they charged us, Wat.'

'Well, he seems to have come by another.'

'Aye, and a better one than I lost,' said Daniel, as he wearily dismounted. 'This one does what I ask him—Cavalier though he be.' The officers laughed.

'Don't tell us you've taken a colour as well,' said Wood.

'Not exactly, Sir, this one belongs to Sir William Fairfax's Regiment. Its bearer was a bit short of breath when I saw him last.'

'Ran, did they?' asked Tyler.

'Like conies.'

'Pox on them—but we didn't do much better,' said Wood.

'This colour, now,' said Tyler with a twinkle in his eye. 'See here, Charley, this puts rather a different complexion on the affair . . .'

'I don't see how.'

'You must be hungry, Abbott?'

'Starving.'

'Come into the barn, and bring the colour. Here, *you!* Take Abbott's horse, and see you feed him well and rub him down.' A trooper who had been looking on led Daniel's horse away, grumbling audibly.

'Another word'll cost you two dozen!' said Wood venomously.[12]

Once inside the farmhouse Tyler sat down in the inglenook. 'Fall to! There's bread and cheese, and a pot of ale for you—not much . . .'

'God bless you, Sir, the Lord Mayor's Banquet would not like me better!'

'You're right welcome . . . Now, listen here, Abbott. There's none of the Troop done better than you this day.'

'It was good fortune, Sir.'

'That may be, and it does you credit to say so, but hark. Mr. Wood here and I, and Corporall King, we've seen service before, and we was swep' away with the worst, pox take it! Now, this touches our honour narrowly, and though you know we're blameless, and I know it too, honour is a touchy thing 'mongst soldiers, and there are always kind friends to cry "Poltroon" if things don't fall out quite aright. You see that, don't you?'

'Why, for sure, Sir,' said Daniel, with his mouth full.

'Hmm . . .' said Tyler, pulling his nose, with a look of simple cunning on his honest red face. 'Now, touching this question of the colour, I am not one to tell a lie, but it might be as well if it appeared that it had been rescued by the whole Troop . . .'

'Mortuary' sword of the 1640s, single-edged and with wolf marks and the names WELMM TESSCHE *and* WEIRS BERGH *engraved on the 31½-inch blade. The guard bears crude masks, traditionally the head of Charles I. (Mungeam Collection)*

'That horse as I came back on,' said Daniel suddenly.

'What of him?'

'I like him. He's better than that unruly brute I had before. He's mine, ain't he? By the laws o' war, an' that?'

'That horse is fit for an officer,' broke in Lieutenant Knowles, who was none too well mounted himself.

'My mother,' said Daniel, inspecting his boots, 'my mother is a very God-fearin' woman, and a good pious Puritan woman as always brought me up to tell the truth . . .'

'That horse,' said Captain Tyler, glaring at his second-in-command with a look that would have shrivelled a less insensitive man, 'is yours, and I will carve the entrails out of any man, officer or other, who says different!'

'You're a gentleman, Sir,' said Abbott. 'And whatever you says, or whatever you desires, for my part it's as good as done.'

ON the morning of 24th October 1642 Old Robin, the Earl of Essex, drew up his army and faced King Charles once more. He had another brigade of foot and several troops of horse which had not arrived in time for the battle of the previous day; even so, his army made but a poor appearance. Some of the regiments of foot looked very thin, and those that had fled seemed to be even worse than those, like Denzil Holles' Londoners, who had stood to it manfully.

Captain Tyler paraded his troop at an early hour. He had had sixty-eight officers and men before the fight, and he still had fifty-seven of whom three were dismounted. He left these in quarters and rode to the rendezvous at the head of the rest. He still had his standard, more by luck than judgement, and that was more than many a troop could boast. Wood, no mean Quartermaster, had managed to feed both man and beast, and altogether the troop, for all that it had run on both the occasions it had seen action, cut a fair figure.

Sir William Fairfax sat his horse at the head of his men. He was in no sunny mood. He was enough of a soldier to realise that the Lord General would scarcely look with favour on his regiment, which was more than 200 short of the numbers it had mustered twenty-four hours earlier. He had ten companies still, with scarce a colour between them. He tugged at his moustache and cast baleful glances at his uncomfortable followers.

'Pamphlet warfare' came into its own in the 17th Century; both Royalists and Parliament issued numerous documents justifying their positions on various issues. The Trained Bands of London, in which many apprentices such as Daniel Abbott enlisted, were among the best troops of the early Parliamentarian armies.

Captain Tyler halted his troop in rear of Fairfax's Regiment and rode on alone to salute the colonel.

'I greet you well, Sir William.'

'Your's is the first cheerful face I've seen today,' said Fairfax, 'though God knows what you can see of cheer.'

'Have you an ensign named Otter, Sir William?'

'Ned Otter? Do you know him? He's missing, I think. Is Ned Otter back?' he shouted over his shoulder.

'No, Ned's still missing,' replied Major Paine. Tyler raised an arm.

'Lost, is he? And his colour with him, I doubt not?'

'I fear so.'

'Well, fear no more.' At this moment Daniel Abbott rode up, bearing the colour in his hand. Sir William was speechless for a moment. Then:

'Captain Rush, here's your colour back!' A stout, middle-aged captain came running up, his red face glistening with glee.

'My colour,' he gasped, 'my colour! Thank you, young Sir.'

'Thank my captain,' said Daniel.

'I do indeed,' said the red-faced one.

'Sir, I am grateful,' said Sir William. 'Though this beats all. I thought you were on the left. We heard all Ramsey's men had fled.'

'Some faster than others,' struck in Wood, who had joined the group, but before Sir William could probe this happy rescue more deeply his quick eye caught sight of an approaching cortège.

'Have a care!' he cried. The regiment stiffened in its ranks as the Earl of Essex halted and exchanged salutes with its colonel. The Earl's placid gaze fell upon Captain Tyler.

'Your place is on the left, I believe, Captain,' he said mildly. Before Wat could reply, Sir William intervened.

'An't please you, my Lord, the captain has just brought me one of my colours, which his troop, it seems, retook from the Cavaliers.'

The Earl looked faintly surprised. 'Were you not with Sir James Ramsey?'

'I was, my Lord.'

The Earl turned to a well-mounted officer who rode at his right hand.

'It seems that not all our left wing of horse disgraced themselves, Sir William.'

'I'm glad to hear of it,' the officer replied in a markedly Scots accent.

'Captain Tyler, I shall not soon forget this,' said the Earl with a polite bow, and passed on.

Tyler, Wood and Abbott rode back to the troop. The captain was beaming.

'The truth, Charley,' he said. 'The strict truth, eh?'

'It can't be denied.'

'Sir William Balfour's no fool. I'd rather have him for a friend than an enemy.'

'Beyond question.'

'Corporall Abney's sore hurt. He'll never ride with us again, Charley.'

'I doubt it, poor shrew.'

'Can you read and write, Abbott?'

'That I can, Sir. 'Prentice to a printer I was, Sir.'

'Then I think we lack a corporall no longer.'

1643

ABBOTT leaned against the barricade and peered diligently into the night, resting his carbine on the side of the country wagon that blocked the road and was secured by chains to posts dug into either verge. It was a fine June night, and he was not tired. This was just as well, for his fellow sentinel, Samuell Gleed, though as old a soldier as he, was one of the most useless men in the troop: idle, dirty, drunken and irresolute, he was the very type that Captain Oliver Cromwell had once described when he told Colonel John Hampden that most of his troopers were decayed serving men and tapsters. It was not a description that could be applied to Corporall Abbott. He was a cut above the average, and though not an unduly immodest man, after a year's soldiering he was well aware of the fact.

In the first place he had discovered that in action he was no more fearful than the next man. It is true that he had run with the best at Powick Bridge—but then he had been upon that unruly beast Petard. And it is true that his bowels had well-nigh turned to water when the ball from the Royalist demi-culverin had slain that poor beast stone dead beneath him at Edgehill. He would relive that moment too often for comfort before he died. But eight months had passed without any serious action and, as is the way with young men of twenty, his balance of morale had had time to get into credit.

When the war began Daniel had been one of the first to leave his name at the Guildhall as a volunteer. There was war fever in London that summer, especially among the apprentices. Most of Daniel's friends had gone into the foot, but he could ride—or thought he could; had he not once accompanied Mr. Roger Daniel to Cambridge and back?—and some instinct told him that war is more attractive if you do not have to wage it on your flat feet. But if wise in this, sweet reason had not really ruled his heart when he first drew the sword for the Good Old Cause. For one thing he was very near the end of his apprenticeship; for another, even as a trooper, he was not all that much better off financially, if only because his pay of two shillings *per diem* was all too often in arrears. His mother's attitude was helpful; she was deeply religious, detested the little Archbishop of Canterbury, and, thorough-going Anabaptist that she was, was proud to have a son in the army of the Parliament. His sister Meg, little shrew, cared little for religion and less for Parliament, and a great deal about an acne-spotted goblin who worked in Pope's Head Alley. She would have liked Daniel to stay at home and lend her support in the constant war with her mother. It was a war in which old Mr. Abbott, a man in his mid-sixties, played no part.

A year's soldiering had taught Daniel several things. He was now a practised and competent horseman, his muscles hardened by endless hours in the saddle. He was a match for most men with broadsword, pistol or carbine. There were only three professional soldiers in the troop—the Captain, Quartermaster Wood, and Corporall King—but Abbott had been diligent to learn anything they could teach him. There were very few in the troop who could read and write, and Daniel, who had gone out of his way to help the Quartermaster with his duties, felt that he had at least one good friend among the officers of the troop. Having been a corporall ever since the Battle of Edgehill, he looked forward to the day when he might too be commissioned. Most of Essex's original captains of horse had been gentlemen, entitled to bear arms, but one could not say so much of the more junior officers or of those in the foot. Daniel did not feel that he was being unduly presumptuous in casting himself for the role of quartermaster, or even cornet.

Still, he did not delude himself; he had at least one rival, Corporall Tom Blackford, whose sanctimonious soul was in harmony with the troop's psalm-singing lieutenant, Ralph Knowles. In truth the troop was a fine mixture of genuine Cockneys, Buckinghamshire husbandmen, and snivelling Brownists and Anabaptists. Daniel certainly did not reckon himself among these last, though his mother might have approved of them. He smiled to think how they would cast their eyes up to heaven if they knew how he meant to spend the early hours of 18th June 1643. His relief was due at midnight, and a soft feather bed awaited him—with the agile Jane Barton therein, and not for the first time. Jane was a witch, and there was an end on't.

Abbott's sharp ears heard footsteps coming down the road behind him. He stepped sideways and gave Gleed a warning kick. 'Stand to your arms!'

'Pox on you, corporall, let me be . . .' Gleed did not budge.

'Earn yourself two dozen, if you choose.'

The Parliament's hard bargain shambled to his feet just before Lieutenant Knowles stuck his long nose and drooping moustache out over the barricade. He seemed to be looking down the road towards Oxford, but he was also taking a good look at the sentries. The psalm-singing lieutenant had his faults, but idleness was not among them. He did not like Abbott, but he could see that he was fully accoutred—helmet, buff-coat, long boots and all. The wretched Gleed had elected to stand guard this warm night in his lousy holland shirt, albeit with baldric, carbine belt and lobster-tail helmet to set it off.

'Gleed, where's your buff-coat?'

'It's been stole, Sir.'

Oddly enough Knowles believed this no more than Gleed had hoped.

'Corporall, we will look into this in the morning.'

It was a good idea, doomed never to be put into practice. Corporall Abbott gave a suitable grunt, and the rounds went on their way. He watched as, with one of the troop's two trumpeters bearing a link,[13] the lieutenant retired to the house where the officers were quartered, the troop's standard projecting from an upper window to mark the headquarters, place of parade and alarm post. Gleed relapsed into torpor and Abbott resumed his vigil, smiling to himself at the thought that Knowles would not altogether approve of his relationship with Jane Barton. No doubt, if he could, the pious lieutenant would have her pilloried, ducked and whipped from the troop's quarters, a treatment Daniel had seen meted out to a 'camp-follower' at Coventry the previous August. Well, he would be discreet . . .

Gleed's snores may have spoiled the local acoustics; however that may be, riders suddenly loomed up from nowhere.

'Stand!' cried Daniel, but they came on. Their leader was practically touching the muzzle of his carbine when he pulled the trigger. Nothing happened—a misfire, curse it! The cavalier was pointing with his rapier and rapping out orders, and some of his men were dismounting to shift the barricade. Gleed, still half asleep, struggled to his feet, and out of the shadows someone lunged at the whitish shirt. A bubbling scream rent the night. Daniel swung the butt of his carbine at two men who were loosening the chain at his end of the cart; then, as the Royalists broke in, turned and ran up the street shouting 'Stand to your arms!' The Court of Guard was in a house a hundred yards away, exactly opposite the house where Captain 'Wat' Tyler was quartered. A few shots rang out, and at least one ball came near enough to make Daniel change course. He darted between two houses, paused, and looked back down the street. The Cavaliers had lit torches and he could see them plain. They had moved the barricade and were coming up the street, some mounted and some on foot. One or two were tossing torches on to the thatched roofs of cottages. With triumphant cries of 'God and King Charles!' they came surging towards him. Abbott ran.

It was not a question of panic, simply a tactical manoeuvre. The street between himself and the standard of his troop was far too unhealthy for him to entertain thoughts of rallying. He spared a thought for Jane, but she lived at the other end of the village and being, as he knew, a light sleeper, would have a few seconds start if the Cavaliers got that far. In truth, Corporall Abbott's most urgent thoughts were for his horse. Duke was picketted with several others in an orchard not fifty yards away, and Daniel had stowed saddle, bridle, holsters and all in a nearby shed where one of the several boys who followed the troop and helped with the horses was wont to sleep. As the sounds of conflict rose behind him Daniel ran to the shed. The boy was up.

'Quick! We are surprised! Saddle up! Where's my saddlery?'

'Here's yours, and here's the quartermaster's.'

'Bring that, too.'

They ran through the wet grass, and with desperate speed saddled and bridled the two horses. There were several houses on fire by this time, and shooting could be heard around the Court of Guard. There was a gate in the corner of the orchard;

as Daniel flung it open men ran down between the houses. One caught sight of the quartermaster's grey and set up a cry,

'There's some of 'em! Give fire!'

But Daniel and the boy were through into the field by this time, urging their mounts into a lumbering canter, and they did not draw rein until they reached the edge of the woods 500 yards away. Daniel dismounted and checked their girths, making much of the two horses, which did not seem to be unduly excited. Silhouetted against the burning cottages he could see scores of men on horses and on foot flooding through the village. He could hear shots and cries, but the noise did not seem very great. *They'd hardly find us here*, thought Daniel, but even as the thought crossed his mind he saw that men were running across the field roughly in their direction. *They must be some of ours*, he thought, but drew his sword nonetheless.

'We'd be safer in the wood,' muttered the boy. Daniel did not answer. He had heard hooves. A horseman was galloping towards them.

'Who's there?' he cried. As the rider veered towards them Abbott gripped his hilt. It was Tom Blackford, riding bareback but sword in hand.

'Who's that? Oh, it's thee, Abbott—who else is here?'

'Only Jake, but I saw others on foot . . . you passed them, did you not? Were they ours?'

'I don't doubt it. Over here! Over here, rally!' cried Blackford, as some shadowy figures passed a few yards away. Abbott rode up to them. Five or six breathless men clustered round him.

'Any of you armed?' asked Blackford.

'I've got my sword,' said a voice—rather a dubious voice, Daniel thought.

'Well, mount the grey,' said Blackford sharply. Jake slipped to the ground and rather to Daniel's surprise the trooper, a country boy named Hodges, mounted without argument.

'Come on!' said Blackford, and started back towards the house where Captain Tyler was quartered.

'What do you mean to do—storm the village on your own?' grumbled Daniel.

'We'll see,' replied the corporall. 'Are thee with me?'

'I wish I weren't' said Daniel.

The three of them cantered down the field and into the orchard, Blackford leading. A man ran across his path, then another.

'Follow, follow!' cried Blackford, and rode down between the houses into the main rode yelling like a fiend   A knot of Cavaliers came out of a house, propelling someone into the street. Duke ran straight into one of them and sent him staggering, and Daniel took a swipe at another, making his helmet ring. Blackford was still yelling—something about smiting Amalekites—and laying about him at the 'men of wrath' with his broadsword. Abbott and Hodges caught his mood.

Daniel turned Duke towards the barricade on the Oxford road; there were riders there in the shadows, beyond the white bundle in the road that had been Trooper Gleed. '*Run, run, we are betrayed!*' he shouted.

'Who's there?' demanded an officer-voice.

'For the King!' said Daniel quickly, adding for good measure, 'The Cropheads have fresh supplies—we are to fall back!'

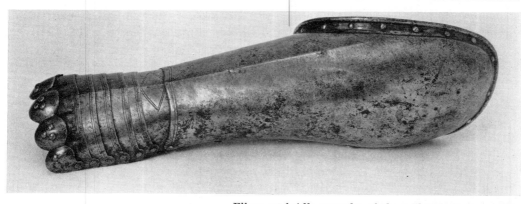

Elbow or bridle gauntlet of the mid-17th Century; this example lacks the finger-plates. A dent, possibly from a sword-cut, can be seen about half way along the central ridge. (Mungeam Collection)

'Pox take that! I will go with the last, and you shall stay with me! Hold hard, Sir!' But Daniel was past him.

It should not be supposed that Corporall Blackford's counter-attack changed the fortunes of the troop; still, it lost nothing in the telling. Captain Tyler was content to have held out, even at the cost of a dozen men and twice as many horses. Lieutenant Knowles was in raptures at his favourite's brilliant feat of arms, but Quartermaster Wood, who enjoyed his Troop Commander's favour in somewhat fuller measure than did the lieutenant, was not slow to extol Daniel's part in the affair. The recovery of his grey steed may have influenced him. For his part, Abbott could not conceal from himself that though he had played his part he had been somewhat eclipsed by Tom Blackford, whose 'madness'—ever a quality admired, if shunned, by the English soldier—was soon broadcast through the troop by Trooper Hodges.

THE sun was up long before 'Wat' Tyler led the remnants of his troop over Gilton Hill. A mile or so to the west he could see Prince Rupert's rearguard, to his front Colonel Mills' dragoons pressed in on the Cavaliers' heels. From every direction, and especially from that of the Earl of Essex's headquarters at Thame, troops of horse, and such officers of foot as had horses, were concentrating to avenge the previous evening's raid. Tyler was no pessimist, but it seemed to him that the gathering Parliamentarian force was scarce equal in numbers to Prince Rupert's brigade. It seemed that the dragoons agreed, for they were dismounting and lining a hedge, sending their horses to the rear. The cavalry were halting and forming a line. A man on a big horse, Colonel Dalbier, came down the line giving orders.

'Captain Crosse is on your right and Colonel Hampden is with him,' he shouted, but Daniel did not hear him; his place was in the rear of the troop covering the cornet. Tyler with his two trumpeters was on the right flank of the troop, and Lieutenant Knowles on the left. They were covered respectively by Corporalls King and Blackford. Quartermaster Wood posted himself a horse's length behind Abbott where he could see the whole troop. Tyler had brought his men forward at a sharp trot, and horses and men were glad of a rest. Duke had hardly caught his breath when, as was his wont, he dropped his head and began to nibble the lush meadow grass; Daniel let him.

Suddenly there was a volley of shots, and to his astonishment Daniel saw first one and then a dozen Cavaliers leap the hedge to their front coming towards them.

'Draw swords!' shouted Tyler in his high-pitched, breathless voice, 'March on!'

Out of the corner of his eyes Daniel could see the flanking troops moving forward. They were going to charge! The horses were all in a trot now. The trumpets sounded and they broke into a canter. There were shots ahead and suddenly Daniel saw that Cornet Bland was slipping sideways out of his saddle. He caught his reins with his right hand, letting his sword fall dangling on the wrist strap. Duke bounded forward, and as he passed the stricken cornet Daniel made a desperate grab for the staff of the standard, and held it. Duke was racing now, and soon they were in the front rank. Ahead was Tyler, making straight for the hedge on his swift charger.

The old man'll never jump that, thought Daniel, and instinctively began to pull away to his right. Cavaliers were coming up on both sides, and the troop was being squashed as in a vice. Tyler took a mighty leap and vanished over the hedge; three or four of the better-mounted followed him. A grey-bearded Cavalier of noble aspect took a thrust at Daniel, who managed to catch the blow on the standard pole. All this time Duke was galloping in a semi-circle towards Wapsgrove Manor and most of the men of the right division were doing likewise.

'Follow me!' shouted Quartermaster Wood, charging in the wake of his captain, but he took the hedge alone. Knowles and his division, or most of it, had wheeled left, and were having a mêlée with some of Lord Percy's Regiment—and getting the worst of it. Abbott, at the end of his wheel, caught a glimpse of this, but there wasn't much he could do about it, especially as most of the troopers were now ahead of him and going pretty fast. An officer with an orange scarf rode up, pistol in hand, and tried to rally them.

'Cornet! Cornet!' he shouted, 'To me!'

'It's Colonel Hampden,' cried one of the men. Daniel pulled Duke up and wheeled behind the colonel, and so did a few more of Tyler's troop. They were all mixed up now with some of Crosse's men who had followed Hampden. Before the few officers could get them into a decent line another wave of Cavaliers swept down upon them, led by a wild-looking officer who was spurring forward with a long rapier raised almost shoulder high. Hampden coolly raised his pistol and aimed at the enemy commander. There was an explosion, and to his horror Daniel saw that the pistol had disintegrated: where the colonel's hand had been there was now only a bloody, mangled stump. The Cavalier charged straight past, and in the mêlée that followed Daniel lost sight of both him and Colonel Hampden.[14] He felt sure that it could only be a matter of time before he lost seat, sword, standard, life and all. Pistols snapped on every side. Swordsmen wheeled about him, every blow seemed to be aimed at him, and several times he felt something hit him on the head or body. One fellow actually got hold of his baldric and tried to pull him off his horse. This was too much; sticking his spurs into Duke he bounded forward, the Cavalier hanging on just too long and pitching over his horse's ears as Daniel lost sight of him.

Daniel could hear himself urging Duke on, and the old horse set off towards Gilton Hill with the bit between his teeth. He passed loose horses and single riders, and even a few dismounted dragoons. They must have really run! Loosing the wrist-strap of his sword Daniel sheathed it, took the standard in his right hand, and began looking around for men of his own troop. They came dropping in gradually until there were a dozen or fifteen; as there was no commissioned officer among them they looked to Daniel for a lead. Two or three riderless horses came up and took their places next to others they knew. Several of the men and horses were wounded, and a bit of rudimentary first-aid was going on when Daniel suddenly spied far off a familiar figure. It was Tyler. He came circling in from the south, head bare and a bloody gash on his brow. Daniel marched the troop down to meet him.

'Your colours, Sir,' he said, with a touch of drama which may or may not have been unconscious.

'Yes, well, Abbott, you've done well again. I shall remember this.'

At this moment the quartermaster came thundering up, his horse utterly blown, and another, riderless, galloping alongside.

'Deuce take it, where's the rest of the troop?' demanded Tyler.

'Pardon me, Sir, Lieutenant Knowles is ta'en, Sir,' said Trooper Hodges.

'Here comes Corporall King,' put in another, as the gaunt veteran came down the line from another troop which had rallied on their right.

'Whose horse is that?'

'Why, it's Blackford's, Sir,' replied Wood. 'He jumped the hedge with me, but was pistolled just before you turned for home.'

'God rest him,' said Tyler, and several said 'Amen', but Daniel's first thought was that his advancement was the likelier for his rival's demise.

The fight in Chalgrove Field had been a rude experience coming as it did in the wake of a night alarum. The troop could not muster half its strength of the previous morning. Yet, as they rode back, they raised their voices in the metrical version of the 117th Psalm,

> *O give you praise unto the Lord,*
> *All nations that be*:
> *Likewise you people all accord*
> *His name to magnify . . .*

And by the time they reached Postcomb some very unlikely adventures were gaining currency. By a happy chance they met with a sumpter horse belonging to Crosse's Troop, and so far from returning it to its owner, they took it home with them. Captain Tyler was heard to utter an obscene opinion to the general effect that a bottle of wine and a good woman would put any soldier back on his feet inside twenty-four hours, and as the sanctimonious Knowles was no longer with them there was none to gainsay him. With the aid of Jane Barton and one of Captain Crosse's bottles Daniel was able to examine the truth of his captain's contention.

Nobody bothered to arrange an exchange for Lieutenant Knowles, and Quartermaster Wood proved a very adequate replacement. And needless to say the Corporall who saved the standard of his troop was promoted Cornet with effect from 18th June 1643.

1660

'GENTLEMEN, you have heard what the petitioner has to say. You have read his certificate. Do you wish to order that his pension be renewed? Ye'll recall that 'twas four pounds *per annum*.'

'Four pounds is a great sum,' said a little old gentleman in a cassock of a cut that had been fashionable in 1643.

'Four pounds would be better spent for a soldier of the King,' said the florid gentleman in the fashionable periwig.

'One who rode with *you*?' enquired the scar-faced gentleman, in a honeyed tone which contrived to be extremely offensive.

'The truth is, Daniel Abbott fought for Oliver and his crew,' said a bearded Justice, who looked low-born and was probably ill-bred, despite his good clothes.

'And which crew did *you* fight with?' asked scar-face, in a tone yet more offensive than before.

'We all know Major Woodville rode with Rupert,' put in a ferret-faced Justice whose eyes seemed to look out of one socket. Scar-face turned a baleful gaze upon him.

'I might have ridden alone, for your part,' quoth he.

'Gentlemen,' said the chairman, 'this is little to our purpose. How do you say? Shall Daniel Abbott have his pension?'

'Let the Roundhead work for his bread, say I.' This from the florid one.

'Spend the money on a good King's man,' said ferret-face.

And some said this, and some said that, after the way of Justices. But oddly enough scar-face, who had ridden with Prince Rupert, and the chairman, whose house had been burnt by Cromwell's troopers, thought for some reason that an old soldier who had lost his eyes at First Newbury was worth a pension of four pounds *per annum*, even if he had fought for Noll.

NOTES

The officers and men of Tyler's Troop are fictitious. Arthur Goodwin, Jon van der Gerish, Sir Charles Lucas, Captain (later Sir John) Smith, Captain Rush, and the named senior officers of the Royalist and Parliamentary armies are historical characters. A young officer of Parliamentary foot, Ned Otter, fought at Edgehill. Mr. Roger Daniel, bookseller and printer to Cambridge University, conducted his business from premises in Pope's Head Alley in the City of London. A quartermaster of Royalist horse was killed by a cannon-shot in the rear of the Duke of York's Troop at Edgehill on 23rd October 1642, and his mount ran free.

1. 'Worcester': he means the engagement at Powick Bridge on 23rd September 1642. 'Kyneton': the battle of Edgehill, 23rd October 1642. 'Cornett' or cornet: a junior officer of horse, of which one served with each troop of sixty men, whose task was to carry the troop colours. '*Morbus campestris*': probably typhoid fever.

2. Roundshot: the commonest form of projectile fired by ordnance during the Civil War. The diameter varied from eight inches (for a cannon royal) down to one and a quarter inches (for a robinet).

3. Dragoons: mounted infantry, who rode into battle but dismounted to fight. Carbine: musket with shortened barrel, intended for use by cavalry, and carried hooked to a shoulder-belt.

4. Demi-culverin: cannon with calibre of four and half inches. These weapons measured about ten feet in length and threw a nine pound ball over a range of 400 to 2,400 yards. Before the integration of the artillery into the army in permanent formations—from 1716 onwards—a 'master gunner' would be given a contract to raise and instruct a

train of artillery from civilians, and the train would be disbanded at the close of hostilities. Sailors from the fleet provided one of the few sources of trained gunners. Linstock: device for holding a piece of burning slow-match carried by artillerymen. They were often fitted to a shaft with a point at one end so that they could be used as weapons in close fighting.

5. Musketeer: a soldier equipped with a matchlock musket, firing a three-quarter-inch ball. The heavy four or five-foot weapon was supported on a rest while being aimed and fired. During the lengthy process of reloading musketeers were protected by bodies of pikemen, the two types of unit often being placed together in the battle line. Ballard's Regiment: a unit raised in Buckinghamshire by Thomas Ballard. He commanded a brigade at Edgehill, in the left rear of the Parliamentary army.

6. Most cavalrymen on both sides wore breast and back plates over a buff coat —a thick oxhide garment tough enough to protect the wearer from sword-cuts. A helmet of the burgonet type, with a pivotted face guard of one or three bars and a neck guard, often of laminated plates (thus 'lobster-tail pot') was common. Elbow or bridle gauntlets were frequently worn; these protected the left arm, so that the rider did not have to release the reins to avoid a cut at that arm. Musketeers did not generally wear armour. Pikemen wore substantial breast plates with plate skirts and broad-rimmed helmets, usually referred to as pots.

7. With certain exceptions, uniforms *per se* were not usually worn at this period, and the various regiments and brigades were distinguishable only by coloured sashes and scarves. As this chapter makes clear, such scarves were often the only immediate means of identifying friend from foe.

8. Pistols were carried in holsters on either side of the horse's neck at this period; the 'personal' holster did not appear until the turn of the 18th and 19th Centuries. Pistols of both wheel-lock and flintlock type were used during the Civil War, although the latter were not common and their issue was probably governed to a large extent by the financial means of the individual or his commanding officer.

9. This was Sergeant-Major-General Sir Jacob Astley.

10. Captain John Smith succeeded in recapturing the Banner Royal, and was subsequently knighted.

11. Ensign: the infantry equivalent of a cornet of horse—a junior officer who carried the colours of a company of foot, usually around 100 strong.

12. Wood was threatening the trooper with two dozen lashes. Flogging 'at the triangles'—frames of wood, or tripods of pikes lashed together—was the standard punishment for military offences in the British army until the mid-19th Century. The cat-o'-nine-tails was the normal instrument, and was traditionally wielded by the unit farriers.

13. Link: torch of tar-soaked wood.

14. John Hampden (1594–1643), one of the architects of the Parliamentary rebellion and a patriot respected by Royalist and Roundhead alike, died a few days after this incident, at Thame. Some sources maintain that he was wounded by two pistol balls in the left shoulder, but the version quoted here is supported by the fact that when Hampden's body was exhumed during the 19th Century by Lord Nugent—a distant descendant—the right hand was found to be missing. His pistol would have been loaded by his servant, and it is not hard to imagine how an inexperienced man might have over-charged the weapon in the heat of battle.

SELECT BIBLIOGRAPHY

Godfrey Davies, *The Early Stuarts*, Oxford University Press, 1959.

Sir Charles Firth, *The Regimental History of Cromwell's Army, Vol. 1*, Oxford University Press, 1940.

Col. H. C. B. Rogers, *Battles and Generals of the Civil Wars*, Seeley, Service and Co., London, 1968.

Frederick Wilkinson, *Battle Dress*, Guinness Superlatives, Enfield, 1970.

Brig. Peter Young, *Edgehill 1642*, Roundwood, London, 1967.

7: Louis Ménade

PRIVATE Louis Ménade eased the strap of the clumsy pack from his shoulder, stretched his aching back, and leant his Charleville musket against the bole of a tree; it gleamed with care, in sharp contrast to the rest of his equipment. With a groan and a chorus of creaking joints he lowered himself to the ground. It had been a long, hard march, and his equipment seemed to grow heavier and more cumbersome with each footsore mile. Louis was into his thirties now, no longer a youngster by the standards of his century, and a harsh life was beginning to take its toll.

He lit his pipe, watching his companions as they spread themselves along the edge of the forest road. *Les Compagnies Franches de la Marine*, the Colony troops[1]—for what they were worth. Their faces were strained with fatigue; some were marked with the pox, some scarred by old injuries, some blotched with insect bites, and all were haunted by the rumours which follow a retreating army. Their grey-white frock coats and blue waistcoats and breeches were patched and travel-worn. Their *mitasses*, the coarse trade-cloth leggings cut in Indian fashion and worn in place of gaiters, were mottled in places where the blue dye had run; some were given a flash of colour by Indian beadwork thongs. Most of the company had long ago lost the black cockades from their battered tricorn hats, soaked off

Soldiers of the Marine Companies. Left, winter campaign dress, with blanket coat, woollen cap and sash, and Indian leggings. Centre, full parade dress, the hat trimmed with false gold and a black cockade. Right, summer campaign dress, the white coat discarded. The sword was often replaced by a hatchet, the gaiters by Indian leggings. (Drawing by Gerald Embleton.)

in a storm or whipped away by a clinging branch, and had replaced them with feathers, or a hank of ribbon, or even bunches of leaves. They wore moccasins in place of boots, and most carried a spare pair tucked in their packs or under their belts; the damp ground rotted the deerskin quickly, and to be caught unshod in the forest was dangerous. The men of the company carried only a minimum of equipment. Their spare clothes and few personal trinkets were bundled into shapeless knapsacks of heavy linen, tied around and with a shoulder strap passed under the flap. A waistbelt supported the socket bayonet, and the hatchets and tomahawks for which they had thankfully exchanged their issue swords, and the leather cartridge-box with twenty-seven loads for the flintlock musket hung on the right hip from a shoulder belt. Some carried canteens of wood, some simply a hollowed gourd on a length of cord.

Down on the lake a flotilla of boats was on the move, full of French soldiers, and far out a line of canoes, paddles flashing in the sunlight, glided swiftly across the dark water. To the south a great pall of smoke drifted across the sky, picking up the colours of the sun, now strengthening as it dipped towards the mountains to the west. Monsieur Bourlemaque, the French commander, had fired the magazine at Ticonderoga before abandoning the fort to General Amherst's British column.[2] Serve the bastards right. . . .

Louis reached for his wooden canteen, fumbled the plug out and took a long pull of *sapinette*—spruce beer. He wiped his moustache with the back of his hand, and smiled as he shook the canteen. Nearly full. How many gallons of the stuff had he drunk since—when was it? January? February, 1756? It seemed much longer than that. He puffed a glow into his pipe and exhaled the blue smoke in slow clouds. They had enlisted at St. Jean, he and old Jacque Prideaux, both over four foot ten and with their teeth—the only conditions of enlistment. Poor old Jacque . . . had his throat cut with a butcher's knife, just by the sawmill at Ticonderoga . . . found him sitting there next morning, with the top of his head gone. It was hard to reconcile that fate with his memories of Jacque back in the days when they had traded for furs in the high country. To think of one of Rogers' Rangers buying himself rum with old Jacque's scalp . . . It all seemed so long ago.

He closed his eyes and leant back against the tree. The last rays of the sun were throwing long shadows out across Lake Champlain. Voices carried by a gentle breeze came faintly to his ears, and merged with the rustling of the leaves overhead as he drifted into sleep.

L OUIS MÉNADE was born in 1724 in a small farm on the banks of the Richelieu River. Around 1670 the land along the river had been divided into large seignioral grants among the officers of the Carignan Regiment, and the settlements still carried their names—Sorel, Chambly, Contrecoeur, Vercheres. They in turn granted out strips of land to their disbanded soldiers. These *Grands Seigneurs* established a feudal system that preserved an element of French aristocracy in Canada, but in many cases the feudal lords were as poor if not poorer than their vassals. The practice did have the advantage of establishing a fairly well organised system of settlement, and provided a ready-made militia in moments of crisis.

Grandfather Ménade, one-legged after the Iroquois wars, had dragged the tree stumps from the ground and exhausted the last of his strength clearing the land.[3]

His son, Pierre, had turned the land into a self-supporting farm, and with a little speculation in the Indian trade had achieved a modest prosperity. He had great hopes for his son, Louis, and had put him into the hands of the Jesuits to be educated. Pressure from the priests and from his parents, who wanted their son to go to the Jesuit College in Quebec, produced a rebel. When he was fourteen years old young Louis packed a bundle, joined a fur brigade at Trois Rivières, and disappeared into the far West.

The bush rangers—or *coureurs du bois*—had been a thorn in the side of New France for years. To escape the rigid controls of the Councils, the Seignorial system and the priests the young and the vigorous had deserted the farms for the beaver trade. The free life of the forest trails was draining the depressed and under-populated settlements of their best blood. Edict after edict was directed against them. Fur trading was forbidden without a licence. When this failed, they were threatened with branding and life imprisonment in the galleys, but the laws were impossible to enforce. There were big profits to be made in the fur trade, and while Governments threatened and priests ranted, merchants and gentlemen grew fat on their efforts, and a chain of forts followed their routes across the Great Lakes and down the Mississippi. (In the bleak wilderness of New France, the waterways were the roads and life-lines on which the sparse settlements depended.)

Montreal was Sodom and Gomorrah to the Jesuits when the *coureurs du bois* returned after a year or two in the wilderness. Outlandishly dressed in fringed buckskin and tattooed and painted like Indians, they rioted and brawled for as long as their beaver skins lasted. The inhabitants of Montreal locked up their daughters and opened their shops to sell rum. Stripped to breech-clout and moccasins and greased with bear fat, these wild men of the woods sprawled in drunken oblivion outside the taverns; with long , unkempt beards and feathers stuck in their matted hair, they fought and gambled and drank their hard-earned profits away.

It was said that two years in the forest spoiled them for civilisation forever; certainly their way of life brutalised them, and many degenerated and became more barbarous than the Indians with whom they had lived. For the most part, however, the *coureurs du bois* were simply a reckless and irresponsible rabble, despised by the farmers, used by the merchants and tolerated by the authorities. In time of war they were invaluable.

For six years Louis Ménade roved the Great Lakes and the rivers of the Ohio Valley. He knew the forest and he knew the Indians. At seventeen he took a wife among the Scioto Shawnees, a step which gave him the only really idyllic time of his life. He called his girl wife Annette, after his mother, and she followed him with a simple animal-like devotion. Her gentleness bewitched and bewildered him completely, and he revelled in this, his first taste of manhood. He took her with him to Fort Michilimackinac, the fur-trading centre on Lake Michigan, and within two years she died of smallpox. There had been many women since, all Indian. He had no experience of white women at all, and had never managed to form any deep attachment after Annette's death.

On his twenty-first birthday he got himself tattooed, an act he had regretted ever since. Among the *voyageurs* tattooing was both an act of initiation and a trial of endurance, and they all carried crude tattoos of animals or plants on their arms and bodies. The symbol was pricked out with a needle and then powder was burned in the holes to print the design into the skin. Unfortunately both Louis and the tattooist were drunk, and all that emerged from the long and painful ordeal were unidentifiable and disfiguring scars on both forearms.

In the autumn of that same year, 1745, news of the fall of Louisberg reached Michilimackinac. Until then the war with England, which had begun the year before, had seemed a long way off, but now the Great Lakes forts buzzed with rumours of an English invasion of Canada. With the whole of Canada in a state of alarm Louis and a friend, Jacque Prideaux, packed their belongings in a canoe and set out for Montreal. When they reached the St. Lawrence River settlements they found the whole countryside up in arms. Louis felt the need to be with his family in this moment of crisis. He had hardly given them a thought in the years that had passed since he had left home. Once or twice, in moments of maudlin sentiment induced by an excess of rum, he had wept a silent tear for them, but now he felt a strong bond. He was harshly disillusioned. He found a farm run by his younger brother, whose shrewish wife and brood of unkempt children were openly hostile to his arrival. His father was dead and his mother grown hard and embittered. There was no place for him there.

There was a coldness in his personality from that day, a hardness about the eyes that discouraged friendship.

All along the St. Lawrence the citizens were under arms. Indians from the missions were arriving daily at Montreal: Abenakis, Iroquois from Sault St. Louis and the Lake of the Two Mountains, Algonquins of the Ottowa, and wild, painted savages from the high country. The partisan leader, Marin, was recruiting among the *coureurs du bois* for war parties to raid the English settlements. Louis and Jacque Prideaux had their first taste of warfare in the raid on Saratoga on 28th November 1745. It was hardly a fight. Five hundred French and Indians fell upon the sleeping hamlet in the dead of night. All hell broke loose as flames from the fort, mills, barns and houses lit up the surrounding countryside. The screams of women and children mingled with the blood-curdling yells of the Indians as pathetic bands of settlers in their night clothes were herded from their burning homes. Louis watched in horrified fascination as a group of Indians, nightmarish in the orange glow of the burning buildings, prodded an old man into an hysterical dance with their knives before breaking his neck with a war club and tearing off his scalp. They left thirty dead in the ashes of the settlement and marched a hundred prisoners back to Montreal to be exchanged or ransomed.

All through 1746 the war parties roved the English settlements. Louis knew little of the real course of the war. He paddled canoes along the great waterways, and marched for days through the dark forest to send a few grain barns up in flames. He grew accustomed to the terrible screams of the prisoners as they were put to the torture by his Indian allies. He watched with a growing contempt the courtly manners of the French noblemen who led him. To the aristocracy war was a game. The French nobleman doffed his hat to the captured British officer, but remained unmoved by the sight of ten common soldiers hung by their feet in the trees to be tormented to death by the so-called Christian Indians from the Mission at St. Francis.[4] At night as they sat smoking their pipes around the camp fire, Louis would address his half-formulated thoughts to Jacque Prideaux. His friend would shrug his shoulders.

'But what can you do, mon ami? It is the way of things.'

His total acceptance helped Louis to dismiss the disquieting thoughts.

A French 'bush-runner' (left) with a group of Indians. Next to the Frenchman is a mission Indian in semi-European dress with an officer's gorget, talking to two Miamis from Lake Michigan. In the background are two Swegache Iroquois. (Drawing by the author.)

'It is the way of things. Some men lead—others follow.'

When the war ended it came as a surprise to Louis Ménade. These things were decided in England and France. Canada had no further need of him; he was paid off.

The two men drifted back into the fur trade, but the old way of life had lost its attraction. Louis had grown used to taking orders—it simplified life. His enthusiasm for the freedom of his younger days had gone. The Indians at Michilimackinac were degenerate, or so it seemed to him. More and more of them wore odds and ends of European clothes, and traded anything they could lay their hands on for rum. Only the Nations of the far West, those who had the least contact with the white man, retained their proud and arrogant bearing and dressed with barbaric splendour. The Indians of the trading posts seemed to be drifting into apathy and squalor.

There were, nevertheless, moments of great joy. The rhythm that vibrated through a master canoe as the *voyageurs* plunged their paddles deep, catching their timing from a song: the great encampments on the plains of the far West: the clear, biting mountain air of the high country. . . . But Louis found his mind continually wandering back to the farms along the St. Lawrence River. On winter nights, as he lay curled close to the fire in a buffalo robe and felt the dull ache in his bones, he found himself thinking of a fireside in a warm log cabin. As he lay in the arms of a greasy squaw in some smoke-filled and stinking lodge, he dreamed of a plump, rosy-cheeked French woman in a clean white apron, baking bread. He sought oblivion in the rum bottle.

One winter's night in a tavern at Detroit he listened to a group of soldiers talking wistfully about the land grant they would receive at the end of their service, and of the war that had once again broken out between England and France. Louis was quiet for several days afterwards, and then, his mind made up, told Jacque of his plans. His friend's reaction was predictable. With a shrug of his shoulder he said, 'Fine. I'll come with you.'

Three weeks later the two men enlisted in the Marine Regiment at St. Jean. Reinforcements for the regiment were slow to arrive from France, and it had been necessary to fill many gaps in the ranks from among the Canadians. The French Colony troops were contemptuous of the new recruits, but on the whole their sense of superiority was good natured.

When Louis Ménade was issued with his equipment he had more material goods than he had ever possessed in his life. One overcoat, one blanket, one woollen cap, two cotton shirts, one pair *mitasses*, one pair breeches and two pairs of drawers: two hanks of thread and six needles, one awl, one tinderbox, one butcher's knife, a comb, a worm and a tomahawk: two pairs of stockings, two Siamese knives, one pair of mittens, one waistcoat: two pairs of deerskin shoes, one dressed deerskin, two portage collars, one drag rope. . . . Jacque was bewildered by so many possessions and declared it impossible for any man to carry that much equipment around with him, but in the weeks of daily routine that followed he learned to fold his blanket and fill his knapsack, and waistbelt, canteen, bayonet and musket became merely an extension of himself. Even the impossible precision of arms drill became automatic.

For the first few months of his service Louis Ménade worked on the new road between La Prairie and St. Jean. It was a welcome task; due to the shortage of workmen the soldiers received extra pay for their labours.[5] After the constant uncertainty and occasional near-tragedies of the forest life, Louis basked in the unaccustomed luxury of regular and varied rations—biscuit, salt pork or cod, dried peas, and occasional fresh vegetables from the gardens of the settlements. In September 1756 Louis's company was ordered to Fort Carillon on Lake Champlain, and joined a convoy of *bateaux* taking men and provisions to the fort.

Fort Carillon, commenced the previous year, was situated at the head of Lake Champlain on a peninsula pointing south between Lake Champlain and Lake George. The unique position of the peninsula, called by the Indians Ticonderoga, had made it a position of strategic importance. Lake Champlain was the gateway to Canada, and Ticonderoga was the gate.

The site of the fort was a hive of activity. Men of the La Reine, Languedoc and Royal Roussillon Regiments were hauling timber and digging ditches. Troops of the Guyenne and Bearn Regiments were laying out roads. Smoke spiralled upwards from the campfires of Indians gathered from the far-flung corners of French Canada, and above the clamour came the monotonous and broken ring of axes as men of the Marine Regiment cleared the forest from around the fort. Every day two well-armed boats left the camp to watch the movements of the enemy on the lake, and small parties of Canadians and Indians trotted off into the forest to patrol the approaches to the fort and reconnoitre the British lines at Forts William Henry and Edward, south of Lake George.[6]

With the approach of winter the forest around Ticonderoga changed colour dramatically. The landscape changed first to a drab green and then to rich gold and red. Winter quarters assignments for the battalions were announced, and Louis heard with some relief that his company of the Marine Regiment would stay at Carillon. The regular battalions were to start leaving for their various destinations on 1st November, although a picket from each of the La Reine, Languedoc and Royal Roussillon would remain, leaving a garrison of 150 regulars, 100 Colony troops and about fifty workmen. M. de Lusignan, one of the best of the Colony troops officers, would be in command.

On 26th October Louis found himself posted for duty on the schooner taking the Marquis de Montcalm to St. Jean. When he returned winter was closing in rapidly. It began to snow in December, and the ships were frozen in as the lake iced over. The men passed their free time skating on the lake. Patrols and guard duty became an agony as the temperature dropped steadily. The forest, blanketed in snow, was eerily silent; a sudden fall of snow from a tree or the cracking of a branch under its weight would send the patrol plunging for cover. Their nerves were stretched taut by the enemy activity around the fort. In spite of the harsh winter conditions they found tracks of enemy patrols around Carillon every day, and once the remains of a meal eaten during the night within its very defences. M. Lusignan was much troubled by the activity of the enemy rangers.

In February Louis, together with fourteen other men from his company, was ordered to Fort St. Frederic for supplies. They were up at first light harnessing the horses to the sleighs for the journey. Sergeant Lebecque was squinting at a supply list in his mittened hand, and urging his men to get the sleighs moving. It was bitterly cold, and a mist shrouded the surrounding hills. The company paraded and, stamping and blowing warm breath into their mittens, set out over the frozen surface of the Lake. There were two men to each sleigh, and their orders were to keep the sleigh ahead in sight and not to close up. Louis' companion, a stout soldier named Martel, was a Frenchmen who had come over with several companies of Marines from France, the previous year. He talked incessantly about his native land, and found it hard to accept the fact that Louis had been born and bred in this bleak and barbaric wilderness. He was leading the horse and Louis followed a few paces to the rear of the sleigh, half listening to the monotonous monologue. Suddenly shots crashed out ahead of them. They were the fourth sleigh in the convoy and they could only see one of the three sleighs ahead of them—the other two were swallowed up in the mist. The sleigh in front of them suddenly turned. More shots crashed out, and Louis saw the horse and the two men go down. Just behind the fallen men running figures emerged from the mist, and Louis saw from their dress that they were not Frenchmen. Martel squealed with fright and clambered on to the horse. Louis began to run. A volley of musket fire thumped out behind them and Louis turned to see Martel pitch from the horse. Less than a hundred yards away a running figure was closing fast. Louis dropped to one knee and thumbed back the cock of his musket. The English ranger had obviously just fired and had had no time to reload. He was coming on fast with his bayonet. Louis waited, squinting along the barrel of his musket. The muffled, fur-capped figure stopped, and for a moment they looked at one another, the ranger hesitating— he could do nothing but hope that Louis would miss. With a yell he charged forward again, and Louis pulled the trigger; there was a puff of smoke from the priming, a split second of hang-fire while Louis's brain cringed with panic, and then a crashing report. The dense grey-white smoke blotted out everything in front of him, and it was only when it drifted away that Louis saw the ranger sprawled on his back in the snow barely a yard from the muzzle. Thank the good God it hadn't misfired. . . .[7]

He sprang to his feet and began running, sheer terror giving him extra speed. Behind him he was dimly aware of running shapes, and expected every moment to hear the shot that would bring him down. But they did not fire. A single shot from quite close reverberated across the lake as one of his pursuers stopped long enough to reload, but the heavy ball whistled past some distance away.

When Louis dared to cast a glance back over his shoulder there was no one to be seen. He dropped to his knees, panting like a cornered animal, and then set off at a steady pace. No one followed.

The other sledge had already arrived when Louis reached Carillon. M. de Basserode was parading about a hundred men on the road. M. de Langlade, an Ensign of the Marine Regiment, was assembling an assorted group of Indians, and called Louis over when he saw him. He was ordered to fall in. M. d'Astrel came out on to the road, cursing that there were no snow shoes, followed by the Commandant and M. de la Granville of the La Reine Regiment. Granville saluted the Commandant, who stood on the road and watched the column move off.

Louis fell in beside M. de Langlade, who questioned him about the sledge ambush. Although no one had said as much to him it was obvious to Louis that they were going after the ambushers. M. de Basserode led the party deep into the forest and ordered them to rest. The going was bad. The powdery snow was four feet deep in places and a rain the previous night had frozen it over with an icy crust. After an hour the soldiers were ordered to move again. After a short march they stopped once more, and M. de Langlade reappeared with some of his Indians. His face was glowing from his exertions in the bitter cold. Louis sat huddled in his blanket coat and watched as the officers conferred over a map. He had learned that in the Army a soldier always waited. Sooner or later someone would give him some orders without giving any reason, and he would obey, without asking for one. Langlade called the men to order and they moved off to a high ridge under his direction. They were told to spread out and take cover. Louis positioned himself in the roots of a stunted tree and with the calm patience of the professional hunter methodically prepared for action. Until this moment he had not had a chance to reload his musket, an omission which he quickly remedied. He pulled the cock back to the half-cock position, pushed the frizzen forward to expose the priming pan, and carefully scraped away some fouling around the touch-hole with the point of his knife. Taking one of the stiff paper cartridges from his case he tore off one of the twisted, thread-tied ends in his teeth and spat it into the snow. He carefully tipped a small measure of the black powder into the pan, and closed the combined frizzen and pan-cover. Then he set the butt on one of the tree-roots at his feet and tipped the rest of the cartridge—powder, ball and paper as well—down the barrel, and rammed it tightly home with the rod which he pulled from its pipes under the barrel. He settled himself again, with cartridge-box and ramrod ready to hand, and as an after-thought replaced the rather worn flint in the jaws of the cock with a new one from his pocket, a fine dark one he had been saving up.

About half an hour after they had arrived on the ridge a runner came along the line. Louis laughed aloud when he saw it was Jacque. His friend punched his shoulder with a surprising show of emotion.

'I thought they had got you with the sledges.'

'Nearly, old friend, nearly.'

'And now we are going to get them, eh? No pipes and no noise, that's the word.'

A group of Rogers' Rangers. Left, winter campaign dress. The rest wear green uniforms with buck-skin additions; the green clothing was issued in 1758. In the background, Rogers and another officer confer with a chief of Stockbridge Indians, a community which provided him with scouts and warriors. Many British officers served with the Rangers for a term to gain experience of forest warfare. Scots bonnets were popular among the Rangers. (Drawing by the author.)

He waved, and Louis watched him floundering off through the deep snow as he passed the word along. He eased himself into a comfortable position and turned inwards to his thoughts.

'They'll be hours yet—and us with no snowshoes. Someone will get it in the neck for that. Still, who'd have expected M. de Lusignan would send practically the whole of the garrison out of the fort? If those English rangers attacked Carillon now they could probably take it.'

It was about three in the afternoon when the enemy advance scouts came into view. Langlade, looking apprehensively at the Indians, signalled to let them pass. Shortly afterwards the main party came into view, bunched together like a mob of raw recruits. M. de Basserode raised his arm as the enemy came abreast, and as he dropped it a great volley crashed out, spilling a dozen of the enemy in the snow. The silent forest erupted with the roar of musket fire and the war-cries of the Indians. As the order came Louis fixed his bayonet, and plunged down the slope as the whole line charged forward. The stricken enemy fell back; they had the advantage of snow shoes, and Louis cursed as he floundered waist-deep through the snow. A return volley from the enemy sent him diving for the cover of a deadfall. The English had gained the high ground and had taken up a defensive position. All through the afternoon and evening they shot it out. The Indians tortured some of the rangers they had captured within sight of the hill, and taunted their companions, promising them the same fate.

When darkness descended firing from the high ground ceased, and M. de Langlade and some of the Indians discovered that the enemy had slipped away, leaving their food, snowshoes and forty-two dead on the field of battle. M. de la Granville ordered his men to light some fires as pursuit of the enemy was impossible, and the rest of the night was spent huddled around them. In the morning twenty-five men together with a Chaplain and a Surgeon came out from Carillon to help with the wounded. Louis accompanied M. de Langlade as he examined the bodies of the enemy dead. They had been stripped by the Indians. Langlade said that he hoped to find Rogers[8] amongst them, but no one knew what he looked like.

Jacque brought a cup of hot rum over to Louis, and pointed out four commissary clerks who had volunteered for the mission. They were clustered around a companion who had been shot through the throat. Jacque smiled wistfully:

'In Canada everyone is a soldier.'

IN the spring of 1757 preparations got under way for a campaign against Fort William Henry on Lake George. As work was resumed on the defences of Fort Carillon after the long winter there was a feeling of optimism in the air. Regular troops and supplies began to arrive from St. Jean where the Army, under the Marquis de Montcalm, was assembling. The war belt had been sent to the Indian Nations and hundreds of them began to arrive at Carillon. The Miamis killed and ate one of their prisoners; they were the first Indians who indulged in this practice that Louis had seen. Heaven help the British if they let them loose at Fort William Henry. . . . The previous year Montcalm's Indians had massacred the survivors at Oswego.[9]

One June night Louis and Jacque Prideaux were on guard duty. It had been a fine, quiet night with no disturbances. Jacque left the guardroom for the last watch. At reveille he did not return. The guard commander ordered the guard to find him, and threatened to shoot him if he had fallen asleep. Louis found him. He saw him from some way off, sitting not far from the sawmill, and called out. There was no reply. He was dead. His throat had been cut and he had been scalped. Louis was stunned. Of all the men in Carillon—Jacque!

A party of Ottowas set off after the raiders and picked up their trail. They reported that the raiders were some of Rogers' Rangers, and it was discovered later that they had butchered a number of cattle grazing near the Fort and taken their tongues for food.

In July Louis was sent to St. Jean where he contracted smallpox. He was nursed back to health by Ursuline nuns at the hospital at Montreal and there heard of Montcalm's victory at Fort William Henry.

During his convalescence Louis saw for the first time the effects of the war in Canada. Horses were being killed in Montreal to feed the populace, and indignant women had thrown horsemeat at the feet of Governor Vaudrueil. His own regiment had stood rigidly on parade and refused to accept it as rations. In Quebec there was bread rationing. Supply convoys from Bordeaux had to run the gauntlet of British privateers, and little of the much needed provisions got through. The few ships which did manage to beat the blockade were often pillaged before reaching Quebec, and unscrupulous speculators in the Commissary made fortunes selling valuable provisions privately.

At St. Jean the position was critical. During the winter of 1757 stores including wheelbarrows, tools and wood supplies were plundered. At Chambly the garrison was near famine. Desertions from the Army were increasing, and a mob of women demonstrated in Quebec demanding bread. Morale throughout the Colony was low. News of English troop movements in the vicinity of Carillon and the threat of an invasion of Canada by way of Lake Champlain added to the growing anxiety. In June 1758 the news that Louisburg was under siege and that a British fleet was at the mouth of the St. Lawrence brought further misery to an already depressed Colony.

French regiments were beginning to move in the direction of Carillon. A British attack on the position was now imminent, and scouts brought in word that a British army was assembling at Lake George under the command of General Abercrombie. Varying reports put their number at between fifteen and twenty-five thousand men.

Louis Ménade found himself aboard a transport carrying reinforcements for the French battalions at Carillon. The regiments had been much weakened by hurried recruiting to bring them up to strength; most of the recruits were well below the required standards, and time was running out.

It had been decided to occupy the heights which dominated Carillon with an en-trenched camp with redoubts and abatis. Louis was assigned to the work party of three companies of *La Marine*. Their job was to cut the trees for the abatis; the trees were felled, then dragged by teams of oxen into position to form a great tangled barrier before the defences. Stripped to the waist under the hot summer sun Louis laboured from dawn to dusk, keeping up his spirits with long draughts of spruce beer. When the trees were in position the Marines cut the tangled branches into sharp points, making a massive, impenetrable barrier in front of the French positions.

On 4th July M. de Langy called for volunteers for a patrol to the British lines. Louis Ménade volunteered to escape the interminable labours of preparing the defences of the fort. The patrol did not reach the British lines. It was a warm night, and the Frenchmen camped on the shores of Lake George. Clouds of mos-quitos swarmed around them and turned the starry summer night into a hell. The following morning M. de Langy sent Louis and two Marines with a few Indians as advance guard. The early morning sun was already hot, and penetrated the canopy of leaves overhead in dazzling rays. The air was alive with the hum of insects. Louis made his way along the shore and, peering out through the tall reeds, saw a shimmer on the lake surface far to the south. As he squinted into the far distance, shielding his eyes with his hands, he saw that it was a line of boats; the others had seen it, and soon M. de Langy was at his side. It was the advance guard of Abercrombie's army. It was led by Rogers' Rangers, their green uniforms now clearly visible, in a long line of whaleboats. Drum calls were assembling the regiments when the war party reached Carillon, and the roads and crossings around the fort were full of moving men.

On the evening of 6th July M. de Langy made first contact with the advance guard of the British army. His patrol of 350 Canadians stumbled into them near the Bernetz River. It was a brief and savage encounter, and French casualties were heavy; the survivors came streaming back to Carillon in disorder. But in the engagement Brigadier General Lord Howe was killed. He was a popular and youth-ful leader, and his death stopped the English advance for several hours.

On 8th July the British army was in position before the fortress. At daybreak the French beat to arms and all the regiments moved into their defensive positions. At the left of the line were the battalions of La Sarre and Languedoc supported by two Light Companies. Bernard's and Duprat's Volunteers guarded the gap by the River of the Falls. The Royal Roussillon, the First Berry and the remainder of the Chevalier de Levis Light Companies held the centre. The La Reine, Bearn and Guyenne held the right. Louis Ménade found himself on the plain between the escarpment of the right flank and the St. Frederic River. An abatis protected the position, defended by 150 soldiers of *La Marine* and 250 Canadians. Along the whole of the front Companies of Grenadiers and Light Companies were held in reserve. The Chevalier de Levis commanded the right, Sieur de Bourlemaque the left, and the Marquis de Montcalm viewed the whole field from the centre.

At about ten o'clock in the morning Louis saw the first British columns move against the left. In the bright summer sunlight musket barrels glinted as the red lines marched on the French position. A cloud of white smoke billowed out from the defences, followed by the sound of the volley. As the smoke cloud dissolved Louis saw red-coated figures sprawled on the ground.

At the same time he saw another column attack the centre, and was suddenly aware of the sound of drums close by. A third column was coming towards the right flank. It attacked the Chevalier de Levis's position and came within range of the Marine position. Louis fired and reloaded until his face was black with powder burn, pouring shot after shot into the ranks of English Grenadiers and Highlanders, who attacked the position time and time again without any trace of discouragement in the face of the hail of fire that thinned their ranks. The position

The Marquis de Montcalm, the much-loved French commander, is cheered by his troops after the victory at Carillon on 8th July 1758. (Fort Ticonderoga Museum.)

held by the Canadians and the Marine Regiment suffered no attack. They poured a deadly fire into the British ranks while being in no danger themselves. The Chevalier de Levis saw that they could take some of the pressure off his position by making a sortie against the flank of the British column. He sent word to their Commander, Sieur Raymond. He and a Lieutenant of the Marines, Sieur Nigon, called upon their men for volunteers. Louis Ménade found himself stepping forward and following the two officers in a charge against the British. The Highlanders stood their ground and delivered a volley against the Canadians and Marines. When the smoke cleared Louis looked round to see Sieur Raymond standing alone, screaming at his men who were running back to their lines in a blind panic. Away in front Louis saw a figure lying on the ground waving his arm to attract attention. It was Sieur Nigon. Louis rushed over to him and saw that his thigh was smashed. He helped him back to the line. Their commander was raving at his men and called them cowards. Sieur Denys la Ronde leapt forward and called upon the men to make another sortie. Once more they advanced, but Louis saw that many of them held back. The advance was falling into disorder. Sieur Raymond raised his sword and called upon them again in the name of France. The Highlanders directed another volley against them, and again the sortie broke up into a panic-striken flight. Louis found himself cursing his comrades for cowards. Some of them crouched in unashamed fear behind tree stumps to the rear of the abatis. Sieur de Trecesson had to order his men to fire from the ramparts of the fort at a large body of Canadians who were fleeing towards the boats at the water's edge.

Towards evening the British attack lost its impetus and the regiments began to fall back. Over 2,000 dead were piled high before the abatis, which in spite of their courageous attack they had been unable to penetrate. Exhausted and demoralised, they began to retreat, and the retreat became a headlong flight. Louis was disgusted to see many of the Canadians who had cringed in fear throughout the battle now cheering and setting off in pursuit of the fleeing British troops.

Louis found a Highlander of the 42nd enmeshed in the abatis as he picked his way through the dead and wounded. A huge, ruddy-faced man with a shock of ginger hair, the soldier was hanging helpless in the tangled mass of spiky branches. Louis hacked through some of the cruel hooks, and eased him clear; a musket-ball had smashed through his ribs, and the terrible wound was bleeding freely. Louis offered him his canteen. The Scotsman swallowed two sips and died. As Louis looked down at him, remembering the courage with which the red-coats had hurled themselves again and again at the French positions, Grenadiers of the Royal Roussillon were straggling past him in search of souveniers; many of them had picked up Scots bonnets.

The French casualties amounted to a little over 400 killed; there was much ill-feeling in the battalions which had withstood the full fury of the British attack over the behaviour of the Canadians and the Marine Regiment. Louis felt a cold fury as he heard the insults. He turned to face a group of soldiers in the red-trimmed coats of the La Reine Regiment and shouted back at them, but his words were drowned by their catcalls and jeers. He turned his back on them and walked away, burning with indignation. The sun was setting as he walked towards the river. Directly in his path a drunken Canadian trailing a red coat in his hand raised an arm in salute.

'Victory, *mon ami*!'
Louis swung his musket and sent the man crashing into the scrub.

Louis jerked from his sleep, slapping at the flies which buzzed around his face. Somewhere a sergeant was ordering the Marines to their feet. He hauled himself painfully upright, and gathered up his equipment; a drum was beginning to beat, and around him his comrades were slinging their knapsacks and shouldering their muskets. The company fell in on the road, and resumed their dispirited march towards St. Jean.

The British armies were converging on Canada from all sides. Louis Ménade found himself wondering whether he would survive the battles to come, or even if he cared one way or the other. It seemed pointless to continue fighting, somehow. But as old Jacque used to say,

'What can one do? It is the way of things.'

Until the lords and ministers in far-away England and France decided that it could end, there was nothing to do but wait.

NOTES

With the exception of the Ménade family, Prideaux, Martel and Lebecque, all persons mentioned by name in this chapter are known to history, and their behaviour is accurately described. The commissary clerk wounded in the throat during the fighting with Rogers' Rangers died the following day.

1. The Marine Companies, which usually operated as independent detachments, had a strength of around sixty-five men each. In 1750 the number of companies was raised from twenty-eight to thirty, and in March 1757 to forty.

2. Fort Ticonderoga, built in 1755 on a promontory commanding the river connecting Lakes George and Champlain, thus controlled the natural route between French Canada and British New York. As described in this chapter, General Montcalm decisively defeated General Abercrombie's expedition against the fort on the Heights of Carillon in July 1758. The two positions were dismantled and abandoned in 1759. Restored by the British, Ticonderoga was captured by Ethan Allen's "Green Mountain Boys" in 1775. It changed hands once more during the War of Independence, was allowed to fall into ruins, and early in this century was bought and completely restored; it is now a museum.

3. The Iroquois tribes obtained arms from the Dutch in 1640 and over many years waged war on the Algonquin and Huron allies of the French settlers, and against the French themselves. The close co-operation between French and Hurons was forged in these conflicts. A famous battle at Long Sault Rapids in 1660, between one Adam Dollard and sixteen companions and a force of Iroquois, secured French and Huron access to Montreal from the western settlements.

4. Certain French missionaries were active in setting their Indian followers on the British colonists. Distorted versions of the Gospel story were spread, including one which described Christ as a Frenchman crucified by the English. Brandy and weapons were distributed, and a bounty offered for the scalps of men, women and children. This latter practice dated back to 1624, when the Dutch first offered scalp-bounty, and was continued by French and British alike until at least 1777, when some British officers advertised bounties for Revolutionary scalps. It is said that the encouragement of Europeans was responsible for the spread of the practice of scalping, originally a ritual act to release the spirit of the victim performed by only a small minority of Indian tribes. As this chapter makes clear, scalping was adopted by groups of European irregulars on both sides during the French/Indian Wars.

5. Details of the pay of Colony troops are obscure; as the administration of New France was riddled with peculation, it is reasonable to assume that wages were less than generous and often in arrears. Coin was replaced by paper as the medium of payment in 1757, a change regarded by the troops with vast and justifiable suspicion.

6. Fort William Henry, a log and earth fortification at the head of Lake George, was first built by General William Johnson in September 1755 in the course

of a victorious battle against 1,400 French, Canadians and Indians under Baron Ludwig Dieskau; it was named after the Duke of Gloucester. In August 1757 the garrison was forced to surrender to Montcalm through lack of food and ammunition, and many were butchered by the Indians despite Montcalm's sincere attempts to keep his unruly allies in check. The ruins of a second fort, built some ten years later by General Amherst, still survive. Fort Edward on the Upper Hudson had access to both Lakes George and Champlain, and fortification of the site dated back to 1708. A new fort was built in 1755, and after the Battle of Lake George was renamed after the Duke of York. It survived attack in 1757, and took in the fugitives from Fort William Henry. It was variously occupied during the War of Independence.

7. Louis was armed with a 1728 model musket, termed a "Charleville" in reference to the arms manufacturing centre on the Meuse. It was not such an out-of-date weapon as might be supposed—many of Louis's comrades carried the 1717 model. The musket was 62½ inches long, with a bore of .69 (16.5mm), and was not accurate much over eighty yards range. The flint had to be replaced after thirty or forty shots. Only the best-trained men, under perfect conditions, could achieve a rate of one shot every fifteen seconds.

8. Robert Rogers, born at Methuen, North-East Massachusetts Bay Colony on 18th November 1731, was the most successful irregular leader of the French/Indian Wars; his Rangers were active between 1755 and 1760, and the French put a considerable price on Rogers' head. Louis thinks of him as "English": the distinction between Englishmen and American colonists of British descent—while very real to the latter—would have been lost on a simple Canadian. Rogers led an eventful life, in which public acclaim alternated with periods of disgrace and imprisonment. He was commissioned Colonel in the British Army in 1769—his great ambition—and his death in England was reported by the London *Morning Press* as occurring on 18th May 1795. (Dates prior to 2nd September 1752 adjusted to allow for the change in the Calendar.)

9. The town of Oswego on Lake Ontario dominated the fur trade to Albany in the early 18th Century. In August 1756 the French and Indians captured the town and dismantled its three forts, Oswego, Ontario, and New Fort Oswego. The original fort was rebuilt in 1759.

SELECT BIBLIOGRAPHY

John R. Cuneo, *Robert Rogers of the Rangers*, Oxford University Press, New York, 1959.

Jack D. Forbes, *The Indian and America's Past*, Prentice Hall, New Jersey, 1964.

Edward P. Hamilton, *Adventure in the Wilderness—American Journals of Louis Antoine de Bougainville 1756–60*, University of Oklahoma Press, 1964.

Francis Parkman, *Pioneers in the New World*, *The Jesuits in North America*, *The Old Regime in Canada*, *Count Frontenac and New France under Louis XIV*, *Montcalm and Wolfe*, *A Half Century of Conflict*. (These standard works have been reprinted many times since their appearance in the last century, and are available in a number of editions.)

Howard H. Peckham, *The Colonial Wars 1689–1762*, University of Chicago Press, 1964.

Lewis O. Saum, *The Fur-Trader and the Indian*, University of Washington Press, 1965.

John R. Swanton, *The Indian Tribes of North America*, Smithsonian Institute, Washington, 1952.

Frederick Wilkinson, *Antique Firearms*, Guinness Superlatives, Enfield, 1969.

8: George Morrison

GEORGE MORRISON was nineteen when he joined the Sussex Militia in May 1809. It wasn't that he had any great urge to swagger about in uniform as did some of his friends, but life in the militia offered an escape from the drudgery and routine of his existence as a farm labourer, and an opportunity to get away from his personal problems. And of course it added to his ten shillings a week pay, which never went amiss at the 'White Hart'. The weekly parades and drilling, followed by the liberal consumption of beer, made life more interesting in general.[1]

About a year before he signed on at Hailsham, George had married one of the local girls, a strapping blonde dairymaid from a neighbouring farm, and life had become, relatively, quite pleasant. It was good having someone to come home to of an evening, and things seemed 'more orderly'. Bliss had been short-lived, however, for both Mary and the baby had died within a day and a half of Mary's being brought to bed. The experience and the loss had deeply affected George's entire outlook on life, and left him very largely indifferent about his surroundings, and particularly about his future. The arrival of the recruiting party for the Sussex Militia in Hailsham one Saturday afternoon therefore presented George with an alternative to the brooding existence he was leading several months after his twin loss.

At first George lost himself in the task of learning the drill manual, becoming adept in the handling of the musket and the numerous parade-ground manoeuvres, and this preoccupation brought results which attracted favourable comment from his officers. But once he had got the routine memorised, and developed as much proficiency at ball practice with the musket as it was possible to achieve, he began to lose interest and to slip back into his mental lethargy. His work on the farm kept his body active but not his mind, and while George was by no means a 'thinking man' he could not avoid brooding over his loss. Religion offered him no solace; what he had seen and heard of preachers had convinced him that what they had to offer, if anything, had no direct connection with him or his feelings in the present situation.

One Sunday morning towards the close of September 1810 a group of recruiting officers arrived on the drill ground of George's company, and, having obtained permission from the officer in charge of the company, proceeded one by one to address the company on behalf of their respective regiments, extolling the benefits of life in the Regular Army and the excitement of campaigning. There were four of them, three in sparkling scarlet and gold, and one young man in a dark green tight-fitting outfit with a pelisse over one shoulder and a black shako with black and silver trimmings.[2] The efforts of the three line officers all sounded very much of a muchness to George's ears, even though they offered bounties from £15 to as high as £35 for transferring from the dull, dreary life of a Sussex Militiaman to the sightseeing excursion offered by the —th Foot. But then this young lad from the 95th Regiment, the Rifles, started to talk, and George's ears pricked up. Here was a change indeed. Lieutenant Chadwick was offering £25 for men willing to join what was not really part of the British Army at all, but a selected élite corps of God's Chosen

Few! The Lieutenant was thoroughly convinced of the superiority of the Rifles; there was no doubt, thought George, that this was just the chance he needed to escape from his pointless existence. So, when the moment came, without further ado George stepped forward and marked his 'X' on the spot indicated by the smiling Lieutenant. Six others from the company followed George's lead.

THE life of a farm labourer had fitted George admirably for the outdoor training he now underwent at Hythe Barracks and Shorncliffe Camp.[3] His keen eyesight proved a boon when it came to ball practice with the Baker rifle, and the year and a half he spent in the militia stood him in good stead so far as marching and drill were concerned. There was a lot to un-learn as well, for the 95th operated on a system largely its own as regards the movement of troops into and out of battle. He was no longer an automaton acting in unison with a mass of other automatons, but an individual forced to act upon his own, to fend for himself and to think clearly and quickly when and if the occasion arose. George found it all a challenge which required attention and effort to meet. Months spent executing battle manoeuvres and exercises up and down and across the Downs, mastering the skills required in deploying from column of march into open order formations, learning to take full advantage of the landscape in taking cover, endeavouring to keep in formation and in contact with others in a given formation and yet to be able to act independently in judging time and distance—all of these relatively intricate processes required George's full attention. Extending into open order for skirmishing, from the left, right and centre, required a great deal of co-ordination on the the part of the individual rifleman, and memorising the bugle-horn calls which governed all their movements meant constant attention to the sounds around him. Independent action when formed into a chain of advanced guards fascinated George. The idea was that small detached parties of riflemen would scour a wide tract of countryside, locating groups of the enemy and clearing them out, and reporting on the condition of the land, logistic possibilities, and practical points for defence and offence. George had no trouble in learning to construct huts of earth or tree branches, nor in accepting the routine of camp life with its various fatigues. His own attention to details and alert attitude resulted in very few disciplinary fatigues falling to his lot.

Ball practice at targets with the Baker rifle proved one of George's strongest points. The firing was carried out progressively from distances beginning at fifty yards and extending out to three hundred yards. When the riflemen were to fight in close order, or in open formation advancing, they learned to load with paper cartridges which contained the powder charge and the patched ball wrapped in heavy paper. These were for rapid loading where maximum accuracy was not so important. Whenever the opportunity arose, however, the riflemen were instructed to load with loose ball and patches, using 'blank' cartridges containing only the powder charge. This permitted more careful loading and resulted in far greater accuracy at the longest ranges. George found that, using this latter system, he was able to strike the target, which was painted in the figure of a man, six times out of ten when firing at three hundred yards in the prone position. Another important part of their training with the rifle included learning to load while running or lying down. The ordinary infantryman loaded his musket standing up and standing still, but the rifleman must master the art under cover and on the move. George found that he was able to load and fire his rifle in the prone position just about twice in a minute, and almost three times in a minute when using cartridges. Although his speed in loading did not excel the average, his marksmanship did, and at the conclusion of his marksmanship training the captain of his company presented him with a silver medal as the top man in the company, which he was thereafter entitled to wear at inspections. This distinction also allowed him to wear a green cockade on his black felt shako—a privilege granted to all those riflemen who were able to place four out of six shots on the target.

George's above average ability with the rifle, the peculiar instrument of his corps, naturally increased his pride both in himself and in the 95th, and his was always one of the smartest turn-outs at inspections and parades. What had before been drudgery now appealed to his vanity, and he took great pains to ensure the best possible appearance of his uniform and equipment. The uniform in which George took such pride—a pride shared by his entire regiment, much to the resentment of their red-coated compatriots—was a considerable departure from the usual British Army uniform of the period, both in cut and colour.

The basic colour of jacket and trousers was dark green of a shade known ever since as 'rifle green', and the stand-up collar and cuffs were black, as was a twisted cord down the seam of each leg of the pantaloons. The collar and cuffs of black cloth were edged with white. The jacket was cut without lapels and buttoned down to the waist, and was shaped to slope off behind without being turned back as was the normal practice. The front of the jacket was adorned with three rows of black buttons, twelve in each row, with two rows on one side and one row and the button-holes on the other. Normally the legs were cased in fitted pantaloons, but loose-fitting trousers were issued for guard and fatigue duty and for campaigning. Short black gaiters of woollen cloth were worn with either, partially covering the short black boots which were standard issue. George's headgear consisted of a cylindrical black felt shako, the front adorned with a bugle-horn in place of the more elaborate brass plate worn by the infantry. The top front of the shako sported a green tuft of wool, and the sides were decorated with a white cockade and green cords and tassels—except in the case of George and other marksmen, who had the green cockade in place of the white.

An officer of the 95th, sketched by a comrade in the Peninsular War. The pelisse is dark green with brown fur trim, the trousers light grey, the sash red, and all leather-work black. From History and Campaigns of the Rifle Brigade, Pt. II, 1809–13, *by Col. Willoughby Verner, published by Bale, Sons & Danielsson in 1919. (Print courtesy Maggs Bros.)*

George's accoutrements on parade consisted of a series of black leather pouches and belts distributed about his person, and a scabbard for the sword bayonet with two-foot blade which accompanied his Baker rifle. His black leather waist belt was secured by a brass buckle in the shape of an S laid sideways. The bayonet scabbard, which was of black leather with a brass throat and chape, hung at his left hip with the round D-guard of the hilt facing forward; just to the right of the buckle there hung a small leather pouch, containing a number of lead balls, known as the ball-bag. Between the ball-bag and the belt buckle a vent pricker and brush were suspended by a brass or iron chain. The cartridge pouch or box rested on the right hip, and was suspended from the left shoulder by a broad black leather strap. When on active service this was filled with from sixty to eighty rounds of paper cartridges. Just above the cartridge pouch was suspended a powder flask (some of the riflemen carried horns instead of flasks) for use when the practice was with loose powder and ball rather than cartridges.[4] The flask or horn was normally suspended on a green cord with tassels. In addition, some men also carried smaller priming horns.

George's Baker rifle was, not unnaturally, his pride and joy. Its polished, oiled walnut stock never failed to shine, either on the firing line or the drill ground, and the brass furniture was kept almost at a mirror-finish. George took particular pains to keep the bore and the lock spotless, and in this respect he was different from most of his comrades in arms who met the requirements of the manual as regards condition of arms and equipment, and little more. Only those men who took a personal pride in their marksmanship imitated George's meticulous care of their rifles. Although in its details it was remarkably unlike the India Pattern Musket used by the infantry, the overall effect created by the rifle on the individual rifleman could not have been very different. When the weight of the two arms was compared the India Pattern smoothbore with its bayonet fixed weighed eleven pounds, while the Baker rifle and its bayonet were only a half-pound lighter. It could be argued, however, that the rifle was not normally fired with its bayonet fixed whereas the musket often was, thereby making the rifle lighter still by the absence of two pounds of bayonet. Quite contrary to popular opinion, the riflemen did almost as much fighting in the light infantry rôle as they did long-range sniping, so that the distinction loses much of its validity. When it came to manoeuvrability, the rifle with its bayonet was just as unwieldy as the musket with its bayonet, being only one-quarter of an inch shorter. In common with most of his fellow riflemen, it must be admitted that George neither cared for, nor excelled in bayonet drill.

Once away from the practice butts or the drill ground, George found that being a rifleman was not all a bed of roses. While the men of the 95th might consider themselves as well above the ordinary run of humanity, and particularly of the infantry, this regimental vanity had the reverse effect upon their red-coated comrades in arms; there was no love lost between the 95th and the line regiments, with the exception of those normally forming part of the Light Division (after it was formed in February 1810)—the 43rd and the 52nd Light Infantry. The 'Light Bobs', although often secretly thanked by many a hard-pressed infantryman, were abused in the open on every occasion, and not always in a humorous way. Since the Light Division operated well in advance of, or well in the rear of, the mass of the infantry, the man in the line had little opportunity to observe the routine existence

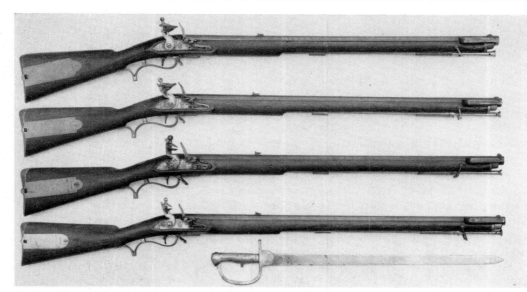

Baker rifles, of designs varying in detail between 1800 and 1815. The top rifle is of musket bore, larger than the normal ·625 inch, with a browned barrel and seven-groove rifling pitched to give one full turn in ten feet. Fittings, including the patch box lid in the butt, were brass. The bottom rifle is of the type produced from 1806, with a smaller butt-trap. The brass-hilted sword-bayonet is the second pattern, used between 1801 and 1815. (Tower of London Armouries Collection.)

of the rank and file in the Light Division, and the swaggering and dash of its officers created envy where respect might have been more suitable.

The routine of camp life, of drills, inspections, parades and the too infrequent hours spent at the practice butts, all came to an end for George and his entire company early in June 1811. It was announced one fine morning that they were to depart for Portsmouth in a week's time, en route for Lisbon, from whence they would join Lord Wellington's army in Portugal, becoming a part of the Second Battalion of the 95th in the Light Division under the command of General Robert Craufurd.[5]

I N all his life, Rifleman Morrison could not remember having been so miserably, completely and abjectly sick. As day followed agonising day he remained convinced that he would never survive for another twenty-four hours of the constant sickening movement which engulfed him. The squeaking, groaning and sighing of the ship's timbers, and the hissing, splashing and pounding of the water against the ship's sides combined with the human sounds and smells which assaulted his senses and reduced him to a thoroughly abject state. For most of the ten days' passage between Portsmouth and Lisbon he lay in a state of semi-consciousness, and it was not until he was manhandled ashore by two unsympathetic sailors and dumped on the quay like a sack of grain, that the thought occurred to him that he might yet live. It must be said in George's favour that there were many of his fellow riflemen in exactly the same state, and that the infantrymen who had been aboard the transport were in little better case. The passage had been unusually rough for the season of the year, and the ship had been overcrowded to begin with. What a ghastly transition it had been from the march to Portsmouth, which had amounted almost to a triumphal procession. At every town and cross-roads the local population had turned out to cheer them, strew flowers in their path, and hand out mugs of beer and cider. It had been almost a holiday, but it had certainly ended when they went aboard ship at Portsmouth!

George and hundreds of other enfeebled men were quartered in a warehouse set aside to receive the convalescent and lightly wounded and after two days on solid ground life began to return to normal. The heat was sweltering, which only made the recovery of the sick men more uncomfortable and protracted. George's basic good health and long experience of outdoor living and hard physical labour made his recovery more rapid than that of many of his companions, and by the second day after landing he was strong enough to set about cleaning himself and his equipment. Having been very little aware of his surroundings for days on end, George felt that a complete examination of his kit was in order, and, finding a reasonable space in one corner of the building, he proceeded to empty his glazed canvas knapsack of its contents. His examination revealed that nothing of any significance had been lost or stolen, and that all the articles with which he had been issued before leaving England were still present. These included two pairs of flannel drawers, two flannel shirts, two pairs of stockings and two pairs of socks, two shirts, a pair of braces, a pair of short boots, a tin of blacking and a shoe brush, a case containing a knife, fork and spoon, a clothes brush, a hair brush, shaving box and brush, razor and case, and the straps for securing his greatcoat and his blanket to the outside of his knapsack. The articles which were carried on the outside of his kit—his hatchet, canteen and tin cup—had all survived the journey. With his gear carefully stowed away in the knapsack, there remained space for carrying three days' rations—that is, three pounds of beef and three pounds of bread. At the moment the heavy frieze greatcoats were with the baggage waggons, and were only issued when the weather seemed likely to turn cold and stay that way.[6] The loose-fitting trousers which had formerly been worn on night watches and for fatigue duty now became the order of the day, and the smartly cut pantaloons were consigned to the knapsack. Some of the men had been issued with brown trousers, but George was very grateful that he had received green ones, as they made a much better appearance. When fully equipped, that is with his greatcoat and eighty rounds of ammunition in his pouches, George carried almost eighty pounds of equipment—and it was a weight which was universally cursed by the men of the 95th. How the hell could they be 'light troops' with a load like that on their backs? Despite this considerable handicap the Light Division had already earned a reputation for speed in covering ground by the time Rifleman Morrison joined its ranks. They were among the best marchers in Wellington's army, and they had to be—for they were normally expected to be in several different places all at the same time.

GEORGE's baptism of fire came soon enough. Some of the men with whom he had marched up from Lisbon had seen action at Vimiero, taken part in the epic retreat to Corunna in 1809, and fought again at Busaco the previous year, so he had heard plenty of 'old soldiers' stories' by the time his turn came at Aldea de Ponte in September 1811. But the stories only prepared him for part of it, and as every man knows who has survived going into combat for the first time, there are parts

of it which cannot be related to another being with any expectation of being understood. His morale had been marvellously buoyed-up by the cocky attitude of the 95th and of the Light Division in general, and he did really feel that when he got the chance he would prove himself to be, indeed, capable of superior feats of valour, just as he had proven that he could keep his mouth shut longer than most about his devilish sore feet!

George's company was amongst those ordered to watch one of the fords of the Coa, and after the tedium of several days' observation of the landscape, word that the French were on the move came as a decided relief to the veterans. The riflemen were spread out in open formation and under cover on and just under the brow of a ridge overlooking the ford. The opposite side of the river formed a gentle slope with little or no vegetation, an invitation for both riflemen and artillery.

What little natural cover was available was hastily improved upon with sword bayonets employed to scoop out the loose soil, bits of timber, and brushwood. George settled himself in position behind a slight mound which he had improved by digging away at its off side. About an hour passed before the first sounds of the French musicians were heard. It was when the music stopped again that eyes narrowed and nerves tightened. George pushed back the steel of his rifle's lock and made certain the priming looked fresh. He loosed the flap of his cartridge box and laid two cartridges down next to his right hand. Looking across the slopes in front of him he tried to fix in his mind the distances to certain points. And then they appeared, loose lines of blue-clad soldiers trotting along in ragged open formation, heading for the bank of the river. The faint rattling of accoutrements came across on the still, warm air, but there was as yet no real disturbance of the quiet. 'Here comes Johnny Crapaud', 'We'll dust their hairy knapsacks for 'em', reached George's ears as he watched the *voltigeurs* draw nearer the bank.[7] The French had seen the riflemen on the opposite bank, as there was no possibility of an ambuscade being laid in such open country, but as yet there had been no shouting or firing. The first of the line infantry now appeared on the crest of the slope, moving in two columns. The *voltigeurs* had paused and formed up ready to cross the ford, and a break had developed between them and the infantry now beginning to form line of battle. With a flashing of swords and shouted commands, the *voltigeurs* waded into the river. Complete silence had fallen in the ranks of the Rifles, but the French lines now began a clamour of shouting and encouragement. The first ranks had come ashore and were waiting for the others to come up when three sharp blasts of the bugle-horn signalled '*Fire!*' George drew back the safety catch of his rifle, cocked, and settled his face against the cheekrest of the stock. His eyes passed quickly along the blue lines over his sights; he selected an individual, and he squeezed the trigger. The lock flashed and the rifle cracked, but there was already so much smoke from the rifles surrounding him that the white drifting clouds obscured any certain knowledge of the results. There were already numbers of blue forms sprawled on the bank of the river, and the rapid firing of the rifles kept any order from developing among the ragged lines which had emerged from the river. Because it was a calm day the smoke hung about the lines and prevented any clear idea of what was going on.

George slid his rifle down alongside him, half-cocking the lock as he did so, and setting the safety bolt. He picked up one of the cartridges which he had laid alongside the rifle, and tore off the paper at the tail with his teeth, spitting out the end.

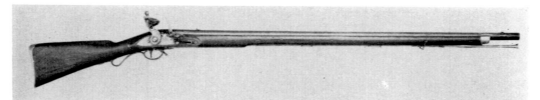

New Land Pattern Light Infantry Musket, carried by the 43rd and 52nd Light Infantry from 1810. With the Portuguese Cacadores, these regiments acted as the 'back-up' for the riflemen in the Light Division, and their muskets were of superior design to those used by Line Regiments. Improvements included a scroll trigger-guard for a better grip; a notched V-block backsight (the India Pattern Musket of the infantry had no backsight); and a raised or 'semi-waterproof' priming pan which increased the efficiency of the lock. The barrel was browned to prevent reflections and to inhibit rusting. Although bore (·75 inch) and barrel length (39 inches) were the same as on the India Pattern Musket, the Light Infantry barrels were more carefully bored and finished, so that with careful loading some increase in accuracy was achieved. (Tower of London Armouries Collection.)

He poured just sufficient powder into the pan to fill it about three-quarters full, and snapped the steel shut, at the same time pushing the rifle further down alongside him so that the muzzle was level with his chest. He poured the remainder of the powder into the muzzle, briefly swinging it upwards to knock at least some of the charge well down the barrel, and tore the remaining paper away from the patched ball at the front of the cartridge. This he quickly spat on before inserting it in the muzzle, for although the linen patch was greased to help avoid fouling the addition of saliva under conditions of rapid firing and a hot climate could not but help. He pulled the heavy iron ramrod from its pipes, and grasping it near its tip gave the ball a short sharp push to get it past the choke of the bore at the muzzle. Reaching up with his right arm he then grasped the rod near its head and sent the ball home with a swift single motion, giving it a tap when he felt it stop on the powder. The rod was then quickly withdrawn and slid back into its pipes, and the rifle pushed forward across the top of the mound, the bolt being slid off and the lock fully cocked in a series of smooth motions. The whole process had taken George about forty-five seconds, during which time it appeared as if the French light infantry were making some attempt to advance up the slope. The sun was blazing down and still no hint of a breeze offered to clear the clouds of white smoke and dust away. George pointed his rifle into the hazy blue line and again pulled the trigger. The rifle had hardly cracked when the bugle-horn sounded 'Advance', and the green-clad men scrambled up from their improvised pits and began to move forward in ragged lines down the slope. Blades flashed in the sun as the riflemen drew their sword bayonets and fixed them on the muzzles of their rifles as they strode along. Now the French were within effective musket range and a ragged volley spattered out, adding to the already deafening din and confusion. Green-clad men as well as blue began to fall, and the screams of the wounded and dying were now clearly audible. The line infantry had progressed down the opposite slope and were about 125 yards distant from the advancing riflemen when their first volley, well timed and aimed, crashed into the advancing green lines. The range was too great for it to have much beyond a psychological effect, but because of the smoke and dust it had not been clearly realised just how close the body of the enemy had advanced.

It now became hand-to-hand between the riflemen and the *voltigeurs*; the latter were still able to fire their muskets at point blank range before resorting to cold steel, while most of the riflemen, having fired their weapons, had to rely solely on their two-foot bayonets. Additional ranks of riflemen had been moved to the crest of the slope behind, and were pouring well-aimed fire into both the lines of infantry on the opposite slope and, where possible, into the mass below them.

In moving forward George had managed to load another round into his rifle, merely tearing off the patch and spitting the naked ball into the muzzle. The whine and hiss of musket balls around him gradually became so accustomed a sound that it made no undue impression on him. When he was about forty yards from the French he threw his rifle to his shoulder and fired, and this time he saw his target fall forward, the musket flying out of his hands. He brought his rifle down with his left hand and drew his sword bayonet, fixing it on the muzzle with his right as he continued to trot forward. His shako suddenly came off, and there was a tugging at the left leg of his overalls; he ignored both. The scene in front of him was now one of red stabs of flame, puffs of white smoke, the icy flashing of polished steel, and splashes of blue, white, green and black, with here and there a face distinguishable in the mass. He literally ran into a Frenchman before he knew quite what had happened, and as his rifle was at the ready it was almost knocked out of his hands by the impact. The blade of his bayonet started into the body of the man facing him, but not being deliberately pushed, it stopped, and it was only when the man roared in pain, anger and surprise that George realised what had happened—and pushed, hard. This time the man screamed and tried to swing his musket at George, but it struck the rifle and dropped to the ground. George stepped forward and kicked the man backwards, drawing the bayonet out. The Frenchman fell forward in a heap, groaning, but George barely noticed, having moved forward into the milling, slashing, clamouring crowd which now surrounded him. The butt of his rifle came up and smashed into a heavily moustached face, its shako flying off as it disappeared beneath him. A sudden blast erupted practically in his ear, stunning him for a split second, and he fell forward on one knee, catching himself with his rifle butt; he felt, more than saw, a movement behind him, and fell forward swinging his rifle around as he did so, automatically parrying the thrust of a bayonet which had been directed at his back. He lunged upwards and caught the Frenchman in the throat; the man's hideous scream was drowned by the raging storm around him, but the blood spurted out down George's rifle and both arms, splattering his uniform. George now became aware of the bugle-horn blaring out '*Fire and Retire*', and of the fact that there seemed to be fewer blue forms at which to swing or thrust. 'Fall back, lads', '95th, fire and retire' came the shouts through the din, and the green-clad soldiers began to withdraw from the tangled mass of humanity lining the river bank.

Briefly looking around him, George started to move away from the river, and pulled another cartridge from his pouch, repeating his earlier procedure of tearing off the patch and spitting the naked ball down the muzzle, and merely thumping it home with the rod. Having loaded, he turned and fired at the group of remaining Frenchmen now half in and half out of the river. As he fired, the sword bayonet jumped off the muzzle of his rifle and fell to the ground. As he stooped to retrieve it, swearing vigorously, a ball passed along his back, tearing a long groove down his jacket but failing to break the skin. George stood up, not really aware of what had happened except that he had been grazed and was bloody annoyed about his bayonet. He sheathed the bayonet and reloaded, walking to the rear. Again he turned and fired, and by this time he was back to the point from which he had started; the Rifles were walking through the lines of their own men who were busily firing at the retreating *voltigeurs*, and at the line infantry who were slowly with-drawing up the slope, providing what cover they could for the shattered light in-fantry.

Having passed over the tip of the crest, George sank down amongst other rifle-men, and took a long pull at his canteen. He was numb, deafened, and only aware that he was damned thirsty. The fact that his hands, overalls and jacket were splattered with dried blood did not register, nor did the fact that in his first combat he could probably boast of having dispatched at least three of the enemy, if not more. He heaved a deep sigh, and looked around him; there was Will Jenkins, clutching his arm and looking damned pale, Jack Mahone cheerfully whistling 'Betty Martin' and looking as if he had just come out of the biggest brawl of the year in the 'Bunch of Grapes', and Dave Orr sitting cross-legged on the ground, his shako propped in two distinct sections over his brow, wiping the blood off the blade of his bayonet with a bit of rag and looking intensely interested in the con-dition of George's equipment.

Seeing this interest, George looked down at his uniform, and received a severe shock. And he had thought Jack looked like the aftermath of a free-for-all! True, the two-hundred-odd miles he had marched since leaving Lisbon had weathered his boots and his uniform, but he had seen men who had been a year out here look-ing better than he did after his first engagement. Christ, what a mess, he thought. He suddenly remembered that he had lost his shako, and his faded green overalls looked as if there would be more patching than original material left by the time he got through sewing them up. He had recovered his knapsack and was devouring mouthfuls of bread and stiff beef when the word came to form up and march. They were a tattered lot of riflemen who moved away from Aldea de Ponte, but at least they had stopped the French crossing on the right of the British lines, and George had survived his first battle.

WHEN they reached their bivouac area the tents had not come up, but as the weather remained warm and clear this did not matter much. George and his messmates spent the evening attempting to restore some sort of order to their clothing and equipment. By diligent scrubbing with cold water and soap George was able to remove most of the bloodstains from his overalls and jacket, and having cleaned and blacked his boots and given his rifle a good cleaning, he spent the re-mainder of the time before it grew too dark to see attempting to sew up the tears in his uniform. It was while he was engaged in sewing that he had time to think about what had happened that day, and it began to dawn on him that he was a very lucky man indeed. He had had a regular succession of hairsbreadth escapes from death, all packed into not more than half an hour. He had killed, not once but at least three times, but it was more his own near-death that affected him. After all, that was what he had joined the 95th to do—to kill Frenchmen—and today had been his first real opportunity. In that way too, then, he had been lucky. It wasn't that George hated the French; he had no reason to hate them. But there were a lot of men who did, and *they* must have good reasons, and besides, that was why he had joined the 95th. He was doing his job, and he supposed, doing it well. He slept like a log that night, the sleep of exhaustion.

The following morning George drew a Quartermaster's fatigue, and marched off with several other men under Corporal Smith to collect rations for his company. It was as well he had been detailed for this task, as it took his mind off the roll call that morning: there had been at least fifteen, probably more, men who did not answer up, and the thought impressed itself upon him, even more forcibly than the previous evening, that he had come damned close to being one of that number yesterday. Although the deeper meaning of the remark might have escaped him, George would have agreed that since he had joined the 95th he had regained a reason for living. It was partly this re-awakening of his own personality which gave special significance to an event which was shortly to occur, and which served even more than his first taste of battle to turn him into an enthusiastic killer.

In the course of their return march as escort to the supplies being brought up for the company, George's detachment came across two squalid hovels. By the standards of his green Sussex they were mere sheds, but out here they qualified as 'farms'. Odds and ends of rubbish and a discarded gaiter by the side of the track indicated that the French had passed this way. George and his companions walked into the yard at the side of one of the houses, intent on a short rest in the shade and filling their canteens from the well. In accordance with their training they approached the buildings cautiously; bayonets fixed and rifles cocked, George and two of his mates plunged through the door, alert for any sign of the enemy's continuing presence. The sight that met their eyes stopped them dead in their tracks, more shaken than they would have been by a blast of French musketry at point-blank range.

Another print from Col. Verner's book, depicting a Private Rifleman of the 95th in about 1810; the sketch by Percy Reynolds is based on a print of 1812. It illustrates clearly the tuft, cockade, cords and silver bugle-horn on the shako, and shows how the leather harness was worn, although the rifle is rather crude. (Print courtesy Maggs Bros.)

The interior of the hovel looked as though it had been struck by a bursting shell; what little it had boasted in the way of rough furniture was smashed to splinters, and the earthen floor was scattered with rags, the shards of broken pottery and other simple household implements smashed or distorted by musket butts. In one corner lay the nearly naked body of a woman, her long black hair caked and matted with blood from a neck wound which had almost severed her head; more blood had oozed from half a dozen holes pierced through her contorted body, and had dried in rust-brown streaks across the dusky pale olive of her skin. Her attitude made it horribly plain that she had been raped, killed with the slash of a sword, and then bayonetted for good measure. To emphasise still further the wish of the French to discourage local co-operation with the Anglo-Portugese armies, two children lay sprawled pathetically on the fouled floor where they had been crudely dispatched with bayonet and musket butt.

George nearly dropped his rifle, and doubled up as his throat filled. His comrades, who had seen such sights before in their campaigning, swore violently and stepped quickly out into the yard. George staggered after them, still retching, unable even to curse. He made for the well, but was brought up short by a rifleman who steered him to a wrecked cart, pushed him into a sitting position, and thrust his own canteen at him. It seemed that the well had been rendered useless by the addition of a human corpse stuffed down the shaft—presumably the father of the butchered family.[8]

As long as he lived George never fully recovered from the scene into which he had blundered in that dim, fly-crawling room. His deep, abiding hatred of the French knew no bounds, and he lost no opportunity of indulging it within the strict limitations imposed by the orders of Lord Wellington. If he had had his way no prisoner who filed past him would have survived, no wounded man have recovered—even in the sight of an officer. The scene was etched on his brain, and his horror at the wanton cruelty of it was mixed up in his mind with his old grief for Mary and the baby who had not lived long enough to be named. Now he knew why he was fighting the French, why they were the enemy, and why as many of them as possible must be killed. Had he been a more educated or subtle man he might have been able to rationalise his feelings; had he been a more experienced soldier, he would have been too hardened by the careless atrocities of war to feel much shock. As it was, the simple reaction of hatred satisfied him, and his company officers remarked on his new zeal in volunteering for patrols, foraging parties, and any type of detail which offered a chance of contact with the enemy.

WELLINGTON'S army moved from its encampments around the Coa at the end of December, and crossed the Agueda in the first week of January 1812. Supplies and artillery were brought up from the assembly point at Almeida, and the Anglo-Portugese army made a surprise attack on the weakly guarded fortress of Ciudad Rodrigo. The siege opened on the evening of the 8th with the storming of a palisadoed redoubt called Fort Francisco by a party composed of volunteers from the Light Division regiments, led by Colonel Colborne of the 52nd. George volunteered as much to keep warm as to kill Frenchmen—the rain and frozen mud made the camp less than attractive. The attack was short, bloody and successful, and George only had a chance to fire his rifle twice, making do with his bayonet for the short time it took to capture the redoubt. Francisco proved an entirely different experience from his first fight at Aldea de Ponte; he found himself huddled in a mass of running, yelling men moving straight into the fire of artillery. They plunged into a ditch and scrambled up the parapets on to the rampart, slashing and clubbing at the French defenders. By the time the garrison surrendered night had fallen, and George found an opportunity to search several corpses before the Rifles withdrew; he added several *napoleons* and a silver watch to his small hoard, and, perhaps more welcome still, acquired a new pair of boots to replace the pair which had deteriorated rapidly in the rain of recent weeks. To replace them was worth risk-

An aquatint from The Martial Achievements of Great Britain and Her Allies from 1799–1815, *one of fifty-one in the book. It is entitled 'Storming of Cuidad Rodrigo Jany. 19th 1813' (sic): W. Heath del^t T. Sutherland aquat^t. It was published on 1st May 1815.*

ing the shell-fire now falling on Francisco from the walls of the town. George and the other men who had fought in the storming-party were excused the duty of trenching under fire, and did not return to the scene until the following day. Despite a careful fire by the riflemen of the Light Division, they were as yet too far from the walls to have much effect, and the bombardment of the working parties constructing batteries on and in front of the Great Teson continued without pause. The smoke, the thunder of guns and the rattle of small arms fire were incessant. On the morning after the capture of Fort Francisco the 1st Division had moved into the trenches, and were relieved by the 4th Division on the 10th. During these early operations George found himself well away from the scene of action, suffering the discomfort and inaction of outpost duty. The greatcoats had come up with the baggage, and hot meals were the order of the day, but he found that the rain and cold still bit into his temper as well as his bones.

On the 12th George was cheered by the news that the riflemen were to move forward of the trenches and dig in for a session of sharp-shooting at the French gunners. They scraped their shallow firing pits under cover of a thick fog, and commenced firing at a range of about 150 yards. It was so cold that loading the rifle was a painfully slow task, as well as being just plain painful, and the fire from the ramparts was so severe that they were withdrawn before many hours had passed. George had tried to scoop out the ground behind a fair-sized rock but had found it frozen so hard that he gave up for fear of snapping his bayonet, and simply lay down full length behind the rock. Loading in the prone position was a nuisance but was no novelty to him; with the dedication of the professional who takes a pride in his work, George reloaded with meticulous care after each shot. As he was in no hurry, and accuracy was all-important in his sniping rôle, he used loose powder from his flask rather than cartridges, and greased patches, which he carried in the butt-trap of the rifle; he paid particular attention to the priming in the pan. The fog did not wholly disperse while the riflemen lay in their improvised pits, and, added to the smoke of the incessant cannonade, made aiming difficult. Despite this George and his companions continued to pour an accurate fire through the embrasures of the walls, trying to catch the artillerymen as they gathered round their guns to reload, when the tight groups of men offered the best targets. It was a hopeless task, however; the thick walls gave sufficient protection from small arms fire, and the constant artillery barrage was so effective that before long the sound of the bugle-horn was heard recalling the Rifles from their uncomfortable task. George's face and uniform were covered with frozen mud and cut in several places by chips of rock thrown up by the exploding shells and ricochetting roundshot. As they withdrew into the trenches George's discomfiture was completed by the explosion of a shell quite close to him; the concussion knocked him face first into the half-frozen, churned up mud, winding him painfully. More infuriating still, his new shako evidently got in the way of a flying splinter; when he retrieved it, somewhat battered, from the mud, he found that the front tuft and badge had disappeared, gone to join the cords torn off somewhere on the ramparts of Francisco. To a soldier who took as much pride in his appearance as George this was the last straw; he clapped on the miserable concoction of wilting felt and stumbled off, cursing steadily and fluently.

The next several days were left to the infantry and the engineers and artillerymen, with very slow progress being achieved in the face of an unremitting fire from the besieged. What time George had left over from outpost or sentry duty was spent in cleaning up his uniform and equipment, mending the tears in his clothing, eating and sleeping. The tents had come up, and despite the continuing miserable weather a degree of comfort was possible. Many of the men's shoes disintegrated completely and the issue of the latest consignment of short boots to come out from England met with almost as much complaint as the collapse of the old ones. Food, at least, was ample, boiled beef and bread keeping the men's stomachs, and to some extent their minds, satisfied. The rum ration helped to keep the cold out, and some of the men managed to keep very warm indeed.

The riflemen, temporarily out of the front line, were roused at the usual hour before daybreak, paraded and told off for the various fatigues and duties for the day. George managed several quartermaster's fatigues, which, although hard work, were considered a prize since there was always an opportunity for an extra tot of rum while it was being issued for company consumption. Those parties sent off for ammunition and equipment were never popular, although George rarely complained about carrying up ammunition. On one such fatigue George was confronted by his colonel, affectionately called 'Old "What's this"' Beckwith, from his normal opening remark. Colonel Sidney Beckwith had the distinction of being much loved by all his men, and an uncanny knack of knowing names and personal points about seemingly every man in his command. He spoke to George by name, asking if he was getting sufficient food and keeping warm, and with something of a sparkle in his eye, enquired if George were finding sufficient Frenchmen to keep his rifle active? As was intended, the chance encounter was a great boost to George's rather mud-splattered and noise-benumbed morale, and the recitation of the interview to his messmates obviously cheered them up as well.

On the evening of the 16th George and his company were again sent forward into the pits in advance of the Small Teson, where a warm fire was kept up on the gunners around a breach which had been battered into the walls at the point closest to the batteries of the Great Teson. For several hours the firing was brisk, and they were now close enough to the walls for most of the riflemen to use cartridges rather than the slower load of loose powder and ball. Just before the signal to retire was heard, George noticed that the barrel of his rifle was so hot that it was painful to touch. On the morning of the 17th the Rifles went in again, this time into a hail of shot and shell, and the signal to 'Fire and Retire' admitted that the casualties from the rain of grapeshot from the walls were too much for them. A fierce artillery duel followed for most of the day, and by the evening the 95th was ordered forward once again. George had hardly wormed himself down into his niche in the ground when he was struck in the left arm by a grape-shot; it was a flesh wound which broke no bones, but it put George temporarily out of action. He managed to work his way back through the storm of thundering guns, both in front and behind him, past the trenches filled with red-coated infantry, until he found a surgeon's mate who cleaned his wound and bound it up.

George was on light duty during the 18th and the 19th, but when by the evening of the 19th it became obvious that something big was about to happen, George gave his sergeant no peace until he received permission to go forward with the rest of his company. The arm was painful, but not disabling, and as George's task would be as part of the covering party for the assault force it would not be strenuous duty— at least, to begin with. George argued, almost to the point of insubordination, to be allowed on the storming party against the Small Breach, but in this he was not successful; Sergeant Evans had too much respect for George's marksmanship—if not for his bloodthirsty attitude—to hazard him unnecessarily.

The attackers went forward at about 8 p.m. that evening, beginning on the right of the line by the Great Breach. The din was incredible, between the roaring of the cannon on the walls, the screaming and whining of grapeshot and the whistling of round shot, the exploding shells and the shouting of the men, the rattling of musketry. The rifles blazed away furiously, all thought of meticulous long-range accuracy now laid aside in favour of covering fire at close range. Without waiting for the hay bags which were to help fill the ditch in front of them the infantry of the Light Division stormed forward across their three hundred yards of open ground, down the edge of the scarp into the ditch and straight at the breach, into a withering blast of musketry and grape from the defenders. The ditch was dark, and the bodies mounted in heaps, but they came on, cursing and snapping shots blindly up at the shouting Frenchmen above them. The signal to 'Incline to the Right' brought the forlorn hope back into line with the storming party, and they pushed on in the face of devastating concentrated fire. The stormers had not been allowed to load their muskets, cold steel being the orders. Those officers remaining unhurt urged the men forward, and with a great surge the breach was carried; the bugle-horn sounded 'Advance' and George leapt to his feet and tumbled down the scarp into the ditch with the rest of the covering party, hard on the heels of the 52nd who were supporting the storming party. The French had only fallen back a short way from the breach, and a constant fire was kept up. The screaming of wounded men mingled with the shouts of those still fighting. The smoke was thick enough to set George coughing, and his eyes watered as he made his way across the piles of bodies lining the ditch, up the bank of rubble formed by the opening of the breach.

He scrambled up the bank, unaware of the cuts made in his hand by the sharp rubble, his senses numbed by the constant roaring of guns, muskets and rifles which surrounded him. He was aware of green-clad men on either side of him, and of the enemy somewhere in front of him. Once through the breach they followed the men of the 52nd round to the left and into the blazing, smoke-filled nest of houses and narrow alleys inside the walls. There was no time for planning or thought, the men simply moved on, looking for flashes of blue uniforms, for a musket pointed their way, for movement which might be hostile. The French were retreating back from the walls in hand-to-hand combat, and were sniping from the houses as they withdrew. George's rifle cracked two or three times, and once he paused long enough to see the Frenchman fall forward out of the window, his musket smashing in the street before him as he tumbled down.

George ducked into a doorway to reload. As he was pushing the ball down the barrel a terrific blast from inside the building seemed to set fire to his left side. Two Frenchmen cowering inside had seen him head for the door from across the alley, and had fired their muskets simultaneously through the door from a distance of not more than six yards. George grabbed at his side, yelling with pain and fury as he staggered out into the street. His rifle clattered to the ground, and in a semi-daze he fumbled for his bayonet, staring vaguely at the two splintered holes in the door.

In a first floor window of the next house along the row a French soldier caught sight of a green-clad Englishman swaying and stumbling in the alley below. He was obviously wounded, and had lost his rifle; but he still had his bayonet . . . and assuredly, there was but one way to be certain in such matters. Steadying his musket on the window-frame he saw the Englishman's waist-belt above the brass blade of his foresight, and pulled the trigger. The musket barked; and as the smoke carried away, he saw the green figure collapse on to the dirty cobbles, twitch once, and lie still.

NOTES

The 'other ranks' named in this chapter are fictitious; all other named characters are actual historical personalities, with the exception of 'Lieutenant Chadwick'.

1. Militia: in 1777 the Militia Act placed control of this defence force in the hands of the local authorities, and the following year the Militia was authorised to accept volunteers. The force was essentially intended for home defence.
2. Pelisse: an extra jacket worn draped over one shoulder; although primarily a feature of hussar uniforms it was effected by officers of the Rifles. *Shako*: tall tubular hat with small peak worn by most infantry of the period.
3. Hythe, on the Sussex coast, was for many years one of the main centres for military small arms training.
4. No conclusive evidence regarding the forms in which ammunition for the Baker Rifle was issued and used by the 95th has been discovered to date. Contemporary accounts from officers and men vary, and official sources are unhelpful. Cartridges for this weapon were certainly issued, and its inventor, Ezekiel Baker, claimed that the powder charge was three times the weight of the ball, i.e. about 100 or 110 grains, less ten grains for the priming. Horns and flasks were both carried by some riflemen but not by others. There is no mention of their official issue. In the early days of the 95th mallets are known to have been used to hammer tight-fitting balls into the rifling, but contemporary sources suggest the early abandonment of an implement so impractical under field conditions. The exact form of the paper cartridges is also something of a mystery: was the patch wrapped around the ball, dipped in grease, and tied up with the powder in the normal manner, or were all patches

carried separately? Officially, we do not know.

5. The official establishment of officers and men for the 95th Regiment (Rifles) in 1809 was 2,283. Three battalions existed by the time George Morrison signed on; the 1st was with the Peninsular Army, and had participated in the retreat to Corunna in 1809; the 2nd had gone to Walcheren; and the 3rd was newly raised. Wellington used his riflemen by breaking up the battalions and attaching one or more companies, as required, to each of his five, later seven, divisions. Not until 22nd February 1810 was the famous Light Division formed; on 4th August 1810 it was divided into two brigades. On 1st January 1812—just before the siege of Ciudad Rodrigo was opened—the Light Division was under the command of General Robert 'Black Bob' Craufurd. The 1st Brigade, led by Barnard, contained the 1st Bn., 43rd Light Infantry; four companies of the 1st Bn., 95th; two companies of the 2nd Bn., 95th; five companies of the 3rd Bn., 95th; and the 1st Portugese Cacadores. The 2nd Brigade, under Vandeleur, comprised the 1st and 2nd Bns., 52nd Light Infantry; four companies of the 1st Bn., 95th; and the 3rd Cacadores. A company of the 95th was composed of 100 men.

6. Frieze: coarse woollen cloth, usually with a nap on one side only.

7. *Voltigeurs*: French light infantry. French infantry regiments of the period comprised 'companies of the centre', '*voltigeurs*' and '*grenadiers*', the two latter being collectively termed '*compagnies d'élite*'. The centre companies, or line infantry, were the main fighting body. The *voltigeur* company, distinguished by yellow uniform trimmings, provided the advanced skirmishing line, while the *grenadiers*, with red uniform distinctions, were basically the heavy assault company and were, in theory and often in practice, the strongest and most aggressive soldiers in the unit. The system was abandoned in 1868.

8. Such atrocities were common in the Peninsular, and the merciless treatment of civilians by French, and of French prisoners by local guerrillas, was a terrible feature of the whole campaign. Joseph Buonaparte remarked to his brother that 'It needs . . . 100,000 scaffolds to maintain the throne for the prince who is condemned to reign over this country . . . Every house is a fortress . . . not one Spaniard will support me, we shall not find a single guide nor a single spy.' A major factor in Wellington's victory was the support of the population for his small and well-disciplined army. Draconian measures kept the undeniably hard-bitten English soldiers in line, and compensation was paid on a generous scale for commandeered goods. Another helpful aspect was the British practice of provisioning their armies as fully as possible, while the French were expected to live off the land. For the sake of balance, one should mention an isolated occasion when British troops did get out of hand—the fall of Badajoz in April 1812. The final assault was successful, but very costly to the tired British regiments—casualties exceeded 5,000 in two hours of unusually bitter hand-to-hand fighting. Maddened by their losses and by the hardships of the long campaign, the troops subjected the town to a sack of medieval ferocity, sparing neither women nor children. Wellington, the supreme realist, knew that any attempt to restore discipline immediately would simply lead to officers being shot by their half-crazed men, and the disintegration of his army. After letting the sack run its course for three days he marched in with fresh troops and brought his men to their senses by a series of summary hangings.

SELECT BIBLIOGRAPHY

W. Y. Carmen, *British Military Uniforms from Contemporary Pictures: Henry VII to the Present Day*, Leonard Hill, London, 1957.

J. Harris, *Recollections of Rifleman Harris* (ed. Capt. Curling), London, 1848.

J. Kincaid, *Adventures in the Rifle Brigade* and *Random Shots from a Rifleman*, combined edition, undated, London.

C. C. P. Lawson, *A History of the Uniforms of the British Army*, Vol. V, Kaye and Ward, London, 1967.

Lt. Gen. Sir W. Napier, *English Battles in the Peninsular*, Chapman and Hall, London, 1852.

C. W. C. Oman, *Wellington's Army 1809–1814*, Edward Arnold, London, 1913.

Maj. Gen. C. W. Robinson, *Wellington's Campaigns 1808–15*, 2 vols., Hugh Rees, London, 1905.

W. Surtees, *Twenty-five Years in the Rifle Brigade*, London, 1833.

9: *Vassili Pavlovitch Zhukov*

THEY were marching. They seemed to have been marching for days, weeks, months. In fact it had been precisely thirty-two days, but Rifleman Vassili Pavlovitch Zhukov of the 4th *Strelkhovy* (Rifle) Battalion of the 12th Infantry Division had lost count of the days long ago. He found it difficult to think in terms of figures over ten, anyway. At first the new sights, the excitement of passing through strange towns and villages with the population cheering them on, the abundance of food and drink, had all made the time pass quickly; but for some time now the countryside had been changing, getting gloomy and more thinly populated, almost desolate. There had been less and less to eat, and now even the bugles and the company choir at the head of the column failed to excite him or keep his spirits up. All the same, there was something in the air this afternoon. There seemed to be more comings and goings by staff officers, more cossack patrols on the hillsides around them; his friend Piotr, who always knew everything before the Colonel did, had said that they would be in Sevastopol that evening—wherever that was. This should have raised patriotic feelings in Vassili; he should have been proud to know that he would be joining the heroic garrison which had resisted the combined attacks of French, British and Turkish soldiers. But all the news meant to Vassili was the possibility of a good meal, some sleep, and, praise be to God, an end to this marching, marching, marching.[1]

VASSILI PAVLOVITCH had been born twenty-four years before in a village in the Urals near the town of Perm. Like most of the population of Russia at that time he was a serf, but as his village was owned by the state rather than by some private landlord he was a state serf. Instead of having to suffer the whims and vagaries of some unpredictable landowner, the villagers had their lives directed by a civil servant, a commissioner, who imposed a strict bureaucratic control.

The country was hilly, and lay on the fringe of the great, dense forests of Siberia. Although there was some farm land most of the population of the hamlet were employed in forestry work; Vassili's father led a team of foresters. They would go off into the forest for weeks on end, and from the age of fifteen Vassili had accompanied his father's gang on these expeditions, first as cook but later as a full member of the team. He had been taught to shoot, and had become adept at providing his companions with something more interesting than *kasha* and pickled mushrooms to eat.

One spring evening Commissioner Denikin had come to Vassili's father's cottage to say that he had received notification that there was to be a call-up of recruits in their area. These came at irregular intervals and affected men of over twenty. Only a limited number were needed and so the commissioner was always prepared to listen to good reasons why certain young men should be exempted, although these reasons generally had to be emphasised by the provision of something of more material benefit to the commissioner. Vassili's two elder brothers had avoided the call-up, the eldest because the eldest was exempt by right, and the second because of certain convincing arguments which their father had pressed into the commissioner's hand. It now became apparent that due to his father's reduced means and the rise in the cost of living, they would not be able to satisfy the commissioner a third time.

The day came, therefore, when with a dozen or so other young men Vassili prepared to leave the village with the commissioner to appear before the recruiting board at Perm. Service in the Army could last up to twenty-five years, and the villagers realised that they were unlikely to see any of the young men again. Their departure was the excuse for a riotous farewell party, with the wilder members of the group driving furiously and noisily up and down the village street in their *troikas*, and the quieter ones holding long, earnest conversations with families and girl-friends. At last there came the tearful farewells; Vassili's mother gave him a new shirt she had embroidered for the occasion, and his father gave him two roubles. A loaf of bread, a sausage, some *kasha* and a small bottle of Vodka were added for the journey.

At Perm, they arrived just in time to watch the recruiting party drive in. There was a troop of mounted gendarmes,[3] several carriage-loads of officials and a column of dismounted soldiers from the Internal Defence Corps. They set up at the Police Station and sifted through the selection of conscripts offered by various local villages, each according to the quota laid down on the basis of its population. A few were rejected by the doctors, but most were passed after a cursory examination, and they assembled before a priest to take the oath of allegiance.

That evening Vassili found himself in a local military depot with fifty or so others,

Russian camp scene in about 1850. Of the two central figures, the left is a line infantryman and the right is a Jaeger or Strelkhoy; they are identified by their white and black belts and straps. (Mollo Collection)

being looked after by a couple of trained soldiers known as '*diadkas*', or 'uncles'. From the uncles they found out that they would not be staying there long. It was not government policy to allow soldiers from the same region either to serve together in the same regiments, or to stay in their home areas. After a week at Perm Vassili and three others were posted to the Ukraine Regiment at its Kiev depot.

It was at Kiev that Vassili had his first taste of the rigid military discipline which characterised the army of Tsar Nicholas I in the 'stick and fist' period. For mistakes in drill or other failings the instructors applied the 'toothpick'—a blow in the face with a cane, a drumstick, or even a fist. They believed that this was the only way of teaching the *muzhiks*. They themselves had been beaten innumerable times, and they were merely perpetuating the methods which had been used, not without success, on them. Vassili and his intake soon learned to keep an eye out for one old *feldwebel*[4] whose favourite ploy was to halt in front of a young soldier and shout, 'What are you scowling about? How many times must I tell you that you must look your superiors cheerfully in the eye?' The demand would be accompanied by sharp blows in the face. 'Look more cheerful, *more cheerful*, I said, blockhead!' he would continue, raining punches on his victim, until the recruit somehow contorted his swelling eyes and split lips into a grimace which satisfied the old *feldwebel*.

Most of the recruits' training consisted of drill, for it was considered that in perfect and unblemished formal parades lay the guarantee of success in war. They were taught the parade march, a form of goose-step in which the knee was bent and then straightened with a jerk; they had to learn the exaggerated postures which they were required to adopt on particular occasions, and an arms drill designed more for its impressiveness on parade than for practicality in the field. They were taught the motions for loading and firing their muskets, but during their entire three months training' they were given only one opportunity to fire live ammunition, and then only five rounds per man. Even this allocation was only made because of the war—in peacetime they had to make do with blank firing practice, or even resort to making clay bullets for themselves. Vassili's shooting experience in the forests around his village stood him in good stead, and his five shots were skilful enough to bring him to the attention of his officers. He found himself posted to the Rifle Battalion of his Division, the 4th *Strelkhovy* Battalion. Here he was taught to use the Belgian-made 'Stutze' percussion rifle, which was still in service with many line *Strelkhovy* Battalions although it was supposed to have been replaced by that time.[5] Here, too, he met Piotr, who became his best friend. They went well together—Vassili quiet and rather earnest, Piotr noisy and irrepressible.

One morning they came on parade to find dozens of carts lined up, each with its peasant driver. They were to set off for the Crimea, where the British and French were threatening invasion in support of the Turks.

'What's the Crimea like?' asked Gregori, the company blockhead.

'Oh, marvellous,' said Piotr. 'Don't you know, that's where the double-headed eagles come from?'

'Go on now,' said Gregori incredulously. The others laughed. Piotr always got a rise out of Gregori.

More important to them than their destination was the fact that wherever it

was, they were not going to have to march the whole way. Enough carts had been impressed from the villages round about to carry the whole battalion. However, by law the *muzhik*[6] drivers could only be forced to carry them as far as their regional boundary, and then the quartermasters had to round up another lot. Once they reached the edge of the Crimea there were none left to take; the foreign invaders paid far better rates than the Russian Army, and the Moslem Tartars who inhabited the region had little loyalty to a Muscovite Tsar.

AND so it was that after thirty-two days of marching Vassili Pavlovitch and his comrades found Sevastopol suddenly coming into view below them. They had been marching along a valley with low hills on either side, one of them crowned by a fort flying the Imperial flag, when the ground fell away to the right and they saw the white buildings of Sevastopol glistening in the afternoon sunshine. They could see the streets of square, classical buildings dominated by the naval barracks on the bay to their right, the entrance of which was blocked by the masts of sunken ships—all that remained of the proud Black Sea Fleet[7]—and they could even see, on that clear afternoon, the enemy ships blockading the port. What attracted their attention more immediately, however, was the bridge at the foot of the hill they were marching down. This was a flimsy pontoon contraption which provided the only means of communication between Sevastopol and the rest of the Russian Empire, and the only route for supplies and reinforcements. The battalion passed the breastworks guarding the approaches to the bridge, and exchanged the predictable comments with the soldiers who garrisoned them: 'What's the food like?' 'What's been keeping you?' Then they reached the bridge, and an officer shouted, '*Break Step!*' What on earth did he mean? Hadn't they learned, with bruises to emphasise the lesson, that soldiers must never march out of step? However, the alarming bucking and rearing of the floating bridge as they marched across it prevented anyone keeping step anyway. A wave flowing in from the sea washed over the right hand side of the bridge and wetted Piotr's boots. Vassili was gawping over his shoulder at the incredible expanse of sunlit water when something came crashing down, and they ducked instinctively as fragments of a bomb fell hissing and splashing into the sea beside them.

On the far side there were shouts of '*Smarten yourselves up!*' and '*Get your step!*', and then they were marching through narrow streets of square white houses, many of which, as they could now see, had been badly damaged by the enemy's cannonade. It didn't seem to have affected the population much, however; men and women were promenading on the streets as if it were a pleasant summer's evening at the height of peace. The column marched on, through an arch which had had one wall blown away, into a square which obviously formed part of a barracks. They were marched over to the far side of the square, and here at last received the welcome order to halt, and pile weapons and equipment where they stood.

Vassili looked around. The baggage wagons were standing in the middle of the square, and the drivers were knocking stakes into the ground for hitching-posts. The cooks had dug a pit and collected bits of wood from various ruined buildings nearby, and were now busy preparing soup. On one side green ammunition boxes were lined up in a row; on another, artillery wagons stood, the teams still in the shafts. Vassili joined a large group who were standing around a huge cauldron of cabbage soup with a few pieces of fat beef floating in it. This was always a favourite spot with the soldiers. They had pulled their trousers out of their boots as a sign that they were now taking things easy, and some had lit up the pipes they had recovered from the legs of their boots. One of the cooks was using his boots as a bellows to fan the wood fire. At last the soup was ready; Vassili and Piotr held out the canteens they had removed from the backs of their packs, and received two ladles of soup and half a loaf of black bread. Things were looking up. They were back by their piled equipment enjoying the meal when the *Feldwebel* came round.

'All right, lads, hurry up and finish that and get some sleep; we've work to do tomorrow.'

After the hardships of the last few weeks they did not mind settling down for the night right where they were, on the barrack square. Vassili took his greatcoat out of its roll on top of the pack, adjusted the pack to form a pillow, wrapped himself up in his coat and lay down. The company storyteller had launched into the tale of Ivan Tsarevitch and the Grey Wolf, and Vassili listened sleepily.

He never heard the end of the story—or rather, it seemed to become merged with shouts of 'Fall in!', 'Time to move!', 'Come on, wake up there!' What was going on? It was still dark; Piotr, who could do educated things like tell the time, looked at the clock tower and announced that it was one o'clock in the morning.

The harbour at Balaclava, the Russian objective at the battle of that name in 1854. This remarkable contemporary photograph is by Robertson. (Mollo Collection)

They had had only three hours' sleep. Their officers were hurrying about in full battle order with their short-swords and pistols, and the quartermaster sergeants were handing out extra powder and ball from a cart. Still trying to shake the sleep out of his eyes, Vassili automatically went through his morning drill of seeing to his weapons and equipment. His Belgian Stutze ('Where is Belgium, anyway?' he had asked Piotr, but for once Piotr hadn't known) needed a couple of pulls through with an oily cloth wrapped round the end of the ramrod. He cleaned the lock mechanism, making sure that the nipple was clean, and then checked his small pouch of percussion caps. His ammunition pouch contained its full load of forty paper-wrapped cartridges, which meant that the extra supply that was now being handed out would have to go in the small haversack which he carried slung over his left shoulder.

He managed to get some hot water from the cooks. In his haversack he had two or three little cloth bundles of tea and sugar, but coming to the conclusion that he was unlikely to get any more for some time, he decided not to use any that morning. Instead he ground up the stale end of a black loaf left over from the previous week, and mixed that with the hot water. (A visiting general had once been very impressed when he saw the soldiers drinking this concoction, assuming that it was coffee.)[8]

Vassili wasn't going to be able to have a wash before going into battle, as he would have liked, but he could at least put on a clean shirt. He spent a little time getting his foot-wrappings just right, so that there were no uncomfortable folds below the foot and it was neither too loose nor too tight at the top of the boot. He hoped he would get a chance to change the wrappings round later in the day, but he could not be sure, so it was just as well to make a good job of it right from the start. The company wagons came round and they were told to leave their helmets and coatees on it. This meant that they would be wearing their caps, which were far more comfortable than the big, leather, spiked helmets, and their loose-fitting greatcoats.[9] Like most *muzhiks*, Vassili hated wearing anything tight.

The greatcoat required some preparation; when it reached down to your ankles it looked fine on parade, but was hopeless for running around the countryside. In the Rifle Company they had fixed hooks and eyes round the bottom so that they could hitch up the lower eighteen inches or so. It also meant adjusting their black leather equipment, which for the last few days they had been wearing over their jackets. He and Piotr helped one another with the straps and buckles, and soon they were ready.

The *Feldwebel* called them to attention, and the Colonel came out followed by the other officers. After a word with the *Feldwebel* he walked to the middle of the square and exchanged the traditional formal greetings with his regiment.

'Greetings, my brave ones.'

'Good health to Your Honour.'

The Colonel went on to announce that today they were privileged to strike a great blow against the enemies of the Tsar and Mother Russia, and that they should all obey orders promptly and do their duty. Even Piotr was unable to deduce much from that.

He did not have much time for conjecture, however, as they were soon called to attention, formed into fours, and marched off the way they had come in the previous evening. As they approached the bridge they halted to allow a battery of artillery to rumble and rattle past them. The weight of the artillery caused the bridge to rock even more than before, and it required some concentration and balance to avoid being knocked into the water. When they reached the other side they turned right down a smaller road which Vassili had not noticed on the way in, a road which wound off down the hill into the valley where it followed the course of a small river. They had been marching for about an hour when the road passed two hills over to their right. As they came around the second the column halted. Vassili's company was told off to attach itself to the Odessa Regiment, the rear regiment in the Division, and they were ordered to take up skirmishing positions on the lower slopes of the hill.

As they trotted over to the position indicated to them by their Captain, they were at last able to see over the crest. From it they could see into the end of the valley which wound away out of sight to their right round two hills. In front and to the left, filling the end of the valley, thousands of soldiers were formed up. Immediately below them were two squadrons of lancers, and over to the left they could see the large masses of men representing the two leading regiments of the division. Next came the Odessa Regiment, with Vassili's company forming the right flank. Behind them the track along which they had come was now filled with cavalry— hussars and cossacks, with horse artillery adding to the apparent confusion. The whole scene was bathed by the early morning sun just rising over the hills on their left.

Across the valley could be seen another line of hills which seemed to have square tops. A puff of smoke from one of these explained their shape—there were field fortifications or redoubts built on top of the hills. In the brightening light they could see a flag flying from the highest of the hill-tops, a red flag bearing the hated crescent.[10] Piotr took the corner of his coat between his fingers so that it formed the shape of a pig's ear and shook it in the direction of the flag. The Turks wouldn't be able to see the gesture which so infuriated them, of course, but it gave Piotr some satisfaction.

For a while nothing much seemed to be happening except for mounted officers galloping to and fro as the two leading regiments began to reform into columns. Then the drums beat the advance, and the columns wound forwards across the valley. They began to diverge, the left hand column heading for the main hill-top with the flag and the right hand one aiming for the two smaller hills which flanked it. From their vantage point Piotr and Vassili had a grandstand view of the battle. They saw puffs of smoke from the redoubts, and occasionally a larger puff which brought in its wake the sound of an explosion.

'They've got some guns up there,' said Piotr. 'I hope they manage to deal with them before our boys get too close.'

The head of the left hand column was obviously beginning to suffer from the intense fire from the top of the hill, and the leading companies started to waver. The right hand column had less of a slope to contend with, however, and more room to manoeuvre. After staggering back from the first volley they reformed, and with a cheer charged into the redoubt. With all the smoke and confusion it was difficult to see what was happening for a moment or two. Then figures appeared, running from the far side of the redoubt, and through the smoke they could see the Standard of the Azov Regiment waving from the middle of the position. Encouraged by this success the left hand column charged again, and they too swept the enemy out of their fortifications.

For Vassili and Piotr a comfortable hillside with a grandstand view out of musket range of the enemy was too good a position to last, and sure enough the bugles for their own company began to sound the rally. They ran back down the hill and fell in on the right of the Odessa Regiment, which was forming up in company columns. They set off along the valley floor, leaving their two hills to the right and the captured redoubts to the left. They passed some wounded from the Azov Regiment; their priest, with his soft

Faces of the Crimean War – a Jaeger or Strelkhoy and a line infantryman. (Mollo Collection)

black cap, long beard and staff, was wandering among them encouraging the more lightly wounded and offering last rites to the dying.

They came round a bend in the valley and saw two or three more redoubts stretching away up on the left hand side. There was some shooting from them, but it looked as if most of the defenders, discouraged by the fate of their comrades, were making good their escape as the Odessa Regiment appeared. Vasseli's company halted at a point in the valley opposite the last redoubt, and spread out in skirmishing positions on the lower slopes of the hill on which it was built. The regiment split up into three columns, each of which moved up to attack one of the enemy positions. After a short burst of firing, shouting and general din from the top of the hill, all became quiet again. A few moments later, with jangling and rattling and clouds of dust, the horse artillery battery swept past the skirmishers and on up to the crest, where they unlimbered between the redoubts and began to lay their guns on a target which the riflemen could not see on the far side of the hill.

Looking off down the valley and beyond it to a sharp crest in the distance Vassili and his companions could see a long thin line of scarlet winding down a slope. 'Angliski,' muttered Piotr. They were distracted by more sounds of rumbling hooves and jangling harness from behind them. Down the valley were trotting squadron after squadron of Russian cavalry; just short of their position the leading squadrons of hussars wheeled left and trotted up to the crest of the hill.[11] They paused for a moment, fanned out into line, and trotted away over the ridge and out of sight. The rest of the column continued down the valley until they too wheeled left about a quarter of a mile past the watching riflemen. The last few squadrons were cossack units; in contrast to the hussars they rode past silently—a cossack always took care that his weapons and equipment did not jingle as he rode, and regarded any noise from his accoutrements as a disgrace. The cossacks began to spread out on the flanks of the hussars in front of them, just as Vassili had seen them do on manoeuvres.

Then everything seemed to happen at once. Over to the left they heard musket fire, then the first column of infantry began to stream back over the hill. This was quickly followed by the sound of bugles, and the second column in front of them

Line infantry in action in 1854. (Mollo Collection)

recoiled as red-coated cavalrymen came pouring over the crest into the middle of them. The Russian cavalry, obviously taken aback by the suddenness and fury of the charge, came galloping back in confusion.[12]

Above the din they heard Captain Kalugin give the order to load and prepare to fire. Their own cavalry swept by and back up the valley, but as the redcoats saw the masses of infantry ahead of them they pulled up and galloped back to the top of the hill. A wounded hussar came limping by, having lost both horse and shako somewhere up the hill. 'Those mad English,' he grumbled. 'They came at us from all sides.'

Now, beyond the English cavalry, Vassili saw that the thin red ribbons he had seen on the hillside had become columns of red coated infantry, and he was rather disturbed to note that they seemed to be coming his way. 'He's come to re-take the redoubts,' said Piotr.[13] This certainly seemed to be the infantry's task, although they were taking their time over it; very deliberately forming into line from column, advancing a little way, reforming column, waiting until another regiment came up on their flank and advancing a little way and forming into line again. It all seemed very impressive, and would have pleased the old *feldwebel* at the depot.

A few skirmishers in green appeared, and started shooting in their direction. Old Sergeant Golovin took off his cap and crossed himself. The sharp cracks of rifle shots could be heard, and the whizzing of the balls as they passed on either side; Vassili and Piotr replied to this fire with an occasional shot whenever a suitable target presented itself. Once a rifle bullet passed between them, struck a rock and glanced off with a whine. 'Watch out, or you'll be getting your discharge in full before tonight,' said the sergeant. By nightfall several of them had got their discharge in full, and others had been wounded, but the rest went on joking just the same.

Looking over his shoulder Vassili saw that the Odessa Regiment was drawn up in line with their left hand battalion in a redoubt and the remainder formed up on the side of the hill. A staff officer galloped up to the colonel, there was a hurried consultation, orders were given, and the regiment turned and marched back down the valley. Vassili's company followed them in skirmishing order, trying to discourage the enemy greencoats from getting too close. They had gone about half a mile past two or three of the now-empty redoubts when the orders came to halt and take up similar positions to those they had held before.

It was now mid-afternoon, and a pleasantly warm and sunny day for the time of year. The redcoats had halted by the first redoubt, and nothing much seemed to be happening; Vassili's company were ordered to stand down for a while. This gave him a chance to explore his stock of black bread and wash down a couple of not too stale chunks with a few swallows of water from his canteen. He also took the opportunity to change his foot-wrappings round so that the damp sweaty part which had been round his foot was left under the upper part of his boot, where it would dry out, while the dry part went under his foot.

What with the early morning start and the heat of the afternoon sun, Vassili was beginning to feel a bit sleepy when Piotr nudged him and pointed down the valley. Across the end they could see a long line of blue-coated cavalrymen forming up. Some of them were lancers—they could see the red and white pennons fluttering quite clearly—and some seemed to be hussars. A hussar officer, gleaming in blue and gold and mounted on a magnificent chestnut charger, had trotted to the front of the line; then the whole force began to move steadily in their direction.[14] Their company bugler sounded the alert. Vassili and Piotr cocked their Stutzes and crouched down behind a fold in the ground. Sounds of gunfire behind them indicated that the cossack horse artillery battery had noticed the enemy cavalry too, and were coming into action. As the line of horsemen reached a point opposite Vassili's earlier position they broke into a canter. Vassili drew a line on the magnificent hussar officer leading the charge, whispered 'To the Father and the Son', and pulled the trigger. The officer swept on past them, unharmed, and, followed by the first line of troopers, now rather brutally thinned by the cannon-fire, disappeared into the smoke which now enveloped the battery position. By the time Vassili had reloaded he only managed to get off one more shot— which brought down a rider in the rear line—before the rest disappeared into the smoke as well.

All that was left on the valley floor were dead and wounded cavalrymen and horses, and a few riderless mounts wandering around. Normally the cossacks would have had these very promptly, but they seemed too occupied up the far end of the valley behind the battery position. A superb grey charger with a gorgeously uniformed lancer officer slumped over his neck stopped at the foot of the hill where Vassili's company crouched; when the horse dropped its head to crop the grass the rider, either dead or unconscious, toppled out of the saddle and lay still. The horse swung its head to sniff at him. Captain Kalugin shouted at Piotr, who was furthest down the slope, 'Antonov, go and catch that horse!'

As his friend stumbled down the hill Vassili heard a shout from further back: 'They're coming back—take up your positions!' Sure enough, small groups of cavalrymen and single riders came straggling out of the smoke. Some were galloping, others were urging wounded horses or holding comrades in the saddle; they seemed to be in a bad way.[15] Piotr, still intent on catching the horse, suddenly realised that he had left it too late to get back to the safety of the hillside. He ran a few yards, saw that a knot of four or five riders were bearing down on him, turned in desperation, and got off one shot with his Stutze. Then the riders were on him; Vassili saw a sabre flash, and his friend went down under the hoofs. From his position on the slope Vassili managed to pick off one of the hussars; he had fired at the group, and could not be sure that the Englishman who tumbled out of his saddle was the one who had sabred Piotr, but he hoped he was. As fast as he could reload there were more targets to shoot at; he even squeezed off a shot at some lancers, only to be cursed by the captain. 'Can't you see their greatcoats? They're ours, you fool!'[16] Then the last of the straggling riders was off down the valley, and all was quiet again. Vassili got permission to go down to Piotr.

Even as he hurried towards him over the scrubby, trampled grass, he could see that it was no use; Piotr had got his full discharge. There seemed to be an awful lot of blood around him, and when Vassili turned him over he saw a huge sabre-wound in the side of his neck. He had put his hand up to save himself, and the wild cut had clipped all four fingers off the bloody paw. Vassili wandered sadly back to the hill, and came across the lancer officer whose horse had been the death of his friend. The Englishman was dead too. Well, if Piotr hadn't been able to get his horse, perhaps he had something else to offer that he wouldn't be needing any more . . . A quick rummage through the officer's jacket revealed a pocket-watch, but before Vassili could continue his search there was a bellow from his sergeant on the slope above, telling him to get back to his position.

The watch was better than nothing, he thought, shaking it by his ear before stowing it carefully away in his boot; it was a pity Piotr wasn't going to be there any more, he could have told the time with it. As he trotted up the slope in the sunshine, Vassili turned to wondering whether the cooks would be there to give them anything to eat that night.

NOTES

The named characters in this chapter are fictitious; the units and incidents described are matters of historical record.

1. Russian invasion of the Turkish provinces of Moldavia and Wallachia—present-day Rumania and Bulgaria—in July 1853 led to the declaration of war by Britain and France, afraid of Russian expansion into the Mediterranean, in March 1854. By the time their armies reached Turkey the Russians had been halted, and it was decided to carry the war into Russia itself—and in particular to remove the Russian naval threat by capturing the important Black Sea naval base of Sevastopol. The Allies landed in September 1854 and by mid-October, having almost completed its encirclement, they commenced siege operations. Sevastopol, never totally cut off from the mainland, held out until September 1855, when the garrison was evacuated and the city abandoned.
2. *Kasha:* buckwheat porridge.
3. The Corps of Gendarmerie was a para-military organisation controlled by the Ministry of the Interior, which supplemented the ordinary police, particularly in the enforcement of political regulations.
4. *Feldwebel:* sergeant-major. Russian military ranks closely paralleled those of the German army. The junior non-commissioned rank was *Yefreter*—in obvious imitation of the German *Gefreiter*—and the senior was *Podpraboshik*, which may be translated as

warrant officer; this rank was normally held by quartermasters, armourers, and other specialist grades.
5. At that time the Russian infantry division included one *Strelkhovy* or Rifle Battalion, which could provide a company of skirmishers for each of the four infantry regiments in the division. (So-called 'Jaeger' regiments performed a normal infantry function.) At Balaclava the 12th Infantry Division, Lt. Gen. Lipramdi commanding, comprised the 4th *Strelkhovy* Battalion, the Azov, Nieper and Ukraine Infantry Regiments and the Odessa Jaeger Regiment. Each regiment consisted of four battalions of four companies each. A wartime company mustered about 200 men, giving a regimental strength of 3,200 and a divisional strength of nearly 14,000. The Liège-made 'Stutze' rifle had officially given place to the Ernroth rifle in 1851, but many units used the Belgian weapon during the Crimean War.
6. *Muzhik:* peasant.
7. Trapped in Sevastopol by the Allies, the fleet was stripped of its guns for use in the defensive works and scuttled in the harbour entrance to prevent any Allied naval incursion.
8. The harsh conditions which the Russian soldier endured were more the result of grinding poverty than of wartime shortages. A private received 2 roubles

Camp scene, Crimean War period. A Cossack reports to an officer while soldiers in caps and greatcoats sit around. (Mollo Collection)

85 kopeks a year; a sergeant, 4 roubles 5 kopeks. These sums were so negligible that it is almost impossible to quote a current equivalent. In peacetime he could earn a little extra by agricultural work, but even with free issues of food and equipment the soldier found it very difficult to make ends meet.

9. The spiked helmet or '*casqua*' had been introduced in 1843 just after the Prussians introduced the *pickelhaube*, and both nations claimed to have invented the style. In 1855 it was replaced in Russian infantry units by a French-style shako.

10. The British had occupied Balaclava and made it their main supply base, and the line of redoubts had been built to guard the landward approaches to the harbour. They were manned by Turkish troops with one British battalion, the 93rd Highlanders, in reserve on the outskirts of Balaclava.

11. This was the Cavalry Brigade of Maj. Gen. Rijoff, comprising the 11th Kiev Hussars, the 12th Ingermanland Hussars, and six *Sotnias*—squadrons—of Cossacks, totalling some 1,600 men. The Kiev Hussars turned off first and encountered the 'Thin Red Line' of the 93rd Highlanders, later immortalised by Sir William Russell.

12. The camp of the British Cavalry Division was just on the Balaclava side of the last redoubt. Early in the battle the division formed up at the end of the valley so as to be able to react to any Russian attack on the town itself. When the 93rd were attacked by the Kiev Hussars, the Heavy Brigade, under Scarlett, was ordered to their aid. They were on their way to carry out this task when they unexpectedly ran into the second half of Rijoff's Brigade, the Ingermanland Hussars and the Cossacks. The success of this action is often overshadowed in the controversy over the handling of the Light Brigade.

13. To the Russian, the enemy is always 'He'.

14. The Light Brigade, consisting of the 4th, 8th and 11th Hussars, the 13th Light Dragoons and the 17th Lancers, were still drawn up at the British end of the valley. Lord Raglan had intended that they should try to prevent the Russians from removing the captured guns from the redoubts. As a result of the famous misunderstanding between the Divisional Commander, Lord Lucan, and Captain Nolan, Raglan's A.D.C., the Light Brigade was sent against the Cossack Horse Artillery Battery of Rijoff's Cavalry Brigade, formed up at the other end of the valley. The hussar officer 'gleaming in blue and gold' was the Brigade Commander, Lord Cardigan; during the charge he wore his pelisse not slung, but put on like a patrol

A Stutze rifle, *as used by the Russian* Strelkhovy *battalions. This weapon was a Belgian-made version of the Brunswick rifle; the example illustrated has the name* P. J. Malherbe à Liège *engraved on the lockplate, the double-headed Russian eagle and the number* 883 *on the buttplate, and the Tsar's cypher on the escutcheon plate. The overall length is 46 inches, and the fittings are of brass. The calibre is .796, with two-groove rifling to take a belted ball. There is a rising leaf backsight. (Tower of London Armouries Collection)*

jacket, and his chest would have been covered with gold lace.

15. A magnificent account of the charge from the viewpoint of an ordinary trooper was published under the title 'One of the Six Hundred in the Balaclava Charge', by J. W. Weightman (17th Lancers) in *The Nineteenth Century*, May 1892. A long passage is quoted in *Rank and File*, compiled by T. H. McGuffie, Hutchinson, London, 1964.

16. This mistake over the lancers was made by both sides; the British mistook Russian lancers for the 17th, although the Russians were in greatcoats and the 17th in their blue jackets and grey overalls.

SELECT BIBLIOGRAPHY

J. Curtiss, *The Russian Army under Nicholas I*, Durham, N.C., Duke University Press, 1965.

F. V. Greene, *Sketches of Army life in Russia*, W. H. Allen, London, 1881.

C. Hibbert, *The Destruction of Lord Raglan*, Longmans Green, London, 1961.

A. Lubinov, *An Account of Balaclava from the Russian Point of View*, unpublished MS.

W. H. Russell, *Todleben's History of the Defence of Sebastopol 1854–5*, Tinsley Bros., London, 1865.

L. Tolstoy (Tr. L. & A. Maude), *Tales of Army Life* (including *Sevastopol* and *The Cossacks*), Oxford University Press, 1963.

The Battle of Balaclava, article from Voyenia Encyclopaedia (Military Encyclopaedia), St. Petersburg, 1911.

Winslow Homer sketch of the 6th Pennsylvania Cavalry in the field in 1862. (All illustrations in this chapter are reproduced from the Library of Congress Collections.)

10: *Alonzo Wayne Crawford*

A PACKET of letters and a number of personal effects, including a uniform, were recently discovered in a trunk in the attic of a house in Philadelphia, Pennsylvania. The letters told the story of a young man named Alonzo Wayne Crawford, who enlisted in the Sixth Pennsylvania Cavalry (Rush's Lancers) after the First Battle of Bull Run in 1861, and fought with the regiment throughout its existence. He joined up as a private, carried a lance throughout 1862, was wounded at Gettysburg in 1863, participated in Kilpatrick's Raid into Virginia in 1864 (when he was promoted to First Lieutenant), and finally marched with the Regiment at the Grand Review in Washington in 1865.

Mr. Crawford was born in Philadelphia in 1838, and lived there throughout his life. He graduated from the University of Pennsylvania after returning from the war, and practised in the city as a civil engineer until his death in 1906. He was a respected member of the Grand Army of the Republic and the Military Order of the Loyal Legion of the United States of America.

Most of Crawford's letters were written to his brother Charles, who had been injured in a shop accident before the war and was unable to serve. These letters reflect a candour that often did not exist in formal correspondence of the Victorian period. The third letter, written to his father, provides a marked contrast to the other letters in the collection. The whole packet, which unfortunately ends in July of 1863, demonstrates the experiences shared by Crawford with millions of other young men who joined the Union Army during the American Civil War.

1.)

> Camp Barclay
> Washington City
> January 27, 1862

Dear Charles

These few lines leave me hale and hearty as ever. Would that I could say the same for all our noble band. Many of the boys are sick with complaints of the bowels, etc. etc. This camp was occupied for several months by another cavalry regiment, and is a stinking, mushy hole. Their leavings are all about. And the weather has been cold and damp. But Thank Heaven we will be away by Spring and we can endure some few weeks more. We reached this place on the train at noon on December 11th.

General Butler gave the 'Plug-Uglies' a smart lesson in Baltimore and we had no difficulty passing through Mobtown.[1] As you will remember when we came here with Father, there are niggers everywhere, but they aren't half bad, if you can stand the *smell*. I think the traitors here are cowed, and Bull's Run be damned. The Union men have set up a Soldier's Refreshment Saloon in Baltimore and the Soldiers' Rest in Washington City, and we were treated royally.

I came to see the 'Elephant'[2] and have yet to see Him, but his tracks are everywhere hereabouts. This old city of Magnificent Distances is all aswarm with soldiers and office-seekers from the loyal states. I sauntered over to the Willard Hotel bar on Pennsylvania Avenue, after having my photographic likeness made at Mr. Brady's Gallery. Charles, you never saw so much make-believe military plumage or so many bogus bigwigs in your life. It makes one roll with laughter to hear the schemes for subduing rebeldom that these gents spout.

Sometimes I wish we were back at Camp Meigs in Philadelphia. Back home the damsels didn't titter if a dashing lancer happened to spill from the saddle—they knew it was just 'an accident' don't you know. But as our training here continues under the eagle eye of the gallant Colonel Rush, we are learning to gallop and wheel in as fine a fashion as Napoleon himself ever saw. When Captain Lockwood orders us 'In each rank count fours! Prepare to mount! Mount!' we can now do it without executing an impromptu dismount forthwith.

When we paraded through Washington on the 1st our lances, with their gay scarlet pennons, were the wonder of all who beheld them, and even the secesh maids[3] must admit that we looked fit to beat all. Our lances are scientifically designed and improved, though we don't yet quite have the hang of them, and General McClellan will doubtless give us good opportunity to prove their worth in rebel-sticking when the time comes. We are the only regiment with this arm to be seen hereabouts, and it naturally excites much curiosity.

Bye the bye, Charles, 'Little Mac' is the man to watch, and anything you hear to the contrary is hogwash. As it was he who first thought to arm us with the lance, we look to him as our patron, though small-minded people think he must advance or face the wrath of Father Abraham.[4] When Mac does move on to Richmond the rebels will beg on hands and knees to live again under the folds of the glorious old Flag.

Some of the boys have spent part of their $13 a month on a bottle of tanglefoot whiskey, and with their infernal yelling, I can't keep my mind on writing. Tell

A group of Rush's Lancers taking their ease during the Peninsula Campaign of 1862.

Father that we are the pride of the army, and kiss Mother, Alice and Fanny for me.
Your Brother,
Alonzo
Write to me care of Capt. Benoni Lockwood,
Company H, 6th Pennsylvania Cavalry (Rush's Lancers)

2.)

PRIVATE   Camp Barclay
March 29, 1862

Dear Charles

Please excuse me for not writing more often, but our camps around Washington have been all astir with rumors and preparations for a grand 'On to Richmond' move, and there has been little time to attend to matters of a personal nature. I have purchased a badge to wear that has a bust of our beloved Mac on it, in the hope that it will bring me good luck when we ride to crush the rebels for good.

We did have a little scouting run (or swim) into Virginia on the 10th through the 16th inst. But it came to nothing more than a lot of rain-soaked clothing and many runny noses. To be truthful it was a grand fizzle out. Nary a secesher did I spy, though it started well enough with our fine mounted band tooting 'Dixie's Land' on their brass horns as we crossed the Chain Bridge into the enemy's country. You need have no fear for the safety of the Capital. As we left the city we saw forts and armed camps all around with the Stars and Stripes floating over all.

Charles, I begin to suspect these lances of ours aren't worth a darky's damn. I'm glad to have my Colt's Army six-shooter,[5] but the light cavalry sabres we were issued are defective in temper, and are the source of much grumbling. Mark my words, the army contractors who supply such shoddy will reap fortunes from this war instead of the several feet of stout hemp that they deserve. On a ride into the field, all kinds of useless baggage goes by the board. We soon learn what we want badly enough to haul around with us. In the name of Christ, Charles, don't send me another canteen for purifying water, though I know you mean well by it. They draw more curses than an abolitionist in Charleston. Drinking tubes, bulletproof vests and nightcaps are about played out in this army. You will oblige me greatly, however, if you can slip a few good segars into your next package. The copies of *The Temperance Letter* and *Satan's Baits* that father put in the box afford the boys great amusement.

One day last week I did manage to find some fun. An officer from a neighbouring regiment, whose acquaintance I have made, took me down to Sal Austin's House in Marble Alley, between Pennsylvania and Missouri Avenues. Her establishment is something to behold, though I have heard others speak more favorably of the Headquarters U.S.A. and Madame Russell's Bake Oven. The battered old Cyprian that Sal introduced me to had a **** the size of a horse collar. I am told that she is a rebel to boot. Charles, there is horizontal refreshment aplenty, and no mistake, but the most sought-after of the fallen angels have a decided taste for shoulder straps.[6] Indeed, the rows of finely appointed chargers and waiting orderlies outside these places has become quite a scandal, and you may expect to read of a large scale bust-up by the provost marshall's men before long.

I have yet to see the inside of one of the famous gambling hells, with their fine carpets and magnificent chandeliers. Frank has promised to point out the entrance of one he recommends highly, where the right password whispered through the grate gains entré to parlors that would be remarkable (he says) in London or Paris. Meanwhile in camp we have games of bluff and chuck-a-luck which are the undoing of many a greenhorn, and some not so green. I lost $3·75 at bluff, but mean to get it back directly.

Tell Mother to put a good pie or two into the next box you send me. The salt pork and hardtack they issue soldiers for food is the most loathsome curse visited on mortal man since the plagues of Egypt. If we waited to soak these crackers so that they could be eaten, the rebels would have time to march to Maine, with a side trip to Niagara Falls on the way. Fry everything, that's my motto. Four of us have formed a mess, and take turns with cooking, etc. I am acclaimed the champion in the coffee-bean grinding department. The government ovens here turn out fresh bread, but on campaign it will be all root hog or die.

I am sending $5 of my pay to Father to put away for me, and right now I wish I was in Philadelphia to spend it. At the noon meal, with grease all down my trousers, I curse the day that my eyes strayed to that lying recruiting broadside on Market Street.

Frank has sent off to New York for a photograph of a damsel in a pose he says is calculated to rouse even old Ned Turner. I hear that he has just received it, so I am off to take a look see.

Your Brother,
Alonzo

P.S. Burn this letter after you have read it.

3.)

> (*This letter is on stationery headed with an engraving of Gen.*
> *McClellan in two colours, and the following verse:*
> '*For McClellan is our leader, he is gallant and strong*
> *For God and our Country, we are marching along.*')

Camp Barclay
March 29, 1862

Dear Father

Your kind favor of the 15th instant was greatly appreciated. We in the regiment are in good spirits, and mean to trounce the rebels soon once and for all. We made a reconaissance into Dixie some three weeks ago, and chased the enemy back into their holes. Jeff Davis[7] can't stand another such fright as we gave him.

You need have no fear of my being caught in the Devil's snares of which you write. Any bad habits of old have been put aside for good. An appreciation of the cause of *humanity* and our *country* can give one the strength to resist temptations. I have shown both *The Temperance Letter* and *Satan's Baits* to my comrades, and they are a great success. Prayer meetings are well attended, and I take especial delight in raising my voice in 'Blest be the tie that binds' and 'Just as I am'. The regular soldiers curse fearfully, but I have tried mightily to cleanse myself of that sin. I do not wish to die in battle with an oath upon my lips.

Your friend Mrs. Harris has been here, and has distributed pillows, bed quilts, blankets, and other comforts and luxuries to our hospitals. I saw little of her as she was quite busy.

How are my old friends from the University? Tell them all 'how-do-ye-do' from me, and make them all write me. When the war is over I intend to go back and take my degree.

Dear Father, if you could, would you please send me a new watch and a pair of braces in your next box? The watch will help me to budget my time to good advantage. My old braces are all frayed.

My love to Mother, Alice, Fanny, and Charles.

Your loving Son,
Alonzo Crawford

P.S. Franklin sends his regards.

4.)

In Camp at Harrison's Landing, Va.
August 6, 1862

Dear Charles

I take my pen in hand to let you know that I am still in the land among the living. We have been so occupied with galloping hither and yon lately, and now and again braving shot and shell, that there has been no chance to write, though I am always delighted to receive your missives.

I've seen the 'Elephant' now, but I narrowly escaped being trunked and trod upon. There have been times since you last heard from me when I was in the midst of a regular carnival of death. Thank God, so far I am unscathed, although I think my legs are permanently bowed from riding so much. We have all lived in the saddle too long and are chafed to a frazzle. I have faced the dews and damps regularly with only my gum blanket to protect me. Thank Heaven for black Coffee! As muddy as it usually is, it keeps us all in the saddle.

Charles, consider yourself fortunate that the mishap to which you lost your hand kept you from volunteering in the first surge of enthusiasm, for if you were here in Dixie you would run a good chance of being served a worse fate. Frank was packed off to a field hospital near Coal Harbor with dysentery, when, out of

An Edwin Forbes sketch of a cavalry skirmish during the Gettysburg campaign.

nowhere, down came the rebel cavalry. The entire hospital, under Dr. Ellis, was taken, and it was off to a wretched prison pen and who knows what else for our old chum. They left Dr. Ellis behind, and it was he who told us of poor Frank.

On the night of the 31st of last month, at half-past one o'clock by my watch, we went through a hellish display of pyrotechnics. A rebel battery on the other side of the James River brought our encampment under a fire of shell and solid shot. Strange to tell, we lost only one man killed, and he was found stretched out without a mark on him! How fickle a reaper War is! By two o'clock our batteries had gotten their range, and they were silenced.

There is nothing good to be said for this camp. It is alive with flies, dust and sand swirl everywhere, and 'Chickahominy Fever' is raging. The heat is worse than I have ever known, and as a capstone to this great pyramid of misery, we are forced to drink the foul water of the river. Now, Charles, don't you wish you were a soldier?

This Peninsular Campaign which has now come to a close will loom large in the historical annals of our Republic. McClellan has brought off a very notable manoeuver when he changed his base in the face of the enemy. This Army of the Potomac has fought a score of great battles, in every one of which it was greatly outnumbered and checked the rebels. If Richmond has not fallen you can blame it on McClellan's enemies in Washington. They are afraid that if he wins he will become a dictator, and they have failed to support him. There is more than one kind of traitor abroad these days.

After leaving Camp Barclay on March 30, we came by ship down to Fortress Monroe, Va., and from there by land toward Richmond. The country we passed through was rich and had plantations and farms filled with cattle and sheep, and fields of grain and grass. Much of the land also contains watery marshes that turn into insect-filled pestholes in the hot months. The women and families were still at home. Many a woolly-headed contraband (as we call the darkies) came into our lines to aprise us of the strength and positions of the rebels.

For much of the campaign we were brigaded with regiments of regular cavalry and together styled the 'Reserve Brigade'. Those regulars are OK, you may depend on that. But they spend too much time combing their horses. We served under Gen. P. St. George Cooke, who is the father-in-law of the rebel cavalry leader Stuart.[8] We spent many weary hours chasing Stuart when he rode around our army, but he outran us. Sometimes, during the chase, we went for days without unsaddling, and several times we passed the whole night standing 'to horse', all of which has not improved my constitution. Many a good horse was ridden to the ground. At Hanover Court House, on May 27, Company 'A' captured Captain Johnson's company of the 28th North Carolina Infantry entire, and the appearance of these deluded wretches as they were marched to the rear aroused much interest. The fact is our own infantry directs almost as many volleys of epithets at us cavalrymen as they fire bullets at the rebels.

It is no secret among us in the ranks that as a service weapon the lance in America is an utter failure. They are useless except in a mounted charge, and not one such charge did I see. One of our carbineers is worth a dozen lancers in our service. Our officers, on the other hand, are very fond of the colourful show our pennons make. They don't have to carry them.

I almost forgot to mention that we got to see a military balloon ascension by a Mr. Hall, who is one of Professor Lowe's people.[9] He went up to spy out rebel land, but descended very quickly, as he was within range of the enemy's guns.

In this momentous campaign we have seen many strange sights and fought in nearly every fight, but it has usually been only a squadron, company, or detachment engaged at each place. Also we have been used on many kinds of service, such as headquarters guard, provo marshall's men, etc.

Before I end this epistle I want to give you a few lines from a spritely song that is sweeping through the army. Its title is 'Kingdom Comin'', and it goes this way—

> Say, darkies, hab you seen de massa,
> Wid de muff-stash on his face,
> Go 'long de road some time dis mornin',
> Like he gwine to leab de place?
> He seen a smoke way up de ribber,
> Whar de Linkum gunboats lay;
> He took his hat, an' lef' berry sudden,
> An' I spec' he's runa-way!
> *Chorus*
> De Massa run, ha, ha!
> De Darky stay, ho, ho!
> It mus' be now de king-dom comin',
> An' de Year ob Ju-bi-lo!

Your brother 'til death,
Lonzo

5.)

In the Field,
Near Frederick, Md.
September 13, 1862

Dear Charles

This short and hurried note finds us galloping pell-mell after the rebel army under Lee, which has crossed the Potomac and is headed for Jesus knows where. He'll not cross the Pennsylvania line if we of the 6th have anything to say about it! Lieutenant Leiper, with Co. 'A', met a party of the enemy some 45 minutes ago and whipped them soundly. His men, though armed only with pistols and lances, charged, routed them, and took several prisoners.

Little Mac is back at the helm, after Pope's fiasco,[10] and the news has shot new life into every man in this army. My sleeves are now adorned with a sergeant's chevrons, as you may already have heard. The bugler is sounding 'Boots and Saddles', so I must break off.

Yours in haste,
Alonzo

6.)

Camp near Frederick, Maryland
October 13, 1862

Dear Charles,

We are encamped once again near Frederick City, about one and one-half miles from the town. Colonel Rush is taking the opportunity to refit the regiment. Tomorrow Lt. Leiper leaves for Philadelphia on recruiting duty, as our ranks are sorely in need of replacements. Write and let me know if any of our friends are contemplating enlistment, for if so they can't do better than our regiment.

You have doubtless by now learned of the raid into Pennsylvania of our old enemy, Stuart. We have been out dogging his tracks since Friday, but it is a damned hard trick, as we have only seven severely depleted companies. Much of the intelligence of Stuart's movements comes to our army headquarters from us. Corporal John Anders of Company 'D' has had much praise heaped on him for a recent exploit in which he entered the town of Woodsboro on scout in disguise, talked freely with the men in the rebel column, and gained much valuable information. As usual, one company has been sent here, another there, and our regiment was seldom all together at one place. Chasing these rebel horsemen is frustrating in the extreme.

We were present at the memorable Battle of Antietam in September where the mighty, invading rebel host was halted. Some of us were with Gen. Franklin, others elsewhere on the field. The 6th made a gallant dash on horseback across a stone bridge over Antietam Creek on the left of our line, under a galling fire. It was some of the most desperate fighting I have yet seen, with horses plunging and rearing, and the frightful shrieks of the wounded and dying making the sloping fields and valley into an inferno on earth. Our own loss, though, was surprisingly light.

The next morning, as both armies lay exhausted on their arms and the burial parties began their grisly work, I took a look around. The bodies were strewn as thickly as cobblestones in a Philadelphia street, some lying in the most curious

A typical camp of Union cavalry in winter quarters – in this case, the 18th Pennsylvania, in February 1864. The photograph is from the Brady Collection.

positions. Some soldiers have indulged in wanton cruelty, but with so much steel and lead cutting through the air, there is havoc aplenty of an impersonal nature.

Charles, if I should fall, I want to be sure that whoever finds me will know who I was, and who my friends were, so I have purchased an identification disc bearing my name, company, and regiment. I wear it around my neck at all times.

Please don't put a fright into Mother, little Alice or Fanny with a recital of the scenes of which I write. The boys were all overjoyed to learn of the exchange of poor Frank, or what the rebels left of him. I hope the generations to come will remember how great were the sacrifices for our beloved Union.

Yours 'til death,
Alonzo

7.)

Winter Quarters,
Belle Plain Landing, Va.
March 11, 1863

Dear Charles

Much has happened since last you had word of me, but thanks to a merciful Providence, we are now safe in our new winter quarters.

Some few weeks after our brilliant but much-abused Little Mac was relieved of command, and the well-intentioned Burnside out in his place, we were set in motion toward Fredericksburg, Va. On the way we stopped by our old campground, Camp Barclay, at Washington City, and indulged in many a lively jest at the greenness we showed in those days.

In the holocaust that was the great Battle of Fredericksburg, we crossed the Rappahannock on one of the pontoon bridges on the left of our line, but were not asked to advance against the withering fire which forced back our splendid army. We guarded the bridge. If the rebels had spent years fortifying their position they could not have made it stronger.

Burnside next thought to try a flanking march, but the pontoons he needed from Washington were delayed and we got started too late. The rains turned our route into a quagmire of mud so deep that I half expected to see the cannon sink out of

sight entirely. Indeed, some swear they did just that. Across the river the rebs
put up signs reading 'Burnside stuck in the mud', etc., and offered to come over
and help us, damn their eyes. Many were the renditions of the new song, 'Give Us
Back Our Old Commander', when at last we returned to camp, thoroughly soaked,
and horses and men covered with Dixie slime from head to hoof. This excursion
has been dubbed the 'Mud March'. Well, Fighting Joe Hooker is in charge now,
so' we shall see what he can do. I wonder how many generals it will take to win
this war?

Our new camp here is arranged in first rate style. It was laid out in what was a
dense wood. The trees were cut down and used to construct our cabins. We used
our shelter tents for roofing. The company streets are one hundred feet wide,
with the officers quartered at the end of each street. Ample provision has been
made for our mounts also. We have the area almost entirely to ourselves and there
are no other troops to annoy us for several miles. We have named it the 'Camp
of Magnificent Distances'.

Our huts are roomy and quite comfortable, with fireplaces and all. The time is
passed with drills, cooking and endlessly grooming and caring for the horses. For
amusement we have had amateur theatricals, snowball battles (though it snows
here only rarely), and what have you. Some of the boys can't resist placing a plank
over the chimney of a neighbor's hut when the fire is going, and watching in glee as
the occupants, with smarting eyes and clenched fists, come pouring out. The
reading matter at hand is generally trash. One of my men is a devout follower of
the *Highwaymen and Housebreakers* series; he has gone through *Captain Heron*,
Claude Duval and His Companions, and *Blueskin Baffled*. Can't you send me
something worthwhile, Charles? A Shakespearian tragedy or a Walter Scott will
do nicely, and an issue of our city's best paper, the *Public Ledger*, is always
welcome. Mittens and scarves would also be appreciated. And any edible to vary
this terrible army diet! I'm sure that hard crackers will get me in the end, even
if I manage to avoid Johnny Reb.

There is alcoholic refreshment to warm the insides in abundance. The home
brew that circulates goes by such names as '40 Rods', 'Oil of Gladness' and
'Nockum Stiff'. When a soldier gets too frisky there are punishments like 'bucking and gagging' and the 'barrel shirt'[11] to give him a temperance lesson he won't
soon forget. One fellow of Company 'L' was found-out stealing from his messmates.
He was served with a shaved head, ornamented with a placard with THIEF in
large letters, and drummed out of camp to the tune of the 'Rogue's March'. Unfortunately, the new men such as he are not of the same calibre as we old-timers.

This war has taken a new turn since Father Abraham's Emancipation Proclamation. Some of the boys don't like the new dispensation at *all*, and they turn the air
blue with curses called down upon all darkies whom they view as the cause of all
our troubles. For my part, I think Abe's in the right. It's time we showed the
rebels that holding the niggers in bondage, and lording it over the free working-
men of the North, is the cause of all their present misery.

A Shylock of a sutler has set up shop near us, and we can obtain a variety of
fruits, tobacco, combs, cutlery, oysters, etc. etc. from him *at a price*. He has no
competition, but his prices are set by the government. For all his guile he is welcome. One item he doesn't stock is the ·54 calibre Sharps Carbine,[12] but I heartily
wish he did. On the 25th of last month each company drew 12 carbines from the

An army sutler's store in winter quarters; a photograph from the Brady Collection.

quartermaster. They are now carried by picked men, but it is high time *every man* in the regiment had one. The lance has to be one of the great fiascoes of this war.

Charles, you must write more often about what has been happening at home. Has Fanny married her Irishman Michael yet? Father's loathing for the natives of the Emerald Isle knows no bounds as you well know, and it will be a hard go if that match is brought off.

All his old comrades send their regards to Frank, and Chaplain Gracey asks to be remembered to Father.

Your brother,
Alonzo

8.)

On Picket near Dumfries, Va.
May 27, 1863

Dear Charles,

It has been quite some time since last you heard from me. I trust these few lines find you enjoying good health, high spirits, and the comforts of our family circle, all of which were denied me recently, for I have only just recovered from a severe attack of the diarrhoea, brought on by the extreme hardships of our last expedition, of which more shortly. Sickness overtakes every man in our army sooner or later, and disease is a worse scourge to our ranks than all the bullets, shot, and shell the rebels can hurl. It has laid low many of the gallant band that started off in such glee from old Camp Meigs in the long ago. Col. Rush himself, as you must know, was incapacitated by the renewed attacks of a case of dysentery contracted in the Mexican War. He has left the regiment, I fear for good, at the entreaty of Surgeon Coover.

The exposure endured on our raid under General Stoneman, from the 24th of last month to the 8th of this, was extreme indeed. At times, in the midst of a storm, we sank down exhausted into pools of water, hungry, without fire or shelter of any kind, and slept soundly with our reins wrapped around our wrists. The raid was bravely conducted, and enabled us to destroy a goodly amount of rebel supplies, as well as railroad lines and a portion of the canal along the James River. Also a great amount of valuable intelligence about the enemy was obtained. But it was all for naught, as our main force under Hooker was even then being driven from the field in the great Battle of Chancellorsville. So all our efforts produced only a successful side-show in the end.

On the ride back we were helpless to prevent the deaths of several of our force when they were swept away by the raging torrent of the swollen Rappahannock River during our crossing. Many successful rescues of men and horses were accomplished, however. There are times, Charles, when everything we do appears to have no useful plan or purpose!

Lt. William Sproul of Company 'F' died of disease on May 19. He was highly regarded by all who knew him. Before his body was sent back to Philadelphia for burial with full military honors, he was carefully embalmed. For my part, Charles, I would rather die instantly in a charge than endure the agonies of a protracted illness, for all the fancy honors and lifelike preservation of corpses to be had in the rear. Truth to tell, I intend to avoid going *either way*.

Why the rebel soldiers continue to fight this war is a mystery to me. The impoverished poor whites who fill their regiments rarely hold slaves, yet they eagerly do the bidding of their slaveocrat officers. I have seen their men perform acts of the most desperate courage, risking life and limb for a cause that would disgrace the Devil himself. I read that the frenzy of some of their attacks is inspired by whiskey. It is a fact that the one captured officer to whom I talked was besotted beyond belief. He must have fallen from his mount several times that day before being taken, for he looked all used up.

The slaveholders must be taught a lesson. Charles, I have concluded that I am

A fine drawing of Union cavalry fighting dismounted with Sharps carbines.

all in favor of nigger soldiers. It seems only just that it should be they who put the arrogant master class in their places. Besides, when it comes to who will stop the rebel minnie balls, I'd sooner it were Sambo than me. Perhaps I could make my entrance into the shoulder strap society as an officer of colored troops. What think you of that? Most of the boys believe that when you give a darky a gun he will think himself as good as a white man, and get other high-falutin' ideas, but I think they will know where to toe the mark, and what they can or can't do. No one in his right mind thinks the nigger will ever be on the same plane as the white.

The lance is now but a memory, as we all finally have been issued our Sharps Carbines. Now that we have some real weapons, Jeff Davis' lackies had best beware of *the 6th!*

My love to you all,
Your brother,
Alonzo

P.S. Please beg Father to go easy on Michael; you might hint that the Dutch and Irish are here to stay.

9.)

Bivouac Near Blackburn's Ford,
Virginia
June 15, 1863

Dear Charles,

This hastily written missive leaves me in good health, and hopeful that we will soon have a share in striking the death blow to the rebellion. The ragged horde of Lee is again on the move north, but we mean to cut his mischief short, and show him that the Yankee boys will put up with no more pranks above the Potomac.

On the 9th of this month was fought one of the greatest engagements of this war, and the most awesome of any we have yet seen. Our Cavalry Corps, with a handful of infantry, met the rebel cavalry corps, supported by infantry and masked batteries, and gave them to know what it is to receive sabre cut for sabre cut in the open fields. No more are the horsemen of our old Army of the Potomac scattered all over creation, but firmly united, and ready for come what may. We are finally done with playing lances, and the bing! bing! of our carbines now greets the foe instead of the ancient polearms of a romance by Walter Scott.

After a frightening night ride through the Bull Run mountains without a halt, our weary men are tonight occupying some cozy cabins which the rebs have abandoned near the famous battleground that proved so unlucky for the armies of McDowell and Pope. The bleaching bones of our fallen heroes which I saw today rekindled my determination to see the war to a successful conclusion, and the so-called 'Confederacy' a prostrate corpse. I only pray my own blood does not join with that river whose flow has made this land sacred.

Convey my warm greeting to Father, Mother, Alice, Mrs. O'Brien and those of my friends who still remember

Your brother,
Alonzo

10.)

Cavalry Corps Hospital Near
Gettysburg, Pa.
July 15, 1863

Dear Brother Charles,

You will see by the heading of this letter that I am wounded. The ball struck the middle of my left forearm, but did not damage the bone. I was struck on the afternoon of July 3, immediately following the repulse of the mighty host of rebels in their final attack of the battle. Our regiment lost only three killed and seven wounded in this fight, although we lost heavily in the campaign as a whole. Many are those whose familiar visages will no longer be seen in our column on this side of the grave, after this invasion.

At Gettysburg, we were under the command of General Merritt, who was to the left of the second Corps. We arrived on the field in the morning of the third day of the struggle, having crossed the Potomac on June 27 at Edward's Ferry, and proceeded by way of Frederick and Emmittsburg, Md. It was all familiar country. When we arrived at the scene of the strife we were thrown in on the left of the line of the army, near the Round Top Mountain.

The ball was opened in earnest about one in the afternoon with an earth-shaking exchange of artillery fire, after which the rebels made the charge to which I referred. We fought dismounted, with horseholders sent to the rear, and that surely is a practical way to fight a war. I am proud to say that I had a hand in saving the country that day before receiving my wound.

I do not wish to increase your anxiety on my behalf by describing the ugly sights to be seen in this hospital. The medical department was overstrained, what with caring for a swarm of rebels as well as ourselves, and the care was none too tender for either, you may be sure. I felt sick when, amidst the blood and gore, I beheld the piles of arms and legs near the amputating table. It seems any wound in a limb, no matter how trifling, was reason for amputation, but thanks to my strenuous protests, my limb was spared. The work of the U.S. Christian and Sanitary Commissions at the hospitals is most welcome, but my heart would leap for joy if you and the family could come out and pay me a visit.

After the surrender of the rebel stronghold at Vicksburg, I am convinced that the celebration of our National Independence on the glorious fourth of July was but part of the 'Grand Design' for the funeral wake of Jeff Davis and his whole traitor crew. My only prayer is that I may return again to my old regiment, so that I may be in its ranks when the final benediction is said.

Love to all,
Alonzo

NOTES

Alonzo, his immediate family, and his friend Frank are fictional; all the other characters named in his letters are historical personalities and are accurately described. The letters are closely based, in tone and content, on actual letters which survive from the period. One of the most important features of the Civil War, from a historian's point of view, is the degree of literacy displayed by the rank and file.

1. Mobtown: Baltimore was notorious for its Confederate sympathies, and a Massachusetts regiment was attacked while passing through the city early in 1861. Gen. Benjamin F. Butler occupied Baltimore to prevent any repetition of this incident.
2. 'To see the Elephant': to experience war.
3. 'Secesh maids': the southern states seceded from the Union, thus a 'secesher' was a person with Confederate sympathies.
4. Father Abraham: President Lincoln.
5. Colt's Army six-shooter: Samuel Colt produced his famous single action six-shot Army Model percussion revolver in 1860, and it was widely used during the Civil War.
6. 'Taste for shoulder-straps': i.e., preferred to ply their trade among officers.
7. Jeff Davis: Jefferson Davis, 1808–89, President of the Confederacy.
8. James Ewell Brown ('Jeb') Stuart, at this time a twenty-nine-year-old Brigadier General commanding the cavalry of the Army of Northern Virginia. Brilliant, audacious and personally brave, Stuart rose to the rank of Major General and commanded the whole Confederate cavalry corps, finally dying of wounds on 12th May 1864.
9. 'Professor' Thaddeus C. Lowe was one of America's leading pioneer balloonists; through the personal support of President Lincoln he had been appointed balloonist to Gen. McClellan's Army of the Potomac, and engaged in numerous ascents to observe Confederate dispositions.
10. The Union Army under Gen. Pope was badly defeated at Manassas, Virginia, in August 1862.
11. In 'bucking and gagging' the victim was tied in a crouching position, often with a bayonet between his jaws. The 'barrel shirt' was a large barrel, often bearing a sign to the effect that the wearer was a thief, coward or drunkard; it was lowered over the victim's body, and he was then paraded around the camp and subjected to the ridicule of his comrades.
12. Christian Sharps patented his breech-loading lock in 1848, and his carbines and rifles gained an excellent reputation in the decades which followed. A large trigger guard moved downwards in a lever action, allowing a block to drop and exposing the breech. A paper —later, metal—cartridge was placed in the chamber, and the returning block sliced the paper and exposed the powder. A separate primer was accommodated on a nipple to the right of the breech and was struck by the external hammer.

SELECT BIBLIOGRAPHY

Samuel P. Bates, *History of the Pennsylvania Volunteers, 1861–65*, 5 volumes, Harrisburg, 1869–76.

John Billings, *Hardtack and Coffee, or the Unwritten Story of Army Life*, Boston, 1887.

Albert G. Brackett, *History of the U.S. Cavalry*, New York, 1865.

Bruce Catton, *Mr. Lincoln's Army*, Doubleday, Garden City, 1951.

Bruce Catton, *Glory Road*, Doubleday, Garden City, 1952.

Bruce Catton, *A Stillness at Appomattox*, Doubleday, Garden City, 1953.

Rev. S. L. Gracey, *Annals of the Sixth Pennsylvania Cavalry*, Philadelphia, 1868.

Margaret Leech, *Reveille in Washington*, New York, 1941.

Francis Lord, *They Fought for the Union*, Harrisburg, 1960.

Francis T. Miller (ed.), *Photographic History of the Civil War, Vol. 4, The Cavalry*, New York, 1911.

John P. Nicholson and Lewis E. Beitler (eds.), *Pennsylvania at Gettysburg*, 3 volumes, Harrisburg, 1914.

Chas. D. Rhodes, *History of the Cavalry of the Army of the Potomac*, Kansas City, 1900.

Bell I. Wiley, *The Life of Billy Yank*, Indianapolis, 1952.

Kenneth P. Williams, *Lincoln Finds a General: A Military Study of the Civil War*, 4 volumes, New York, 1949–56.

11: *Isham Randolph Harrison*

Weisiger's Brigade stood in regimental front along the Lynchburg Road, tattered, mud-caked and powder-grimed. The men were at 'Rest', carrying only their muskets, cartridge boxes, cap-pouches and bayonets. As General Weisiger rode down the line he shook his head when he saw the commander of the 6th, the right flank regiment, start to call his exhausted men to attention. As he rode, his eye automatically took in the details of the regiment. The men almost starving: clothing of every shade of brown: here and there a pair of captured sky-blue trousers and, surprisingly, one man wearing a captured overcoat dyed dark brown. Only a few of the officers still had grey uniforms, and most of them wore short shell jackets in place of regulation frock tunics. Officers and a few ranking non-commissioned officers still had brass uniform buttons, but most of the men fastened their jackets with buttons of pewter or wood.

When he approached the 12th, the second regiment of his brigade, Major Jones, now commanding, and Surgeon Claiborne, one of the two surviving regimental staff officers, joined him. The other, the adjutant, was on foot at the right rear of the regiment, as specified in Hardee's *Tactics*.

As they rode by, the three officers came under the gaze of Pvt. Isham Randolph Harrison, Company E, 12th Regiment Virginia Volunteers. Numb with fatigue in spite of a night's exhausted sleep, still hungry in spite of an adequate meal the night before and a hasty breakfast, Harrison found himself reflective. He knew Brigadier General David A. Weisiger, had known him ever since he could remember. A Petersburg businessman, now not quite fifty, he had commanded the 12th from the beginning of the war until well after Isham himself had joined in late 1863.[1] Yes, he knew that stern, bearded face with the high cheekbones and high forehead. Harrison had the same cheekbones, as had his father, his two brothers and his sister. They were a common inheritance of the Harrisons, the Weisigers, and at least half a dozen other Virginia families from Rebecca Rolphe, the Indian girl, daughter of Powhatan, who married the English planter John Rolphe more than two hundred years before. More than half the regiment must be related in some degree—the inbred white society of Virginia assured that.

As the three officers rode out of his view, Isham looked down. God, what a mess. . . . He shouldn't say that. Sissy wouldn't like it. '*Thou shalt not take the name of the Lord. . . .*' But then Sissy didn't like much of anything. She was well on her way to becoming a bitter old maid. But it was true—it was a mess. Everything was a mess. He wished the sun would come out and dry his clothes. Still, even though it was a chill, grey day, at least it wasn't raining as it had been the day before, and the day before that. And he was better off than most—his brogans were in fairly good shape and almost fit, he had a pair of trousers that had no holes and a good flannel shirt under his threadbare brown jacket.

His sartorial elegance was the result of his brother Wyndham's largesse, he mused wryly. He had never been able to take to Wyndham. He guessed the final straw had been Christmas of 1859. The family had gathered at Chippax, the home of his branch of the Harrison family since it was built in 1660. Never wealthy, never poor, they had never built a grand house as had other branches of the family. When the need arose some ancestor merely added a frame wing to the older brick structure; the furnishings, equally, reflected changes of style over two centuries. Home from Washington College was Isham's oldest and favourite brother, Frank Lewis Harrison. Brother Wyndham, as usual full of himself, was home from the Virginia Military Institute. Isham himself was on holiday from Hanover Academy, the small school a few miles north of Richmond. Completing the gathering was Mother's much younger brother and his bride.

Isham's mouth watered as he thought of that Christmas dinner: oysters, blue-fish, home-cured ham, goose, turkey. . . . His last Christmas dinner, in the Peters-burg trenches, had been provided by the ladies of the town. The troops had looked forward to it for days. Isham's share had been one slice of bread and a tiny portion of ham. . . . He smiled as he thought of the church service that Christmas, six years ago. Reared a Baptist, remaining a Baptist throughout her life, his mother accompanied her husband to the Episcopal church on occasions of state, but the formalism always grated upon her. Her back, Isham remembered, always got stiffer and stiffer the closer she got to the church. Sissy—his sister, Ann Lewis Harrison—was completely in her element, however.

But it was after church, after dinner, that Wyndham finally infuriated Isham. Talk during the holidays had been of John Brown, the bloody-handed old murderer who descended upon Harpers Ferry with a band of cut-throats, seized the United States arsenal, killed the mayor of the town, the free Negro baggage-master and a number of others, and tried to persuade the slaves to revolt. Nobody revolted. The local militia was called out and Brown was finally captured by the Marines, tried by the Commonwealth of Virginia, and hanged. A lot of Yankees claimed they were going to rescue Brown, so the militia was again called out, and with it the well-armed battalions from Richmond and the Virginia Military Institute cadets, Brother Wyndham among them.

Wyndham had already driven the distaff members of the family from the room with his description of the hanging, and had angered his father in so doing. To change the conversation Isham mentioned that Captain Wickham had sent over officers and sergeants of the Hanover Troop to drill the Hanover Academy students. Wyndham, typically, replied, 'Ha—a lot you eleven-year-olds know about the army. And those cut-down Virginia Manufactury muskets you're using aren't worth the powder and ball to blow them to hell.'

'Wyndham!' his father cut in.

'It's true, Father.' And the irrepressible Wyndham added, 'Why wasn't the Prince George Troop mustered, Father?'

That was something Isham hadn't expected, even from Wyndham. His father loved the troop and accepted the captaincy as a trust as important as that of raising good tobacco on Chippax's thousand-odd acres, or his duties as Justice of the Peace.

'I thank God we weren't called, sir,' his father said quietly, 'and I mean that devoutly. I would suggest, sir, that the troop is half armed, some of the men less well drilled. Not quite up to *your* standards, sir, nor quite up to mine.'

Isham remembered that he left the room immediately. He thought, too, that that had been where all the trouble began. If the Damnyankees hadn't made such a martyr of that Goddamned John Brown, if they hadn't forced on the South the

A garrison of South Carolina troops in 1861, smartly uniformed and equipped. (*Library of Congress*)

realisation that as long as the South was tied to the United States there would be just one such attempt after another, if . . . he wouldn't be here, shivering in the clothes Wyndham had provided. It hadn't taken long after that, he remembered. Lincoln elected: the South seceding: Father riding off at the head of the Prince George Troop: Wyndham getting himself elected lieutenant of some new cavalry troop. Frank Lewis had written home that he had enlisted in the Rockbridge Artillery along with other College students. Hanover Academy closed, the masters and older boys going into the army and the younger ones going home.

Isham remembered visits to his uncle's house in Richmond. He remembered the camps around the city, and the troops perpetually drilling. There were a lot of soldiers on the streets, too, many of them in right fancy uniforms. He remembered the Louisiana Zouaves in their red and blue North African uniforms— Irishmen, he had been told, serving under French officers. Whatever they were, black eyes and broken noses seemed to be as much part of their dress as their baggy red pants. He heard the patois of the Louisiana Acadians; it brought to mind the master at the academy who doted upon Longfellow's *Evangeline*, but the French was unlike anything he had been taught at Hanover Academy. He looked with awe upon the tall, rangy Texans, and found he could hardly understand the English of the back-country Tennesseeans and Arkansawyers.

It had been pleasant visiting Richmond, if only to stay out of Sissy's way; she had taken over the running of Chippax and everyone in it. Then Isham's mother died. Sissy badgered the local mason until he got the gravestone up. Isham believed that he would never forget the look on his father's face when he came home, weeks after the funeral, and saw the inscription she had ordered: '*Sacred to the Memory of Elizabeth Lewis, Beloved Wife of Major Wyndham Bolling Harrison. She died as she lived, a consistent member of the Baptist Church, but her children sorrow not as those without hope.*'[2]

Not many weeks later Isham's father lay beside his mother, dead of some camp disease. And so it went: Sissy running the farm, running Isham, keeping his nose to his books and his hands to any convenient task. So it went until October 1863, when Frank Lewis was brought home, dead from a shell fragment at Bristoe Station; the gentle Frank, who had written home after Malvern Hill, '*We were exposed to the most terrific cannonade I have ever seen. God in His mercy saw fit to spare me, for which I owe Him a life of service.*'

Sissy laid down the law. Isham was not to consider going off to any fool war; Wyndham was already riding round trying to get himself killed, but Sissy and Isham would stay at Chippax, keep it going, and hand it over to Wyndham when he came home. Later Isham would realise that Sissy's scorn was born of horror and fear; horror at Father's and Frank's deaths, fear that their line would cease, fear that Chippax would pass to strangers. But now Isham was in a complete rage, a rage against Sissy, against his bereavements, against Wyndham. A month after Frank's burial he went into Petersburg, found Cousin Benjamin, and declared he was going to enlist.

Benjy had a few sharp words to say about petticoat rule on his own account. He was ready to go, and the 12th Virginia was the logical regiment. It was mostly from around Petersburg, and Cousin E.B. was a sergeant in Company E. If they tried to enlist in Petersburg they would probably be sent home; once with the regiment, however, they had a good chance of enlisting. The 12th was in winter quarters somewhere around Orange Court House. They would get passes from the Provost Marshal to go to Richmond, buy a ticket on the cars, and see what turned up once they were in the city. They had gotten their passes easily, so easily that in Richmond they tried again and secured passes to Hanover Junction, and from there to Gordonsville, the end of the line. From there they hiked, asking their way to the 12th Virginia, Mahone's Brigade. Generally the answer was vague: 'Dunno rightly. Up the road a piece, I reckon.' Sometimes it was a little more helpful: 'Somewhere between Mt. Pisgah Church and Barnett's Ford, I think.' As neither Isham nor Benjy had the faintest notion where either church or ford were situated, they were beginning to think that they might spend eternity wandering the road between Gordonsville and Orange Court House, somewhat in the manner of the sea captain in Captain Marryat's novel . . . Or was it the captain in the German opera that Mr. Jones, back at the Academy, used to talk about and sing snatches from?

'Isham! Benjy! You Harrison boys!' The shout came from the first of two escort wagons which bore the words *12th Regt. Va. Vols.* over an imperfectly daubed-out *U.S.* A bearded soldier riding the near wheel horse and wearing the chevrons of a Regimental Quartermaster Sergeant was evidently the man who called.

'What's the matter—don't you recognise me? Joe Spottswood.' They didn't. Not with the beard.

'Where you all headed? Down to the 12th? Well, come on, climb up.'

They knew Joe, a member of a hotel-keeping family descended from one of the colonial governors. As often with innkeepers, Joe could be cheerful and still keep a good eye on the accounts, which was probably a good qualification for being a Quartermaster Sergeant in what was now a poverty-stricken volunteer regiment. He passed the journey by asking for news of the latest doings in Petersburg and Richmond, and on arriving in camp directed them to the thirteen log huts occupied by Company E.

At the end of the street they found the hut; over its door was a crude sign, *The Indian Queen*.[3] They pushed the door open and were greeted by a haloo and an invitation to enter from a tall man in his late twenties who was standing, spoon in hand, by the fireplace. He introduced himself as Will Johnson. The voice was country, and the boys summed him up immediately. The hickory, homespun shirt was not government issue or town bought; the hearts stitched into the points of the collar betrayed loving pains in the making. Sister? Wife? Mother? Anyway, the shirt was obviously the product of a small farm whose owner may have possessed two or three slaves; the type of farm whose yeoman owner and his sons worked the fields alongside the servants. Johnson told them to 'come on in and set'; the regiment was out doing battalion drill, but would be back any time.

The boys 'set', and gazed around the hut while they answered his queries about their homes and their relationship to 'Ol' E.B.' The hut was about twelve by eight feet, with a fireplace at one end, bunks double-decked at the sides, and a home-made table built into the wall opposite the door. There was a ration-box stool, and pegs around the walls were hung with packs, haversacks and canteens. On the bunks grey U.S. issue blankets, worn civilian blankets and patchwork quilts and waterproof blankets were thrown over loose straw. The door and roof were of planks—probably taken from some barn, Isham thought. On one of the pegs hung a threadbare brown jacket with three worn blue chevrons on each sleeve. In answer to his query Will Johnson confirmed that he was a sergeant, 'by grace of God and lastin' two years', as were the other three occupants of the hut: E. B. Harrison, Will Taylewe, and Al Ferguson, an orderly sergeant.

With some embarrassment he asked the boys if they had any rations with them. 'I hate to seem inhospitable. . . . Things ain't too short here, but it's going to stretch it a mite to try to feed six of us tonight out of that pot.' Silently, Isham handed over a bag containing the remains of the food they had bought, and Johnson sorted it out; items he considered luxuries went on one pile, those he didn't on another. The luxuries went back in the bag.

'Them things yours or E.B.'s, if you brought 'em for him. Fancies is private property—grub ain't. Sorry I got to ask you all.'

After adding potatoes and onions to the meat in the pot, he drew a reed-stemmed clay pipe from his shirt pocket, broke a chunk of tobacco from a home-grown twist, crammed it in the pipe and lit up with a hot coal from the fire held between two twigs. As he puffed contentedly the boys heard the sound of a fife and drum in the distance.

The regiment marched up abreast of the long axis of the company streets, halted upon command, brought the muskets down from the right shoulder shift to the shoulder arms, faced left, the second and fourth files diagonalled into position to form the two-rank line of battle, and then came down to the order arms. Isham noticed that despite the ragged condition of the clothing, the exercise was conducted with precision as the orders proceeded from the colonel through the company commanders. Some companies, he noticed, had brightly polished arms; others didn't. After puzzling over it he realised that some companies had the long Springfield rifles which, as issued by the government, had bright finishes. The shorter English Enfields had a browned finish. He noticed that Company E had the Enfields, which were supposed to be better, more accurate weapons.[4]

Isham saw Colonel Weisiger ride down the line, then back to the centre of the regiment, where he gave the order to retire the colours. The boys were familiar with the ceremony. The colour-guard of a sergeant and eight corporals marched off towards the officers' row with the colour, preceded by the drummers and fifers and followed by Company F, the colour company.[5] When they had passed out of sight the officers brought their swords down from the salute, and the men ordered arms. After the colonel left the companies were dismissed, and the men of Companies D and E streamed down the street to their huts; the sergeants remained behind for brief words with their orderly sergeants, and as they broke up Will Johnson called out, 'Hey, E.B., you got company!'

The youthful sergeant glanced over, let out a yelp of astonishment, and walked quickly towards them, demanding what in hell they were doing there as he came.

They were spared having to answer by Johnson's bustle, as he introduced the other two occupants of the hut, fetched extra tin plates, cups and spoons, and began dishing up the skillygallee (a stew of beef of uncertain quality) with a running commentary on its complete deliciousness and the source of the onions and extra potatoes.

He raked out the ash cakes—corn meal cakes baked in the ashes—and dusted them off with a none-too-clean rag and his knife, flipping one on to each plate. He handed round a canteen which Isham found was filled with molasses. The coffee came from a tin can suspended in the fireplace.

After they had eaten, Ferguson got to his feet and said he was off to attend sergeant's call, and that he would tell Captain Patterson that E.B. had kinfolks visiting. He suggested that the boys bed down in the bunks of men who were on leave. At the door he turned.

'Isham, Benjy: when the ladies and the old gentlemen come up here to visit, we treat 'em like guests. But you're kin, and ablebodied; I don't reckon you all will object to pullin' your weight around here.' With that he left, followed shortly by Taylewe and Johnson.

There was a silence, and then, from E.B., 'Now will you all tell me just what you're up to?'

Benjy and Isham told their stories, or as much as they wanted to.

'I figured that might be about it,' E.B. said. 'Isham, Sissy will skin you and me both if she gets wind of this—and Benjy, I don't aim to face Aunt Mary. But we'll talk about it later. Let's get you all bedded down.'

He took them to a hut with two empty bunks. Of the two young soldiers in the lower bunk, Isham recognised one immediately; Henry Cousins, from Hunter's Rest, a farm near Petersburg. The other, they learnt, was Tom Gilliam, from Burnt Quarters in Dinwiddie County. Having made the necessary introduction E.B. left them, and Gilliam immediately asked if they were visiting, or come to join. On hearing that they planned to enlist he shrugged and lapsed into silence. Henry Cousins said that they might as well know something about the company. Its complete strength was forty-seven officers and men; the survivors of the original company were now all NCOs or had been commissioned, the rest were newer volunteers or conscripts. There were three men on leave, two detailed to duties elsewhere, and four in hospital in Richmond, leaving a duty strength of thirty-six. The full strength of the company would be sixty. Isham asked about the conscripts. Cousins told him that some were 'pretty fair', but few had their hearts in soldiering.

'What can you expect?' Gilliam asked. 'Some poor devil of a poor farmer or a mechanic with a wife and a passel of young 'uns at home trying to live on his $15 a month. Course his heart ain't in it. Particularly when he don't get that but about once every three, four months. And the way this war is goin' ain't calculated to inspire great confidence. Oh, sure, confidence in General Lee—he'll lick 'em if anybody can. But the trouble with this war is, there's just too many damnyankees.'

'What do you mean by that!' Isham bristled.

'What I'm tryin' to tell you is that we're fightin' for time. Fight long enough and hard enough and maybe those Yankee Peace Democrats will force Yankeedom out of the war and let us go in peace. All of us here have something to fight for.

All our families have some sort of property. If we don't live through the war, and if the Confederacy wins, even a stalemate, our families and land will survive. If we lose, we might as well all be dead. Now, you take the man without property; he ain't got nothin' to lose but his life, and gen'rally there ain't nobody to look after his wife and children.'

Isham heard him out. Perhaps . . . yes . . . this was what Sissy had been talking about when she said he wasn't to go off to any fool war. Gilliam had obviously thought things out, and felt deeply about them, else he wouldn't use that country idiom. When a member of the Virginia gentry really wanted to express conviction, he lapsed into country speech.

Conversation abruptly halted as the regimental drummers beat 'Attention'. As the field music struck up 'Assembly', Cousins and Gilliam left the hut; it was 8.30, time for evening roll call. Outside the boys heard Orderly Sergeant Ferguson calling the roll: 'Atkins, Allis, Cousins, Cowles . . .' Each name followed by a 'Here'. Then they heard 'Harrison.' 'Harrison! . . . BENJAMIN HARRISON—ISHAM HARRISON!'

The two boys looked at each other, jumped up, ran out, and took their places at the right end of the company. Sergeant Ferguson looked at them coolly.

'You young gentlemen have been invited to pull your share of duty in this company. As long as you all are here, you will. That means putting in an appearance at every roll call, and performing whatever other duty is assigned you. I trust you understand me. In the meantime, you have usurped the position in ranks of the captain and the fourth sergeant. GET DOWN THE OTHER END OF THE COMPANY!'

Red-faced, and accompanied by the chuckles of the soldiers, the boys headed for the left of the line. 'NOT out in front—go BEHIND the Company!' They dashed around the rear and took position. At the end of roll call the officer out front—Captain Patterson, Isham wondered?—dismissed them, and Isham heard him say, 'Sergeant Ferguson—about those two Harrisons . . .' He heard Ferguson reply, 'I'd like to speak to you about them, Captain.'

For the next four days the boys' lives were regulated by the rattle of drums. 'Drummers Call' was followed by 'Assembly', 'Reveille' by 'Breakfast Call', 'Fatigue Call' by 'Drill Call'. The latter delivered them into the hands of Corporal Walsh, going through the School of the Soldier. Isham began to remember it from Hanover Academy; the commands, the monotonous, flat explanations of the Position of a Soldier . . . 'Heels on the same line . . . Heels more or less closed, because-men-who-are-knock-kneed-or-who-have-legs-with-large-calves-cannot-without-constraint-make-their-heels-touch-when-standing . . .' Two days of that routine found the boys drilling with Company E in the morning and doing battalion drill in the afternoon. The fourth day, a cold, unpleasant, rainy day accentuated by the warmth of previous weeks, saw Isham on guard duty; two hours on, four hours off. He got through the day tolerably, clad in a borrowed overcoat with oilcloth wrapped around his shoulders; but that night the rain turned to sleet, and he was so cold, wet and stiff he could hardly move. A coat of ice covered his hat cloth. He didn't begin to thaw out until the next day, when it was his turn to cook and oil for the hut.

After about ten days in camp—Isham could never remember just when, but he knew it was a few days before Christmas 1863—he and Benjy were told to remain in ranks after Reveille. Captain Patterson and Sergeant Ferguson walked up to

The Chickahominy bridge. (Library of Congress)

them. 'Rest', the captain commanded quietly, and in the same quiet voice, 'Have you all had enough now?'

'Sir?'

'Have you had enough? *Will* you go home?'

'No, sir.' Isham wasn't quite sure which question he was answering, but he meant no to both.

'Alright. The regiment is moving up to the river for picket duty. We can't take you unless you are regularly enlisted—and, frankly, Colonel Weisiger isn't happy about taking you under any circumstances.'

'We want to, sir,' Benjy said.

'We'd thought of that . . . Alright, you can go, but you wouldn't be going if the Orderly Sergeant hadn't said you all are worth three conscripts apiece, and if I didn't believe that none of us has much to lose anyway.'

With that they were sworn into the Confederate Army, and were sent to the Regimental Quartermaster Sergeant to draw their gear.

'One piece of advice', said Captain Patterson on parting. 'In fact, it's an order. Keep your own clothes as long as they last—they're warmer than anything we can give you. Just get your overcoat, blankets, waterproof, musket, leather equipment, canteen, haversack and pack.'

The next morning the regiment began its march to the Rapidan for its three days' stint on picket. Isham soon learned the routine; a third of the regiment advanced to the river, with a third about thirty yards behind as picket supports, and the rest 300 yards back as guard reserve. It was not onerous duty. The men were on two hours, off four, and the lines were rotated. Holding a river line, when both

A Confederate casualty in the Wilderness.

armies were in winter quarters, was not a dangerous occupation, and there was little need to take cover. The men simply did not shoot at each other, unless their opponents tried to force the river. On quiet days pickets even traded tobacco—plentiful in the South—for coffee—which wasn't. Small boats made from pieces of board would be sailed across to the enemy's bank; the freight of tobacco would be removed, and the toy sent back with a cargo of coffee.

Christmas came while they were on picket. Dinner consisted of hardbread, brown rice, and a two-inch square of salt beef for each four-man mess. They drew lots for the meat, and Benjy won. On New Year's Eve there was an issue of coffee, sugar and dried peaches, a memorable feast.

And so the months dragged on. As January stretched into February, March, and April they repeated the pattern; three days on picket, then back to camp for more battalion drill—but always on shorter and shorter rations. The only relief from the monotony came in the prayer meetings, held once or twice a week. They varied according to the persuasion of the chaplain or lay preacher who led them, from Episcopalians to baying Cumberland Presbyterians and Baptists; they swept through an army of hungry, desperate, apprehensive men not by command, but by popular demand.

When early May came, the two armies began to move. The 12th Virginia, along with the rest of Anderson's Division, was detached from Hill's Corps to Longstreet's and began to march toward the Wilderness—a huge area of forest and thicket, so thickly choked with brush that troop operations were almost impossible. Apart from a few clearings hacked out by dirt-poor subsistence farmers, the depressing battleground lay under the endless gloom of the forest. As they pushed forwards into the Wilderness the broken and fleeing remnants of Heth's and Wilcox's divisions passed them, to hoots of derision from Longstreet's veterans, and uncomplimentary comparisons with Bragg's battered Army of Tennessee—a formation held in little esteem by Longstreet's men. Anderson's Division did not jeer; these men who had been routed were their own comrades from Hill's Corps. As Longstreet's regiments moved forward Isham's division was held in reserve in the second line. It was impossible to maintain a cohesive line—the fighting degenerated into savage engagements between clumps of Federals and clumps of Confederates, as both sides struggled through the thickets. As evening drew on the Federals reached the safety of hasty breastworks thrown up some time before; the disorganised Confederates could not hope to drive them further, and withdrew to dig in. The next day they faced one another, both apparently utterly exhausted.

With this began, for Isham and his comrades, a month of unadulterated hell.

Out of the smouldering Wilderness, set afire by the fighting, they marched; an hour for breakfast, then more fighting. Day after day, marching and fighting, defending the line here, attempting to counter-attack there, then the inevitable race southward to get between Grant's flank marches and Richmond. Spotsylvania Court House, the Po River, the North Anna, Totopotomoy Creek—all melted into one huge horror. Isham lost track of time, distance and geography; he became an automaton, incapable of rational thought. At one country store he found paper and pencil. He wrote Sissy, '*Grant never seems to weary of this frightful slaughter. He seems determined to wear us down. I have never been so exhausted in my life. I pray God that it may end soon.*'

That letter he wrote in the first period of relative rest he had known in a month. They were in a country of sandy soil, cut by ravines, and as soon as the forced march ended they had begun to dig trenches and throw up earthworks, using tin cups, plates, bayonets, anything to hand. Isham's recollections of the battle were hazy. He remembered hordes of Federals being cut down by artillery and infantry fire as they hurled themselves against the Confederate trenches. When the blue-coats could go no further they, too, began to scrape out trenches, and for ten days the armies faced each other; each night they strengthened their lines, each day sharpshooters picked off the unwary. Isham heard that he was at Cold Harbor. Day and night the artillery kept up its fire. The Yankees brought up Coehorn mortars; the Confederates had none. Isham's two clear recollections were of the dying Federals between the lines calling for water, and of 24-pounder howitzers being dismounted from their carriages and dug in at an angle to serve as mortars.

Then they were on the march again; the rumours said that Grant had side-stepped once more. Down across the Chickahominy, across White Oak Swamp, to the old battlefield of Malvern Hill; more scraping of hasty trenches, then probing at the Union line, only to be driven back by the heaviest concentration of fire from cavalry Isham had ever seen.[6] Again the Confederates waited, and again they were ordered south, this time to Petersburg, south of the James and Appomattox Rivers. The Federals had shifted south of the rivers and were attacking the city; the defenders had already been driven back a mile to hastily constructed works in the rear. The 12th Virginia led Hill's Corps on the march, and as they passed through Petersburg Isham saw the faces of the townspeople. The first glad cheers of re-cognition subsided into shocked disbelief. Later a cousin would show Isham her diary entry: '*. . . what regiment should come first but our own gallant Twelfth Virginia—but oh! so worn with travel and fighting, so dusty and ragged, their faces so thin and drawn by privation that we scarcely knew them.*'

There was no time for a welcome; the 12th moved through the town into a line now strangely quiet. Apparently the Federals had had enough for the moment. But less than a week later the enemy was on the move yet again, trying to extend his line south, and Hill's Corps moved after them. The new Division Commander—peppery Billy Mahone, their Brigade Commander until the week before—pushed them forward, and Isham remembered the sound of firing far off to their right. It died as they moved forward again, into a scattering of fire along their front—surprisingly light fire.[7] Then came the order to bring their rifles down from the *Shoulder Arms* to the *Charge Bayonet*. The speed picked up to a trot, and then to a full run. In seconds, it seemed, they were among a group of frightened Federals, shooting, clubbing, stabbing until the Union troops began to lay down

Wounded Federal troops trying to escape the fires which swept the wilderness.

their arms. Isham saw more than 1,500 blue-coated prisoners marched back through the city.

Another week, and again they were marching south, to Ream's Station on the Petersburg and Weldon Railroad. Wilson's Union Cavalry was rampaging along the line, destroying the tracks. The division halted, formed line of battle, and waited—and Confederate Cavalry drove Wilson's men straight into the arms of Mahone's Infantry. As the firing died away and the grey horsemen herded a thousand prisoners off the field, Isham watched the Union wagons burn. Then back to the Petersburg lines, each man lost in his own thoughts; idle chatter had stopped at the Wilderness. In spite of his weariness, Isham was elated. *If this just keeps up, we stand a chance . . . a bare one, but a chance. . .*

A month of tedious, backbreaking labour on the fortifications south of Petersburg followed; the 12th suffered more from the heat than from the sporadic Federal fire. Occasionally Isham and Benjy managed to get into the city for a bath, a meal and a night's sleep at Aunt Mary's. She was visibly appalled that sixteen-year-olds could be so silent, so gaunt. There was no news of Chippax, far behind Union lines, and only the occasional word of Wyndham, now wearing the three bars of a captain. At the end of the month the strange lull was broken by a single, distant roar; the Federals had finally exploded their mine under Elliott's Salient, east of the city. It was not unexpected. Tension had been growing for weeks, but when the explosion came it seemed to paralyse both sides with amazement. Then came the mutter and boom of a heavy cannonade.

Within minutes Mahone's Division had formed and began to march at the double through the ravines, emerging in a swale between Blandford Cemetery and Elliott's Salient. The infantry quickly cleared the Federals from trenches north of the new crater, then paused while guns and mortars pounded the enemy troops packing the crater. When the artillery fire ceased they advanced again, firing, reloading, and firing again. The tempo picked up as the Confederates realised that Negroes were among their adversaries, and the high-pitched scream of the Rebel yell became a scream of rage. *John Brown all over again*, thought Isham, as he was swept into the mêlée. He clubbed a blue-coated soldier to the ground, then felt his leg jerked from under him. As he spun he felt a jolt to his shoulder. Flat on his back, he saw a Yank looming above him, aiming a blow at his head with a clubbed musket—then the Federal was lifted completely off his feet and crashed limply down on top of Isham, his weapon smashing against the boy's skull.

Later, Isham was barely conscious of a weight being dragged off him, of a voice saying, 'Hey, this one's alive.' He remembered a jolting litter, an ambulance, and pain in his head, his shoulder and his leg. As the surgeon's probe went into the shoulder wound he passed out again.

Consciousness returned in a hospital ward. A surgeon told him that he had suffered some muscle damage in the right leg from a ball which had passed clean through it; a shoulder wound from a pistol ball, which had been removed and which, he was gravely assured, he would probably carry on his watch chain for the rest of a long life; and a nasty, scarring blow on the head from a musket lock.

HE remained in the hospital for two weeks. He heard the matron telling one of the surgeons that she had never seen such vindictiveness on the part of Confederate troops as she saw in the survivors of the Battle of the Crater. Wounded men treasured their muskets, the locks encrusted with blood and hair. 'It used to be,' she said, 'a matter of "we fit them, they fit us". But those Negro troops changed all that.'

From the hospital he was moved to Aunt Mary's; his chances of recovery in the care of 'kin' would be much greater, and the army needed his bed. As the surgeon had assured him, he was able to creep about on crutches inside a month, exercising the leg-muscles painfully back to strength. Soon he could manage with only a cane, and was detailed for light duty with the Quartermaster Department, keeping accounts in a warehouse. His leg continued to gain strength, and the cane was discarded in its turn. Wyndham visited him twice; his attitude implied that Isham was malingering, and despite the Union shells which tore into the town daily he was disdainful of his brother's existence as a 'bombproof' in the Quartermaster Department.

Conditions in the city deteriorated, and Isham's military ration did little to ease the strain on his aunt's household. He knew he was a burden, and for that reason was glad to return to the trenches in December 1864. He found Company E literally starving on their feet, unable to work for more than thirty minutes at a stretch on repairs to trenches constantly weakened by the cold December rains. The mortaring and sharpshooting had increased considerably during his months away; desertions were rising, and handsome rewards were being offered to men who turned in potential deserters. Christmas came and went, with its pittance of a dinner; few grumbled, for they knew that even that mite had cost the people of the shell-torn city real sacrifices. Life was a grim struggle for survival in the face of shelling, mud, snow, sleet and starvation. It was the harshest winter Virginia had known for years, and thousands of hunger-weakened men died of exposure and were buried in Blandford Cemetery. When March came—balmy one day, freezing the next—the desertion rate increased to 100 men a day. Others, no longer able to face trench life, climbed the parapet and waited for a merciful Federal bullet.

The 12th were released from this grim duty early in March, when Mahone's Division were sent north to the Howlett Line, across the Bermuda Hundred peninsula. It was like a different world. On the line between Richmond and Petersburg they were faced by the Federal Army of the James, not nearly as aggressive a foe as the Army of the Potomac besieging Petersburg. Isham watched men of a nearby battery, long in the line, prepare to plant their spring garden, while their chickens and milk cows wandered at will. Only the mutter of guns to the south reminded them of the desperate struggle being fought out almost within sight of them. The rumour circulated that Lee was going to try to break out of Petersburg to the east, to get between the besiegers and their supply depot.

One day in mid-March Wyndham rode up to the camp behind the trenches and thrust a bundle into Isham's hands, saying, 'More where that came from, young feller—and now, if you don't mind, I'll return to the gentlemanly way of fighting this war.' With that, he was gone.

'Right persnickity, ain't he?' observed Benjy.

'Who ever saw a dead cavalryman?' Tom Gilliam muttered.

A Confederate prisoner after Gettysburg. (Museum of the Confederacy)

Untying the bundle Isham found a new pair of sky-blue trousers, a grey flannel shirt, a waterproof blanket, two grey blankets, two pairs of socks, and a pair of slightly worn brogans, all Yankee issue. There was also a selection of canned food from a Yankee sutler's wares. Isham allowed that it was thoughtful of Wyndham, but Benjy was of the opinion that he had just been showing off at the cost of a short ride. The food, shared out with other members of the company, relieved the tedium of the dwindling rations, but not the hunger.

At dawn on the 25th Isham heard heavy fighting east of Petersburg, and guessed it was the attempted breakthrough. By nine o'clock it subsided, but broke out again to the south at noon. The Federals were counter-attacking. For nine days the division occupied the Howlett Line at full strength, listening to the firing and waiting with growing tension. It was dusk of 2nd April before they themselves were attacked. The assault was easily repulsed, but after dark came orders to move back, quietly. They marched silently west through the night, and by early morning reached Goode's Bridge, where they formed line of battle and lay on their arms. Just after noon Isham was shaken from a hungry sleep; they were to march again.[8]

Isham only retained scattered impressions of the rest of that march. Marines and sailors marching westward: artillerymen with smoothbore muskets but no cartridge boxes: Joe Spottswood, standing by the road with a few barrels and telling them to help themselves to as much corned beef as they could carry. Forming for line of battle to fight off Yank cavalry intent on capturing the wagons . . . forming for line of battle to receive the pitiful remnants of Ewell's Corps at Sayler's Creek, where one third of the army had gone down the drain . . . forming for line of battle to try to retake an imperfectly fired bridge . . . forming for line of battle over and over again. Then there was the dead Yankee artillery captain, lying screened from the road by bushes. Isham gulped down the food from his haversack and idly went through his saddle-bags, until the daguerrotypes of his wife and children sent him fleeing in horror.

He remembered the stubborn rearguard fights which held Yankee infantry at arm's length. He remembered a young lieutenant—Isham didn't know him—who announced that he'd damn well run far enough; they left him standing on the Yankee side of a fence, sword and pistol in hand, calmly firing at the oncoming bluecoats. He remembered men falling by the roadside from exhaustion and starvation, and he remembered waiting a full day at some nameless place for rations which never appeared.

A ND then they had arrived here. Firing and still more firing, and the realisation that they were surrounded; then a flag of truce, and rations which seemed to arrive from nowhere, and a night of undisturbed sleep. And now, here he stood; damp, shivering, knowing what was going to happen, and waiting in a long drawn out agony.

'*Attention—REGIMENT!* . . . *Attention—COMPANY!*' All down the line. Precious few in any company now. Company K had fourteen, E had twenty-eight. Not 200 men in the entire regiment. '*By twos—COUNT OFF!* . . . *Shoulder-ARMS!* . . . *Right—FACE!*' The two ranks automatically formed column of fours. '*Support—ARMS!* . . . *Forward—MARCH!*' The regiment moved forward, lacklustre, dispirited. Not a sound, except the crunch of feet on the clay road. The surviving musicians, Tench and Josiah Birdsong, carried muskets. Isham kept his eyes down. The man in front had the heel of his shoe split, and blood was oozing out. A bugle sounded '*Attention*', and Isham looked up to see blue ranks on each side of the road straighten and then come to the *Shoulder Arms*, the marching salute. *Damn them. Damn, damn, damn.* Back through the column came the order, and automatically they returned the Federal salute.

The column halted, faced left, and, upon the order, fixed bayonets, stacked arms. On the out-thrust bayonets they hung their cartridge boxes, belts, and cap-pouches. The colour sergeant furled the colours and placed them on top of the stacked arms. Isham stood there mutely. It was over. For what reason? Two hundred years of fighting for a piece of land. Two hundred years of service to the crown and the two republics. And now it was over. He felt E.B.'s hand on his shoulder.

'Come on, Isham. Let's get our blankets and get out of here.'

As they walked he thought of General Order No. 9, read to them that morning.

He could remember snatches of it now; in years to come he would read it and reread it until it became part of him:

'After four years of arduous service marked by unsurpassed courage and fortitude, the Army of Northern Virginia has been compelled to yield to overwhelming numbers and resources.

I need not tell the brave survivors of so many hard fought battles, who have remained steadfast to the last, that I have consented to this result from no distrust of them; but feeling that valor and devotion could accomplish nothing that could compensate for the loss that must have attended the continuance of the contest, I determined to avoid the useless sacrifice of those whose past services have endeared them to their countrymen.

By the terms of the agreement, officers and men can return to their homes and remain until exchanged. You will take with you the satisfaction that proceeds from the consciousness of duty faithfully performed; and I earnestly pray that a Merciful God will extend to you His blessing and protection.

With an unceasing admiration of your constancy and devotion to your Country, and a grateful remembrance of your kind and generous consideration for myself, I bid you all an affectionate farewell.

R. E. Lee
Genl.'

NOTES

Isham R. Harrison and his family, their home, history and experiences are composites of several actual families. The other officers and men of the various Confederate formations mentioned are accurately named and described, as are the incidents in which Company E was involved.

1. Weisiger had seen service as a lieutenant of Virginia Volunteers in the War with Mexico, and had been Officer of the Day at the hanging of John Brown. Major Jones was a descendant of Captain Peter Jones, whose 17th Century trading post grew into the city of Petersburg.
2. The tombstone—a memorial to a member of an actual family—stands in St. Peter's Churchyard, New Kent County.
3. 'The Indian Queen' had been one of the finer hotels in Richmond, but had fallen on evil days.
4. The only problem lay in the differing calibres of the two weapons; the Springfield was .58, the Enfield .577. The Confederate ordnance developed a ball which could be fired from either. Many Confederate rifles had been captured, many run in through the blockade from Britain, and a few manufactured in Southern arsenals.
5. Officers' row: the line of quarters for commissioned personnel. The colour was mounted in a socket outside the colonel's quarters.
6. The Union cavalrymen were armed with Spencer repeating carbines; the Spencer, patented in March 1860, held seven metal cartridges in a tubular magazine in the butt. It was a reliable weapon, and very popular with the troops. More than 100,000 rifles and carbines of this type were manufactured before the company was acquired by Winchester after the Civil War.
7. The Union command had unaccountably left a gap between two corps, which Hill's understrength corps exploited to the full.
8. The 12th had been covering the bridge, which was on the projected route of Ewell's Corps; in the event Ewell used another bridge, and the 12th had to move fast to rejoin the army.

SELECT BIBLIOGRAPHY

In several cases this chapter has sources in common with that on Alonzo Wayne Crawford. The author also acknowledges his debt to Lee A. Wallace, Jr., editor of the *Military Collector and Historian*, for access to his notes for Francis Lord's forthcoming title *They Fought for the Confederacy*; to McCarthy's *Detailed Minutiae of Soldier Life in the Army of Northern Virginia*; to Berkeley's *Four Years in the Confederate Artillery*; to the letters of Ethelbert and Randolph Fairfax in the collection of the Confederate Memorial Literary Society; and to the kind assistance of E. M. Sanchez-Saveedra of the Virginia State Archives.

12: *Thomas Henry Ovenden*

THE bright moonlight gave the barren mountain landscape a strange luminous surface, cut through with the jagged black lines of nullahs. On an isolated hilltop, in a low stone sanger built before sundown by the picquet, Private Thomas Ovenden, 1st Battalion The Buffs (East Kent Regiment) stood guard. He was of medium height and stocky build, with the clear, observant eyes of a countryman. To be strictly accurate, he was leaning against the dry stone wall of the sanger; sentries in this country did not march about stamping their feet. They kept as quiet and remained as inconspicuous as possible. 'Hobserve this rule', the sergeant had said, 'and you might—Hi say *might* live to get your pension.'[1]

His eyes travelled watchfully over the slopes of the hill, pausing for a second on the twisted shape of a stunted bush some fifty yards away. Don't watch it too long, he thought. Watch anything long enough in the moonlight and it will seem to move. If there's any bloody thing you're afraid of, that bloody bush will be it if you watch long enough.

The rest of the picquet slept in their greatcoats, heads pillowed on their packs, waistbelts undone, rifles and helmets beside them.[2] A cool breeze, which would have been more than welcome in the heat of the day, rose suddenly and as suddenly died away. Ovenden shivered slightly. From the main camp 600 feet below in the wide dry bed of the nullah he could clearly hear the clop, clop of a restless mule pawing the ground, the whinny of some horse annoyed by its neighbour, the long-drawn belch of a camel. Before dawn he must rouse the rest of the picquet for stand-to. He looked across the sleeping figures. Suddenly one staggered to his feet, stumbled over the others, and proceeded to relieve himself over the wall. In the silence the breaking of wind sounded like the last trump. The man stood staring at the moon as if stunned. 'Cor, bloody 'ell', he muttered, and staggered like a drunk back to his place, collapsing again into oblivion like a marionette. Sergeant Brewin raised his head, looked quietly around, and went back to sleep.

Ovenden's mind turned to sergeants. Funny how the whole of nature seemed to be on their side. Their bootlaces never bust, their bloody buttons never came off, nor their bloody puttees never came undone neither. He imagined himself a sergeant. Room to himself in barracks; jolly evenings in the Sergeants' Mess, and two and fourpence a day to spend in it. Envy encompassed him as he thought of the unutterable boredom, the wondering what to do with time off in cantonments, and the long years ahead before the battalion could hope to go home. He was lucky in some respects. Major Moody[3] was daft on theatricals, always organising suchlike, and giving him walk-on parts—like the footman whose big moment, always good for a cheer from his mates, came when he said 'Yes, me Lord' or 'No, me Lady'. He got time off for rehearsals, and what with all them officers and wives, why, what went on behind the scenes was better by half than what they saw out front. Many a good laugh on that lark . . . Like the time him and two 'volunteers' detailed from 'C' Company to move the scenery had bored a hole in the door of the ladies' dressing room . . . Cor! Of course, that was in a big cantonment, but

Field Service equipment as worn by the British soldier serving in the tropics at the end of the 19th Century. The Slade-Wallace equipment consists of belt and harness supporting two forty-round ammunition pouches: a glazed leather valise (distinguished by the regimental badge) behind the shoulders, containing field kit and twenty rounds of ammunition: and below the valise, the mess-tin and rolled greatcoat. Cross-belts support a haversack on the left hip – here rolled into a pad – and water canteen on the right. The bayonet scabbard is slung on the left side of the belt.

These photographs are, obviously, posed; the model appears to be a long-service soldier with a musketry proficiency badge. In the field the white Slade-Wallace harness, pouches, and haversack were darkened to a neutral shade – sometimes by staining with tea – and a khaki-coloured cloth cover was worn over the white tropical pith-helmet. Distinctively coloured puggris – the scarf-like cloths wound round the pith-helmet – were affected by some units, but the Buffs wore a plain khaki puggri.

Malakand was a frontier post: no wives, no families, nothing. Anyhow, they were always on the move.

His mind reverted to sergeants. He'd got his first Good Conduct stripes and the extra penny a day that went with them, and Colonel Ommanney had recommended his application to extend his service from seven years with the Colours and five with the Reserve to twelve with the Colours.[4] He felt the stir of ambition as the concept formed in his mind, the possibility dawning that he might become a sergeant—even (imagination running riot) a married sergeant. He'd been on fatigue often enough, delivering coal or rations to the married quarters and pictures came back into his mind of those snug billets. A wife and kids . . . ah, there's the rub. Finding a wife in this bloody country, where the men outnumbered the women about a hundred to one. Course, there was a few girls in the Railway Cantonment, and glad enough to marry into the Regiment. But with only three married quarters allowed for every hundred men, what hope was there of getting married on the strength? Chapman had got married, and him only a Private. Pretty, she was. She had come out on the 'Euphrates' in '90, specially to marry him, though what she saw in him nobody could make out . . . He grinned suddenly, remembering the story of the gunner orderly bugler who copped it for sounding *Reveille* round the line until he reached the married quarters, where he sounded *Dismount.*

A British troopship on its way to the East passing through the Suez Canal in 1880.

He shifted the weight of the rifle.[5] Sergeant bloody Parsons, the Musketry Instructor, said it was four foot one-and-a-half inches long and weighed nine-and-a-half pounds. Well it ain't and it don't, he thought, this bloody thing is four yards long and weighs nine hundredweight. The straps of his equipment gave him a gnawing arthritic pain in his left shoulder, like toothache.[6] His mouth felt dry, but even so he longed for a smoke. Fumbling in his pocket he took out a small, smooth pebble, and putting it into his mouth began to suck it, feeling the saliva start to flow and the tautness fading from his throat and tongue. Saves your life on a long, hot march, that does, he thought.

His eye fell on the subaltern's sword, thrust into the ground beside the sleeping figure, the topi covering the hilt. Fine lark they had when he first joined the platoon. He come out with a batch of recruits, and his first job was a rifle inspection. For some reason there had been no NCO present, and they had straggled out on to the verandah in a wide variety of costumes, come to attention after a fashion, and each man had straggled back into the barracks without a by-your-leave when his own rifle had been inspected; and there they had sat about on the cots, laughing fit to bust. But he had never batted an eyelid. He came into the barracks and called for attention. 'No prizes for fancy dress today,' he says. 'Rifle inspection in ten minutes, on the verandah in marching order.'

A fine life for an officer, he thought, what with their hunting, and shooting,

A typical meeting of foxhounds in North India on which Ovenden reflects. Master of this hunt at Daodzai in February 1899 was a Captain B. R. K. Tarte of the East Kent Regiment (The Buffs).

The hill fort at Ali Musjid in the Khyber Pass, 1898.

their polo and bloody dinner parties, and all them goings on at the Club. Every evening you'd see them driving up and down the Mall in their carriages or gigs, or on horseback, bowing and bloody scraping to each other, the young 'uns chasing the few unmarried girls, and some of the married ones too, for that matter, like hounds after a bloody fox. Then into the Club for a booze-up, while the band from one of the regiments played on the lawn till it was time to change for their grub.

He pondered vaguely about officers. What was it gave even the youngest the ability to . . . he fumbled in his mind, but the train of thought died without conclusion.

Some scent on the night air transported his mind home. An hour before dawn, he thought, they'll be stirring now—he gave no thought to the difference in time. His father, mother, three brothers and two sisters would be moving about the cottage with candles, a lantern in the kitchen, while his mother bustled about the

Fort Jamrud at the foot of the Khyber Pass, 1898.

hearth and one of the boys worked the pump in the yard, filling buckets for her cooking and washing. He remembered the quiet of the Marsh, the moonlight reflected on the dykes, the soft cry of lambs in the night. It had been hard work all the year round, and little enough to show for it. Meat on Sundays, if they were lucky, and at Christmas a rabbit. One bad year their only Christmas treat had been a raisin pudding. When working they had been paid mostly in kind, and coins

Landi Kotal, a semi-permanent camp site near the Afghan border.

had always been a rarity. As the youngest he had never had any new clothes, always something handed down from his brothers, carefully washed and mended by his mother or the girls. Certainly he had never had anything so good as the khaki tunic and breeches and stout boots he wore now.[7] He remembered the old pack peddlar who had come round once a year in the spring, with his box of ribbons and trumpery trinkets, from whom his mother replenished her stocks of needles and thread. Once he had walked all the way to Newchurch with him, while the old man told him stories of when he was in the Army. True or not, they had fired his imagination, and the thought of strutting the world in a red coat, the Lord of Creation, had taken root. Sevastopol, that was what the old 'un had talked about—one of the Regimental Battle Honours.

Come Easter he had spent his day's holiday walking along the Canal bank to Hythe. Rum go, he thought. If it hadn't rained, if he hadn't sheltered in the porch of the 'Red Lion', he wouldn't have met the recruiting sergeant in his red coat, with the red, white and blue ribbons streaming from his cap.[8] That did it, mate; that did it.   But to be fair, the sergeant hadn't fooled him; he had been more than willing to listen before the couple of pints the sergeant stood him, and as for the Queen's shilling, he had never held so much in his hand in his life.   Not that there was much left after he had stood treat to the sergeant and the hangers-on, always willing to drink the health of a likely lad, at his own expense.   The sergeant was an old time-expired regular from the Regiment, and he had swopped yarns about the Crimea with an old pensioner who kept returning to some long tale about how he rescued Lieutenant Cox, who was wounded at the taking of the Redan. To hear him talk he had taken it single-handed, and if he had his rights would be a Field Marshal.   But when he started on how awful conditions had been, the sergeant had shut him up with another pint.   He wasn't having a likely recruit scared off by tales of hardship.

His mother had taken it badly, crying her eyes out in the chair beside the fire, her apron thrown over her head in a timeless gesture of grief.   His brothers had thought him touched in the head, and his sisters had wept in sympathy with their mother.   His father, who rarely said anything, said nothing at all, but placed a hand on his shoulder in understanding.   On Sunday the family had attended Church, and at the end of the service the Rector had made a few patriotic remarks

The road through the Khyber Pass.

about 'one amongst us going to serve his Queen and Country', and afterwards
chatted with them all in the porch.   The Rector had taken him across the churchyard to the rectory, and there presented him with a small Bible; sitting at the desk
in his study, he had inscribed it in a careful, spidery hand '*To Thomas Ovenden
from the Rev. William Charles Lockwood Wingham, Ivychurch, April 17th, 1889*',
while the cawing from the rookery filled the room through the open window, and
time stood still.   That evening he had met Mary behind the oast-house opposite
the 'Bell', and she had cried bitterly, and promised to wait for him.   She had
written once, the phrases stilted, the handwriting childish.   After a year he had
heard from his mother that she was to marry a well-set young chap from Snave, a
Trooper in the East Kent Mounted Rifles.[9]   Bloody Yeomanry!   It slowly dawned
on him that his mental expressions of resentment lacked conviction, were merely

A Khyberi village. The watch tower served as a fortified block house during attacks by tribesmen.

habit.   He tried to recall Mary's face, but the image was blurred and indefinite.
It don't matter no more, he thought, and felt a growing sense of freedom, of
burden removed.   It don't matter no more.   The little tide of elation ebbed, leaving
a faint sadness.
    On the steep hillside a pebble gave up a thousand-year struggle and surrendered
to gravity, the sharp staccato sound of its impact shattering the stillness.   He
froze, every faculty alert, every sense directed on the sound with the concentration
of a searchlight.   His eyes strained, his mind searched and analysed with the cool
calculation of the trained soldier.   He slipped off the safety catch of his rifle; for a
minute, for a year, he remained frozen.   Nothing, he thought.   Nothing there.
Slowly he relaxed, his breath a long exhalation, and slid on the safety catch.   In
the aftermath of tension his eyes prickled as though he had sand in them, the lids
heavy, and an overpowering drowsiness washed over him.   He pulled himself up

sharply. The banshee cry of a jackal, faint in the distance, swelled nearer, passed, and receded into the far silence. They said that once one of them started they passed the cry on from one to another right across bloody Asia, he thought. A phrase from one of the Chaplain's sermons came into his mind—'Lost souls crying in the wilderness'. Ah, that's it, mate; lost bloody souls crying in the wilderness, me an' all.

Pity Ginger weren't there. He thought of his mate—bloody fool. He would go, and no argument would stop him. Bribed some bullock-cart wallah to smuggle him into the native city from the cantonments under a load of hay, so now he was in hospital, God knows how long for, and a VD entry on his record. *Bloody* fool. He thought with envy of the clean sheets and the comfortable bed, the punkas swinging overhead. Still, not bloody worth it, he thought.[10]

In the east the first indications of dawn could be sensed rather than seen, and gradually the hilltops seemed darker against the sky, the stars slowly paling. He became aware of faint points of light in the camp below, lanterns moving about, flickering flames as the cooks kindled their fires, the first sounds of movement as the transport wallahs began loading up, the indignant complaints of camels and the thwack of an exasperated camel-driver's stick. Time to wake the sergeant.

The Caravanserai at Peshawar City in 1898.

He patrolled the perimeter of the sanger, listening, watching. A nice quiet night, no sniping, nothing. The 'Fridis were crafty bastards. Sometimes they would rush a picquet at dawn, the way the Bengalis copped it up near Jamrud.[11] Most times you never saw them. At best they looked like an old bundle of rags, and when they took cover you might look for a week and see nothing, not right between your feet. And they were not to be trusted as prisoners neither. The Rajputs had caught and disarmed some and took them to RHQ.[12] One old bastard had sat down and had a wash in a bit of a stream and then, quiet like, walked up to the Colonel, whipped out a knife from somewhere in his rags, and stuck him in the guts. The Rajputs soon finished off *that* little lot . . .

He bent down and placed a hand on the sergeant's shoulder. Brewin sat up, instantly awake, instantly alert, his white forehead in stark contrast to the weather-beaten face. 'All right, lad', he said. He stood up and stretched, adjusting his equipment, putting on his helmet. When the others awoke he would be, as always, immaculate. He began to waken the others, starting with the subaltern, his voice subdued. The platoon took up its defence position, half manning the walls, the remainder crouching in the centre, bayonets fixed; if the picquet was rushed, they were ready. In the camp below troops manned the perimeter, the reserves kneeling in dark blocks behind, while the dawn patrols moved quietly out through the gaps. Ovenden watched the patrols circling, the smoke rising from the fires, while the sharp, clear notes of the Brigade Trumpeter's bugle echoed through the hills. In the pale blue sky the rising sun turned the circling kite-hawks to gold. He noticed heavier and darker shapes among them. Vultures—bloody vultures, he thought, and searching the sky he became aware of others approaching from all quarters. Something died, he thought, and then remembered with a shock the Mountain Gunner. A mule carrying a gun-barrel had fallen down the khud-side right on top of the poor bastard, crushing his chest. His mind veered sharply, unwilling to contemplate death. The kites were bad enough, he reflected; bloody things would have the grub off your fork between mess-tin and mouth. He remembered the laugh they had had when old Ginger tied a string to a bit of meat with a bloody great stone on the other end, and hid it under his mess-tin as he walked out in front of the barracks. Bloody bird came down out of a clear sky like a streak of lightning, hooked the meat, and flew straight into the ground as Ginger let go of the stone, all dust and feathers! Still, the kites kept the cantonments clear of garbage and leavings; he supposed that was why they weren't allowed to shoot at them.

Below them the camp stood down; and after much searching of the hillsides with his field glasses, and earnest confabulation with the sergeant, the subaltern stood the picquet down too. Sentries were posted, and the remainder relaxed, conversing in low voices while Martin and Greenslade, the Signallers, indulged in a frenzy of flag-waving with their cronies down at RHQ.

'Here they come, the lazy bastards . . .' He looked down to the camp, and saw halfway up the hill a bird's eye view of helmets, heard the scrunch of boots as the relief picquet climbed up the slope. 'Here comes the idle squad!'—and a shower of catcalls and ribald remarks, immediately quelled by the sergeant, greeted the approaching relief. Not long now, thought Ovenden: not long now, then breakfast, and a cup of char.[13] His spirits rose, and the weight seemed to go out of his equipment . . .

NOTES

Thomas Ovenden and Mary are fictitious—although the family name is not unknown on Romney Marsh. All other named persons and places are accurately described, and the specific incidents mentioned are all factual, although in some cases they have been transposed in time.

1. *Nullah*: a ravine or dried-up water course; sometimes these were of considerable width. The usual practice on the Frontier was for the main body to move along the nullah while picquets advanced ahead and on the flanking hills, and brought up the rear. The numerous transport animals were thus well protected. Camps were similarly protected by picquets on the surrounding hills, in visual communication with the main force.

   Sanger: a small dry-stone walled enclosure built to give temporary cover.

   The Buffs. Originally raised as a body of 300 men by the City of London to help the Protestant cause in the Netherlands, and known as The Holland Regiment, this unit was taken on the strength of the British Army in 1665 as the Third Foot. In 1682 they saw service as marines, being known as The Admiral's Regiment. Some time prior to this a detachment had been sent to America, where they helped lay the foundations of the State of Virginia. In the late 17th Century the unit was known as Prince George of Denmark's Regiment, and later as Churchill's Regiment. Early in the 18th Century they became known as 'The Buffs', from the colour of their uniform facings. The title of East Kent was conferred on the unit in 1782, and this county connection has been retained ever since. The present Colonel-in-Chief (an honorary post) is the King of Denmark, in memory of the historic connection. The regiment's nickname—'The Resurrectionists'—is taken to refer to their ancient origins, in the same way as the Royal Scots are known as 'Pontius Pilate's Bodyguard'.

2. A picquet might consist, as here, of one section and an officer. A Battalion, commanded by a Lieutenant-Colonel, consisted of eight Companies, each commanded by a Major or Captain; the senior Major was second-in-command of the Battalion, which had an establishment of 29 officers, 2 Warrant Officers (the Bandmaster and the Regimental Sergeant Major), 45 sergeants, 16 Drummers (in practice, buglers!), 40 corporals and 900 privates. For practical purposes the Company was divided into two Half Companies, commanded by subaltern officers, and further into four sections led by sergeants.

3. Maj. R. S. H. Moody was the senior Major and second-in-command of the Battalion.

4. Lt.Col. A. E. Ommanney took command of the Battalion in May 1896. A soldier's pay was a shilling a day, and for every good conduct stripe earned an additional penny a day was received. A soldier was entitled to a stripe after two, four and six years' service without any crime entries on his record sheet. If he served longer than seven years with the Colours he could earn further stripes at two-year intervals.

5. In 1897 progressive re-barrelling conversion to Lee-Enfield Mk. 1 standard was being carried out, but many units, including The Buffs, still carried the ·303 Lee-Metford Magazine Rifle Mk. 1*. This was a sturdy and popular bolt-action weapon, with an eight-round magazine. It was normally loaded with single rounds placed in the chamber, fast magazine-fire being reserved for emergency situations. Loading the magazine with loose rounds was an irritating procedure, and contemporary reports mentioned the need for some kind of charger-clip. The sword-bayonet weighed just under a pound and added just over a foot to the overall length of the rifle.

6. Ovenden would be wearing the Slade-Wallace equipment, weighing about 50 lb. It consisted of a waistbelt with two

Detail from an action sketch by E. Hobday (dated 1899) illustrating the charge of the 13th Bengal Lancers at Shabkadar, August 1897. Although not an action directly involving British foot soldiers, the 51st Field Battery, R.A., was in action in support of the Lancers. The picture does however give a graphic idea of the nature of the fighting and of the terrain.

40-round ammunition pouches: canteen and haversack worn on the right and left hips respectively and supported by shoulder-belts: a glazed leather 'valise' or pack on the back, supported by shoulder braces: a mess-tin fixed below the valise: and his rolled greatcoat attached to the back of the waistbelt, which also supported the bayonet scabbard on the left hip. When not in use the haversack was rolled up and fastened into a small pad.

7. Khaki clothing was first worn on the Frontier in imitation of the tribesmen, who appeared to melt into the landscape. It was adopted widely by Irregular troops raised before, during and after the Indian Mutiny, and was also used by Regulars, who returned to the traditional red coats after the Mutiny. It was re-introduced for the Afghan campaign of 1879, and retained in various shades up to the present day. The 1st Bn. East Kents first wore the khaki uniform in 1887, having used white clothing until 1879. The word *khaki* means earth- or dust-coloured; the changing of the last vowel to *-a* alters the meaning to another but more unpleasant substance of similar colour, to which exasperated Tommies have also been known to compare their uniform. The white pith helmet issued for tropical service was fitted with a khaki cover for field use, sometimes with a distinctive puggri wound around it; the Buffs, however, wore plain khaki puggris.

8. Regular sergeants could be employed in recruiting on their transfer to the Reserve, provided they were recommended by their Commanding Officers and their names and addresses were notified to the O.C. of the recruiting area in which they lived. Recruits for the Buffs would report to the Regimental Depot in the old barracks at Canterbury.

9. There were two Yeomanry Cavalry units in Kent: the Royal East Kent Mounted Rifles and the West Kent (Queen's Own) Yeomanry.

10. Discipline: for such misdemeanours as drunkenness a soldier of the day could expect fairly lenient treatment—fines of between two and ten days' pay were normal but only imposed in cases of repeated violation. Deductions from pay were made for loss or damage to equipment, and a Battalion Commander could inflict up to fourteen days' imprisonment, with or without hard labour. More serious crimes were tried by Court Martial, and a soldier might face discharge with disgrace or, in the case of cowardice in the face of the enemy, death. For such offences as desertion within six months of joining the service, leaving his post as a sentry, or threatening a superior, the peacetime sentences for a first offence would range between 28 and 56 days' imprisonment. At the other end of the disciplinary scale, a serious crime on active service might lead to Field Punishment No. 1, in which the soldier was chained in a rigid position for two hours a day for three or four days, or up to a maximum of 21 days. To be chained across the wheel of a gun-carriage in the Indian sun was not an experience a man would wish to repeat.

11. The North West Frontier was inhabited by many tribes of Semitic origin, generally referred to as the Pathans but divided into sub-tribes such as the Wazirs, Mahsuds, Afridis, and so forth. They were, and are, extremely hardy, brave and resourceful fighting men, whose effectiveness was reduced by constant internecine feuding. They could assemble and disperse with extraordinary rapidity, and were masters of concealment by use of terrain and light. They were armed with assorted weapons, but made every effort to steal rifles and ammunition. On the occasion of which Ovenden is thinking, the Bengali sentry challenged the tribesmen in the dawn, but was shot down. The picquet turned out smartly, to be met with a devastating volley, and the tribesmen then rushed the position and seized arms and ammunition. The picquet was reinforced under the gallant leadership of *Jemadar* Ram Sri Khan, and the enemy were driven off.

12. RHQ: Regimental Headquarters.

13. A normal ration on service would approximate 1 lb. of fresh or preserved meat (which often accompanied the column 'on the hoof'), 1¼ lb. of bread from the field bakery, fresh or preserved vegetables (supplied by local purchase), tea, coffee, sugar, salt and pepper. Food was prepared on a Regimental basis, each Company supplying a cook and fatigue parties to fetch the Company allotment. Each man carried an emergency ration of just over a pound of meat and biscuit. Typical meals in barracks might consist of tea with bread and butter and perhaps bacon or egg for breakfast; meat, vegetables and a heavy pudding at midday; and tea, bread, and perhaps sausage in the evening. Further items might be obtained locally and paid for out of Regimental funds. In severe conditions rum might be issued, and lime juice was issued as an antiscorbutic when fresh vegetables and fruit were hard to obtain. Tobacco was also issued on payment.

SELECT BIBLIOGRAPHY

The British Army, Sampson Low, Marston & Co., London, 1899.

The Army and Navy Illustrated, George Newnes, London, 1897–98.

Queen's Regulations and Orders for the Army.

General Orders of the Commander-in-Chief, India, Government Press, Simla, 1890–97.

The Army List and *The Indian Army List*, H.M.S.O., 1897.

13: *Henri Gautier*

SOLDAT *premier classe* Henri Gautier, 66ᵐᵉ *Régiment d'Infanterie*, tried to concentrate on wiping the bolt of his Lebel rifle with an oily rag, but found that his gaze kept wandering out over the shattered and ravaged landscape which only months before had been clothed by the pleasant woods of Camard. Now, nothing could be seen under the wet skies of early May but a nightmare expanse of tortured earth, water-filled shell holes and crazily splintered tree stumps. The damp breeze was tainted with the smell of death, and the churned, blackened morass, streaked here and there with the grey-white stains of chalky soil, hid corpses uncountable.

More literate men than those who now lived here said that it had become like the surface of the moon, and Henri could well believe it.

The shell hole where Henri and his squad were lounging in uneasy expectancy had been enlarged and shored up with wooden *facines de couronnement* by the previous occupants, and was linked to the fox-holes and rough trenches on either side by communication ditches—little more than rat-runs in the muddy soil, intermittently roofed with odds and ends of timber, *facines* covered with earth, and anything else which might give protection against air-bursting shells. In the forward slope each man had scooped himself a shallow hole for further shelter; and Henri sat close to his own pathetic dug-out in the sticky earth, chewing absent-mindedly on his cold pipe and glancing frequently to the north—the direction from which the *boche* must soon come. The date was 5th May 1916, and it was almost exactly ten years since, as a young man of twenty-one, he had first donned the *pantalons garance* of a French soldier. Now his country was fighting for its life, and Henri, and his comrades on Hill 287 and Hill 304, faced undreamed-of demands on their courage and endurance as they guarded this vital sector on the left flank covering

Verdun. The whole army was being fed through this witch's cauldron; and apart from the common determination that the *boche* should not pass, Henri and his comrades were fiercely resolved that the 66th would not falter or fail in its duty.

He was a stocky young man, whose unremarkable features were unnaturally aged by the heavy moustache he wore, in common with many of his contemporaries. His strained face and red-rimmed eyes bore evidence of sleepless nights, but not yet of any killing exhaustion; for the 66th were newly arrived up the Sacred Way, and awaited their blooding. His eyes were shaded by the rim of an Adrian helmet, well shaped and comparatively light and comfortable; the steel was painted a dark smoky blue. His *capote*, or greatcoat, his tunic, trousers and mud-streaked puttees were all of horizon blue cloth, and the coat carried dark blue insignia at collar and sleeve, less visible than the yellow distinctions he had worn a few months earlier.

Although some of his squad had taken off their heavy leather and canvas equipment, Henri preferred to put up with the weight for the sake of convenience. It gave him something to lean against on the damp slope of the shell hole, for one thing; and one of his few personal fads was an unwillingness to risk leaving any of his kit lying around if he had to move suddenly. There was no telling what things would be like when the *boches* gave their full attention to the 66th, so Henri bore the long-accustomed burden without resentment—the big pack with blanket, spare boots and tin plate strapped to the outside, the leather Y-straps supporting his belt and three cartridge pouches, the two-litre canteen or *bidon*, the small haversack on his hip, the bayonet in its thin steel scabbard, and the entrenching spade.

Among the personal kit in his pack were some small luxuries sent by his wife in her latest parcel, to supplement the monotonous hard-tack biscuits and 'monkey'. Henri pondered idly on whether he should dig out one of his precious tins of sardines, or perhaps some walnuts, and try to barter with the young corporal for his tobacco ration. Henri had finished his own the night before, as he huddled in the corner of his hole listening to the occasional bursts of firing from the slopes of Hill 304; the corporal was a non-smoker, but always drew his ration and held out for a high price from some improvident comrade. Henri strongly disapproved of this departure from the good old tradition of share and share alike; but then, there were few enough in the *peloton* who remembered the old days. And tobacco was, after all, tobacco.

As he shifted his weight on the damp earth Henri reflected that at least his feet were dry; he had an old soldier's respect for the importance of a good pair of boots, and was careful to keep his well greased, and to rub his feet and both pairs of socks with tallow each night. Even the youngsters in the squad knew enough to follow his example, as *M'sieur le lieutenant* carried out frequent inspections, and reserved his iciest wit for idiots who neglected their feet.

Henri was stirred out of his reverie by a whiff of hot coffee. Some of the boys in the next trench had acquired a spirit stove, and the squad had each contributed some of their two-ounce ration to a common pool. Giving the action of his Lebel a final rub, he stuffed the rag back into the *musette* on his hip, and slung the rifle on his shoulder; then, fumbling for the mug he kept hooked to the strap of his *bidon*, he trudged over to the squalid ditch which led to the next position. He found that the proprietors of the stove had named their muddy hollow *Café du Rat Mort*, but despite the good-natured ragging this inspired among his friends as they clustered around the stove, Henri felt too preoccupied to join in, and soon drifted back to his place under the lip of the shell hole. He found himself gazing once again at the mutilated slopes of Hill 304, and remembering the inferno which had burst upon it two days before.

On the 3rd and 4th eighty enemy batteries had concentrated a frightful weight of high explosive and jagged steel on Hill 304, in an attempt to succeed where the Bavarians had failed in March. The men of the 66th had seen the hill erupt like a volcano, a huge pillar of smoke and debris rising nearly 800 metres into the sky. Henri had felt sick as he watched the ground torn to fragments, the very fragments to be further pulverised by the endless stream of shells. He knew that in the midst of that inferno men like himself were struggling to survive. He had been brought up as a good Catholic, and he wondered if God knew what was going on.

On the 4th he saw the dark masses of the enemy infantry moving up the slopes behind a continuing barrage, confident that no living soul could still stand in their path. He was a kindly man, and had a grudging respect for the personal courage of his foes; but nevertheless he felt a surge of exhilaration when the advancing waves themselves vanished from view amid the smoke of French artillery fire from the flanks, with the unmistakable music of twenty round per minute drum-fire from the 75mm. guns blotting out all other sounds. A faint murmur had risen from the companies of the 66th, which grew to a cheer as horizon blue figures were seen rising from the quivering ground. Ah, the gallant *bonhommes*, those tobacco-merchants of the 68th from Chateauroux and Indre, they were still there!

It had been difficult to see as the evening extended into night, but the lines of attackers were clearly breaking up, while darting groups of men who should have been insane, or dead, had replaced the agonising roar of the artillery with crackling volleys of rifle fire and the thud of grenades. During the night only an occasional signal flare had been seen, to be followed at once by savage bursts of rapid fire from the tireless 75s. What would they do without *Charlotte* and her crews, still known to the Germans by the name they had won in the days before the uniform changed—'the black butchers'?

Now, as Henri sipped his strong black coffee and gazed out towards the enemy's positions, Hill 304 was silent; but the atmosphere on Hill 287 and along the Camard Wood defences was charged with grim expectancy. The 35th Brigade were holding an important link in the Chain, and after the 304 affair there was no doubt that it would soon be the turn of the 32nd and 66th Regiments to endure torments such as they had witnessed over the past two days.

Private Gautier, the product of years of personal and national sacrifice, waited patiently to play out his final part in the history of his country, and the world. Gone were the flags, gone the traditional uniforms of blue and madder red, gone the officers in white gloves; but France could not have hoped for better men than these who now barred her gates, although the sufferings they would endure could never have been imagined in the days before they were plunged into a conflict for which naked heroism was all the training they had.

F RANCE's position as the foremost military nation in Europe was destroyed during *L'Année Terrible* of 1870, but calling on her tremendous recuperative powers she imposed on herself the task of regaining something of what had been

1914: cheered by crowds, a regiment leaves for the front.

lost. The Laws of 1872 and 1873 established the principle of universal conscription, and by the stroke of a pen every male citizen became a potential soldier. The heavy burden was accepted as a necessary evil, and soon a new army was in existence, intent on blotting out the dreadful sense of shame which clouded the memories of past military glories. On 14th July 1880 the moment came to proclaim to the world that the period of mourning was at an end, and the drums rolled throughout the land as every regiment received its first Colours or Standards for ten years. The outward symbols of martial pride once again flew proudly in the wind, and the *Jeune Armée* had reached maturity.[1]

The small and static population of forty millions was, however, a major cause for concern, especially in view of the ominous increase in the armed might of Germany; and in 1890 every able-bodied Frenchman was declared liable for twenty-five years military service. This was normally made up of three years with the Active Army, ten years on the Active Reserve, and twelve years with the Territorials and Territorial Reserve. Special cases of hardship were considered, as were students and men required for vital government work; these categories could have their active service period reduced to one year. Exceptions to the general liability were allowed only after rigorous examination of circumstances; as reduction of service meant extra taxes in addition to those borne by the nation as a whole, only a small proportion of the young men involved avoided the full commitment.

By 1895 Germany's population had grown to fifty-five millions, but the French, by their sacrifices, had struggled back to join the ranks of military powers to be reckoned with. The doctrine of the *Offensive à outrance* was accepted without question, and the compilation of the manuals was the monopoly of the Napoleonic theorists, whose only basis for instruction, whether for company or Army Corps, was attack. Never again would a French Army flounder and blunder into ignominious retreat, and if the German Emperor became too ambitious he would be hurled back to his teutonic lair by the descendants of the *Grande Armée*.

Henri Gautier, as the eldest son, hoped to inherit his father's business on the outskirts of Tours, where the family had lived for generations. They made their living by the sale of ornamental pottery and glassware, mainly from the factories of Tours itself; but Henri had plans to develop local production, so that his own designs could perhaps restore the Gautier stamp not seen since his grandfather's time. His little brother Jean Paul was a bright child who showed early signs of artistic ability. As their parents could never hope to afford a formal art education for him, he would be a useful partner in the exciting years to come, when the products of the Gautier workshops might even decorate the *bourgeois* homes of Paris.

Unlike Henri, Jean Paul longed for the day when he would be old enough to be a soldier; and every year, during the Summer or Autumn Manoeuvres, he would listen excitedly for the clatter of hooves in the street which heralded the passage of gleaming cuirassiers or sky-blue hussars. The rhythmic throbbing of the drums and the staccato notes of the *clairons*[2] echoing back from the old houses sent him running into the road to follow the tramping columns of red-trousered infantry, until his disapproving mother dragged him inside.

Rumours of secret treaties, or the political arguments in Paris made little impression on the Gautiers, and Henri made plans to prepare himself for his ambitious future. The family lived a normal life based on Catholic standards and hard work, and enjoyed enough food and good wine to allow independence from the complaints of their countrymen in the large cities.

In 1905 a new law established military service at two years in uniform with eleven years on the Active Reserve, and in that year the twenty-year-old Henri presented himself at the Town Hall to be registered in his military class. In 1906, after a period of unsettled anticipation, he received the inevitable call-up papers; and saying farewell to his parents and the envious Jean Paul, he set off to find the Depot of the 66th Regiment of Infantry. The 66th consisted of three battalions, and, with the 32nd, formed the 35th Brigade in the military region of Indre-et-Loire, with headquarters at Tours.

Henri's first contact with the military proper came in the leathery person of his squad commander, a regular corporal who regarded the intake of *bleus* with the exaggerated dismay of a ten-year veteran faced with a mob of mere civilians.[3] It was these NCOs, enlisting and re-engaging for five-year periods, who, with the professional commissioned officers, formed the backbone of the huge citizen army, and it was they who had the task of turning civilians into long-term soldiers.

Each section had its own living quarters within the barracks, called a *chambree*, and after being issued with blue *capote*, tunic, red trousers, *képi*, canvas fatigue clothing and a mountain of equipment, Henri was instructed to write his name above his bedspace, and to report to the '*double*' or sergeant-major, so called because of the two gold stripes on his sleeve. Under the most senior NCO, the *adjutant*, these men were to be the main instruments of authority throughout Henri's service, as commissioned officers were somewhat remote even in the army of a Republic. Officers were nevertheless held in high regard, as there was no doubt that they could do anything they asked of their men.

For the first few weeks recruits learned the regimental routine. Reveille was at five o'clock; a cup of black coffee was followed by four hours of gymnastics, marching and drill, until *la soupe* at ten. This meal consisted of endless *pot-au-feu*[4] and bread, but it was sufficient to sustain Henri through more marching, lectures and drill until the main meal of the day at five in the afternoon. Considerable rivalry existed between the four companies of each battalion, and this spirit of competition existed right down to the two sections which formed each *peloton* or platoon. Rifles were not issued at once, and until the section was reported fully able to function efficiently no shooting practice was included in the training. When the rifles were issued a further period of hard work followed while Henri and his comrades learned to handle the nine-and-a-half-pound Lebel with easy familiarity, to load quickly and fire with accuracy. The 1886 Lebel, an 8mm. weapon with an eight-round tubular magazine, was the first small-bore smokeless powder military rifle used by any army in the world. Nobody in the 66th called his rifle anything but *la Belle*—'the beauty'; and Henri sooned learned to refer to his twenty-inch *epée* bayonet as *Rosalie*.

Private Henri Gautier received one *sou* per day for the honour of serving his country. This sum was paid out by the squad corporal every ten days, together with one and a half ounces of tobacco, for which three *sous* were deducted from the pay of those who elected to take it. One pint of wine was issued free every day, but as gluts of wine were common this generosity with *pinard* did not cost the President of the Republic very much. Like everyone else Henri used the canteen with the aid of pocket money sent from home, but no French regiment had any paupers; unwritten tradition, with almost the weight of semi-official regulation, ensured the sharing of resources by squad-mates.

Henri's two years in uniform passed happily enough; he was a healthy young man leading a vigorous life among boisterous comrades of his own age. Marches of fifteen to thirty miles in a day were commonplace, and although these were always carried out in full marching order weighing some sixty pounds, Henri thrived on the experience. The *Grandes Manoeuvres* were always interesting, if exhausting, and there was a certain excitement in debouching from woods to see long lines of blue and red figures spread like flowers over the green fields of France. Other blue and red figures were always selected as invaders, and being so designated fled at once, to be furiously pursued by squadrons of cavalry, practising their evolutions to the sound of a barrage of trumpet calls. Everyone was physically tough, potentially brave, and able to shoot off the eight rounds from his rifle with reasonable effectiveness; and when Henri passed to the Active Reserve in 1908 and returned to his home as a *soldat premier classe*, he felt that he had at least done his best. For the next ten or eleven years he faced the prospect of two annual four-week training periods, but if this would help to keep the peace then Henri was content to do his bit.

In March 1913 there was a political crisis over the introduction of the Three Years Service Bill, and simultaneously a panic over the forces actually under arms caused the call-up of men of twenty as well as the twenty-one-year-olds of the 1913 class. Henri paid little attention to the newspaper accounts of the controversy; in March 1913 his life revolved entirely round Marie Deschamps, niece of an old friend of his father. They had met at her uncle's house in Tours, and Henri had been blessing his luck ever since. The chaperoned meetings had grown

more frequent; her mother approved of the rather serious young man with his careful manners, and after conversations had drawn from Henri his plans for the
Gautiers' business, Marie's textile worker father had remarked that he seemed to
be a boy of some promise. The family meetings of impeccable respectability had
led to Sunday walks, Henri promenading his young lady proudly but uncomfortably
in his best suit. They were married in September 1913, and by February 1914 Henri
looked forward to the prospect of fatherhood. In August the blow fell; Henri
looked out his mobilisation book and left the weeping Marie in the care of his
parents. It was worrying to be called away so near her time, but no doubt he
would be back before too long.

The French Army stood at sixty-two divisions; and among the 1,650,000 Frenchmen who stood to arms was another Gautier, young Jean Paul, serving with the
77th Regiment at Cholet in the Department of Maine-et-Loire. He was already a
corporal, earning four and a half *sous* a day, and Henri feared he would try to get
to Berlin alone, to justify this large increase in income.

Mobilisation was carried out fairly smoothly, the railways in particular being
well prepared; every motive-power superintendent and station-master had sealed

Infantry soldier, 1914. His appearance had changed little since the days of Louis Philippe and Napoleon III.

orders to be opened in the event of hostilities. Little country stations which
handled a few hundred passengers a
week in peace-time suddenly unveiled
mysterious sheds which could accommo-
date a battalion, and all civilian traffic
gave way to carefully worked out time-
tables for the movement of reservists and
the transportation of existing formations
to their points of concentration.

Henri took note of the mobilisation
instruction which said all reservists had to
take an extra pair of strong boots, and
extra shirts for which he was promised an
allowance on joining his unit. He would
return to one *sou* per day, but Marie was
entitled to a separation allowance equivalent to a shilling a day, with an extra
fivepence when their child was born.[5]
As she lived with his parents, and had
been employed by one of the woollen
goods firms at Tours, she would have
no difficulty in finding work in an
industry switching to large-scale production of military clothing after the child
was old enough to be left with its grand-
parents.

The 35th Brigade entrained, and the
seemingly aimless journeys familiar to all
soldiers began, to end without apparent
reason in nameless places. Masses of

troops were everywhere, but the 66th Regiment lived in their own tiny world, and marched off singing, or swearing, on the assumption that someone, somewhere, knew where they were supposed to be going. Halts were frequent, and they lounged in the roadside ditches under the hot summer sky, smoking or eating their haversack rations of army tinned meat, known universally as 'monkey'.

Stories filtered through the ranks about battles, and great victories; some miserable people talked of German troops having got into Belgium, but this of course was nonsense. Fritz was going to get a good thrashing, so there was no point in repeating silly rumours. The *Chasseurs à pied* were into Alsace, were they not? Henri hoped that Jean Paul would not be foolish enough to get himself wounded in what must be a very short campaign. The prophetic statements from those who claimed to be 'in the know' soon became a bore, and it was just a matter of wondering when they would see some Germans.

Suddenly the alarming tales became too persistent to be ignored; the Germans, it seemed, were pushing back French troops, and the Captain took it upon himself to say that not only the certainty of victory, but the very nation was in danger. The enemy might even threaten Paris itself, and every man must die rather than give an inch of ground. Name of God, they had not yet *seen* a German, and here was talk of last stands . . .

On 7th September the 35th Brigade moved out to assault the enemy; the Divisional Commander was true to his creed, and the engagement took the form of a bold frontal attack.

The Brigade advanced in splendid order from the edge of the woods; colours flying in the centre of each regimental column, they deployed into line, then extended, and slowly the pace changed from a trudging walk to a jolting run. The officers were well out in front with drawn swords, their bugler orderlies by their sides, stabbing out sharp notes on their *clairons* as the companies carefully aligned with the whole. What a brave sight they were, with shining bayonets, and red trousers moving over the fresh grass. Suddenly Henri saw them—rows of grey heads with spikes on their skulls—and at the same time he saw a ripple of tiny flashes and a splutter of reports. Immediately afterwards a regular burst of firing broke out all along their front as the Maxim machine-guns opened up on them. Every officer in his view went down, and the red and blue lines faltered; a sergeant shouted '*En avant, en avant à la baionette!*', a ragged cheer went up, and they stumbled on towards the twinkling line of flashes. Under the implacable lash of the Maxims the ranks swayed and withered, and the impetus of the charge died; Henri found himself almost alone, and bewildered, his rifle and bayonet poised in the 'charge' position by numbed hands while he looked around in confusion. A few men of the 66th reached the enemy lines, but the blue and red was soon submerged in the grey ranks, and it was with a mixture of baffled anger and relief that Henri heard the Recall being sounded on his left. He brought his rifle up, fired two shots at the spiked heads, then turned and ran. He joined up automatically with four other running figures, all strangers to him; by unspoken agreement they stopped, kneeled, and, holding their breath to steady their shaking arms, emptied their magazines at the receding line of flashes, before bolting for the woods. It took only a few minutes, and Henri, with his breath sawing in his dry throat and his limbs aching, found himself clambering back among the trees, as others crashed and tumbled for cover beside him.

Shells began to howl into the woods, and the plateau of Rochelle was covered with the dead and wounded of the 35th Brigade, scattered in broken swathes on the summer grass.

On the following day some 200 men of the 66th and 32nd were hemmed in among the trees near the Vause. There was not an officer among them, and command was assumed by Sergeant-Major Guerre of the 66th. This fine old soldier, with the strangely significant name, gave his orders with calm authority; and when his turn came Henri crept out of the woods with one of the small groups which left at intervals. Two men, Malvau and Bourgoin, were entrusted with the tattered remnants of the Colour of the 32nd. When the last party had slipped away Guerre, with a handful of volunteers—most of them regulars—turned his face to where the enemy were strongest, and charged out followed by his squad of heroes, yelling and firing as they went.

So died the 35th Brigade of 1914, except for the handful who managed to make their way back to their own lines; among them, Henri Gautier.

Paris, France, and the allied cause were saved when, to an angry chorus from the deadly French 75s, the field-grey masses were pitched back over the Marne— but Henri wept. He mourned not only his lost friends on the plateau of Rochelle, but also for his little brother who had wanted to be a soldier.

The 77th Regiment earned its fame when, on 9th September, with bugles sounding the charge, it tumbled the invaders out of the Castle of Mondemont in the teeth of murderous fire. Corporal Jean Paul Gautier led a section straight at the gates and was among the first inside the defences, where he died before he knew what it was to live.

By 1915 all thoughts of an early peace had vanished, and the authorities, anxious to maintain morale, introduced regular leaves for the first time. Each man was entitled to six days every three months, and the soldier's basic pay was increased to five *sous* per day, although some members of the Assembly thought that to die in battle was sufficient reward; these protectors of the public funds were fortunately overruled. Henri was now able to visit his family, and to hold the daughter he had never seen. He did his best to comfort his mother, still stricken by the loss of her younger son, although caring for *la petite Gabrielle* while her daughter-in-law worked long hours in the clothing factory helped to ease her sorrow. One of the two tricolour rosettes in the parlour window was draped with black crepe, a proclamation of pride and grief common to many families with menfolk at the front. Henri's father did not enjoy good health and it was obvious that a new start would have to be made after the war, if the business was to survive at all. At least his people were spared the horrors suffered by those whose homes were now a battle-ground.

The old uniform was now being replaced by one of *bleu horizon*, and the elegant and serviceable *Casque Adrian* was on general issue by the middle of the year. Few soldiers had ever used the futile steel protector meant to be worn under the *képi*; if they did, it was as a reasonable cooking utensil.

It was not only the appearance of the troops which altered, but their attitudes as well. Hundreds of thousands had died or were maimed, and the best officers and NCOs had been swept away in gallant—but too often useless—sacrifices to a God of War who had changed the rules without their knowledge. The losses of the enemy were also enormous, and the nation resigned itself to a long and bitter struggle. The jaunty *piou-piou* had been transformed into the cynical *poilu*, whose acceptance of his chances of personal survival was notably fatalistic. He did, how-ever, object to the translation of his affectionate nick-name as meaning 'bearded' or 'hairy', preferring the sense of 'good fellow' or 'plucky chap'. There were, of course, profiteers and shirkers, but as the call-up regulations became stricter many of these were scooped into the net, much to the delight of the established *bon-hommes*.

The British contribution had risen from ten to thirty-seven divisions of excellent quality, but France's 107 divisions still bore the brunt of the mortal struggles on the Western Front, and some voices were raised in protest over the amount of assistance provided by an ally with a population of more than forty-five millions and a large Empire. The war had now deteriorated into a series of bloody at-tempts, by both sides, to penetrate networks of trenches protected by forests of barbed wire, which scored across the Continent from the Swiss border to the sea, and tactics had given place to shattering artillery competitions. Unprepared as they were for such a situation field commanders, and governments, could only call for more manpower to be sent like moving human walls into the hail of metal which was hurled every attempt to break the stalemate. The old military virtues of courage, discipline and self-sacrifice were more important than ever before, as men fought and died without the elation of victory or the satisfaction of re-cognisably successful defence. Advances were measured in yards, and campaigns were, to the participants, isolated com-bats for the possession of tiny pieces of ground, won and lost several times in a day.

1915: even before the issue of horizon blue and steel helmets, trench warfare had its effect on the colourful uniform.

French troops attacked again and again during the battles of Artois and Cham-pagne, charging through a storm of artil-lery and machine-gun fire with astounding *élan*, only to fall back to their start-lines, leaving more and more of their fellows hanging like broken puppets in the *boche* wire. German counter-attacks met with ferocious resistance, and at the end of the day no flag moved on any headquarters map. Countless deeds of bravery were performed by friend and foe alike, but the unknown heroes who died were often among the one in three who found no known graves, disappearing for ever into the loathsome slime over which their duty demanded that they fight.

By early 1916, although France was proving more stubborn and her soldiers more battleworthy than they had dreamed possible, the German High Command concluded that she could not accept such a drain on her manhood for ever; and as they had good reason to be concerned about their own terrible casualties a plan was therefore conceived which, with minimum cost to the German Army, should either result in a collapse of French morale following a German breakthrough of spectacular proportions, or cause the French Army to destroy itself in attempts to prevent such a threat. The scheme had to succeed before the increasing British forces could bring decisive aid to their hard-pressed ally, so the place chosen was Verdun and its associated forts. For historical as well as military reasons, it was believed that here, of all places, the French would conveniently place themselves on an anvil, to be shattered once and for all by well-prepared hammer blows.

In February 1916 Henri Gautier was a *permissionaire*, enjoying one of the all too brief spells when the war seemed far away; now the noise of battle was exchanged for the prattling of his little girl, and the rough comradeship of the trenches for the loving concern of his wife. Marie was granted a special paid holiday from her war work on these occasions, and she was proud to hold her husband's blue-clad arm as they strolled along almost forgotten lanes, talking of their life together after the war.

She asked about his new *galons*, which he explained did not mean that he had been promoted, but simply indicated that he had one full year of active service plus two periods of six months. She asked him what his prospects were of becoming a *sous-off*—the term for an NCO which she had heard used by the girls at work. Henri smiled, and pointed to the single stripe on his cuff.

'We are needed to nurse the poor little boys they send to the regiment now, and that is responsibility enough, *ma mie*.'

Henri Gautier senior was not such good company as he used to be, and worried a great deal about the war, wanting to know how long it would last, and asking endless questions about matters his son wished to forget, if only for a short time. He also had strong, if ill-informed views about the inactivity of the British, and descriptions of their excellent equipment and reliable military qualities did little to remove a not uncommon impression that France was fighting virtually alone. Henri did agree that such good soldiers would be welcome in larger numbers, but assured his father that the only really objectionable things about 'Tommy' were his pay of one whole English shilling per day, and his execrable attempts to speak French.

On 21st February the leave ended, and after saying goodbye to his parents Henri went with his wife and daughter to wait for the motor lorry, belonging to a training unit, the driver of which had agreed to take him part of his way. On its arrival he made his last farewells and clambered aboard; as the vehicle moved off, its solid tyres rumbling over the cobbled street, he waved to the two bravely smiling figures, dressed in their best clothes for his benefit. They receded from sight, and as he settled back he became aware of the familiar grip of his shoulder-straps and the weight of his pack, and felt that he was already back in the war.

While Private Gautier travelled to join his battalion, the 51st and 72nd Divisions were cowering in their trenches while the greatest bombardment yet known to history rained down upon them, and Verdun. At 4.45 p.m. on that day six German divisions advanced on a front of six miles, in the first act of the great plan to destroy

the French Army. The battalions in the most forward positions were wiped out almost to a man, although surviving sections and platoons fought like tigers, and inflicted heavy casualties on the close formations of the enemy. On the 22nd the assaults were resumed with greater intensity, and Colonel Driant became a national hero when he died rifle in hand among his *Chasseurs* who, fighting desperately for every foot of ground, made the grey columns pay dearly for their gains.

By the 24th the soldiers of the German Emperor were already feeling the strain, and, exasperated by the furious defence in the face of what they thought was their overwhelming power, they made a supreme effort and advanced three miles. Some French units broke under the colossal weight of shells; but others were always there to block the path of the temporary victors, who, in their confident progress, became the helpless targets of point-blank artillery fire and machine gunners who refused to fall back.

France's situation was critical, however, and the fall of Fort Douaumont to the Brandenburgers on the 25th cast a great gloom over the nation. The appointment of General Pétain recreated a feeling of optimism, and soon very heavy reinforcements were pouring into the Verdun sector. The anvil on which the French were to have been exterminated quickly and efficiently now became a ghastly stage which not only the intended prey, but the hunters too, were to stain with their blood in a Satanic tragedy. By March it was clear that French valour, and very considerable organisation, had ruined the German timetable, but desperate battles were daily events, during which massive siege-pieces, field-guns, automatic weapons and grenades made the approaches to Verdun a dreadful slaughterhouse from which, each for their own reasons, neither attacker or defender could escape. German divisions had to endure their agony for long periods, but the French tried to relieve front line formations before they became too exhausted, and for this reason every French soldier knew that sooner or later his turn would come.

Henri was not surprised when, at the end of April 1916, word went round that the 32nd and 66th were about to 'have their jaws broken'. The regiment which paraded in the streets of Bar-le-Duc, between thirty and forty miles south of Verdun, was vastly different from the one which had marched away in 1914. Only a handful remained who had worn the red trousers, and among the tough old soldiers were pink-faced boys, and men who had seen little real action. At the age of thirty-one Henri Gautier was addressed as '*Papa*' by most of the boys in his squad.

Relationships between officers and men had changed, usually for the better. Although commissioned ranks were still the supreme authority in every formation, *cameraderie de combat* had created deep feelings of devotion for certain officers, while those who had proved less worthy received only the bare respect due to their grade. No better compliment could be paid to an officer than to be accepted as a *bonhomme* by his men; and while the term '*mon brave*' was accepted as a compliment from a fellow soldier when used by such an officer, this form of address from a green *Marie-Louise*[6] was considered insolence.

Discipline was severe, but of a character which mystified Teuton and Anglo-Saxon alike. Orders were carried out at once, and without question, but in such a seemingly casual manner that those trained to different standards of personal smartness failed to understand it. Obedience and individualism were jointly encouraged from basic training upwards, and recruits were traditionally addressed by their sergeants thus:

'If I march, you march. If I run, you run. If I fall wounded, what do you do?'

In response to confused replies about offering assistance, the *bleus* were told: 'No, you run right over me and keep going!'

Henri had on more than one occasion been fined, or lost evening liberty, for being late on parade or returning to barracks after hours, but had kept clear of real trouble. Two men in other companies had been awarded five years hard labour for insolence to a sergeant, and for a forty-eight hour overstay of leave, which amounted to desertion. These sentences began with six months in the military prison at Orleans, but in both cases the men had accepted the offer to serve the rest in the field. This meant transfer to the *Bataillon d'Afrique*, now serving in France; but good conduct in this penal corps could result in a reduction of sentence, and, in cases of outstanding behaviour, in the removal of the crime from the records.[7]

While waiting for orders to move, Henri saw all around him more military material than he had ever believed existed. Great dumps of artillery ammunition were everywhere, and the streets of Bar-le-Duc were crammed with lorries, ambulances and staff-cars. At last the waiting regiments were ordered to fall in by squads beside a long line of trucks, and after the roll had been called the men of the 66th and 32nd squeezed themselves into the vehicles, pushing and cursing as they tried to find room for themselves and their equipment. After harassed-looking junior officers had made final checks, the mechanical serpent moved out with a loud screeching of chain-driven transmission, and they were off on the legendary *Voie Sacrée*—'The Sacred Way'.

The road was only twenty feet wide, and as it was used by 6,000 motor lorries every day in each direction all horse-drawn traffic was banned. Gangs of Territorials slaved night and day to keep the surface in some kind of order, but the journey was a lurching, heaving nightmare, as drivers jolted into the ditches to avoid south-bound convoys. Abandoned trucks stood like forgotten toys in the fields, as all breakdowns were pushed off the road; and Henri wondered where they would go if their overloaded conveyance came to grief. As the trucks snaked along the rutted road bursts of song welled up; the popular *Sous les Ponts de Paris* became monotonous, but somewhere along the convoy there was an enthusiastic rendering of the *Chant du Depart*—'*La Victoire en chantant nous ouvre la barrière, la liberté guide nos pas . . .*'. Gradually the singing spread from lorry to lorry, as each squad joined in its favourite of the moment; for some, it was the sheer pleasure of singing, for others, a way to keep their minds off what they were travelling towards. *Le Madelon* could be heard, and snatches of *Sambre et Meuse*; Henri smiled to himself as he heard their irrepressible lieutenant somewhere up front, bursting into *La Galette*, the song of St. Cyr.

At last, to a shrilling of whistles and shouts from the *sous-officiers*, the journey came to an end, and the men clambered stiffly from their uncomfortable transport and formed up in weary, grumbling ranks. Morale rose rapidly when they were marched in files towards steaming stew-pots; reinvigorated by the hot food they almost ignored their first taste of the shelling to which the town of Verdun was regularly subjected. The area had been cleared of civilians in February, and although damage to buildings was extensive large underground dwellings had been constructed, serving as rest areas for units from forward positions and as dressing stations for wounded. Red Cross flags fluttered from many trucks, as they started the southward journey to Bar-le-Duc.

As they marched through the town Henri saw the *fanions*[8] of every Arm of the Service and Staff appointment displayed on the battered buildings, and he noticed a sentry in the khaki of the Colonials outside a Divisional Headquarters. He saw the old Bishop's Palace, now badly damaged, and the Cathedral itself, which enemy bombardment had not yet completely destroyed. As they moved on to the Esplanade de la Roche he got his first clear view of the Meuse Valley, and thought what a beautiful place this must have been, once. They were ordered to fall out, and filed down into the vaults of the ancient citadel in which the townspeople had taken shelter during the first bombardments. It was now a surprising haven of dry floors and walls, with space for canteens and even for proper beds. As the hours passed in this ante-room for battle most men took advantage of the post-box and wrote letters home; others played cards, and from several little groups around him Henri could hear the click of draughts and dominoes, which almost every *poilu* in the Army seemed to carry in his knapsack.

The following evening the 66th filed out under a miserable drizzle of rain, and as night fell they found themselves groping through a series of communication trenches, led by a guide. After ages of sliding in the mud, and colliding with each other in the darkness in what was now a heavy downpour, the order was passed to halt, and, with a clanking of equipment, each man subsided gratefully on whatever glutinous patch seemed least uncomfortable. More time passed, and as the officers peered expectantly at their watches the ground seemed to lift under them, and the air was filled with loud reports and blinding flashes from flanks and rear. A boy next to Henri leapt to his feet like a frightened child experiencing his first thunderstorm, to be pulled down at once with a soothing assurance that it was 'only us, bandaging the eyes of the *boche*'. At that moment the column moved quickly up to make contact with the troops they had come to relieve, and under cover of the French barrage the operation was completed without incident.

The 66th settled down in what was left of Camard Woods, and, like the 32nd on Hill 287, wondered what was in store.

The rat-runs of Verdun—more a series of improved shell-holes than a formal trench system.

H IS coffee finished, Henri resumed his watch over no man's land. From somewhere behind him he could hear a muttering of voices as the signallers tested
the company's field telephone lines. The defensive positions in the Brigade sector,
like those on other approaches to Verdun, were covered by an interlocking system
of artillery support, linked by telephone. The signallers laboured round the clock
to keep communications in good order, and, like the artillery spotters, their deeds
of personal courage went unrecorded.

The testing of the 66th's lines was still going on when the first ranging 150mm.
shells fell in front and rear of the regiment's positions, to be followed almost at
once by a stupefying roar, exactly as if hundreds of trains were speeding across the
sky, to reach their destinations with shattering explosions.

The crouching men were showered with earth, fragments of trees, a hail of stones
and shards of hot metal which rang on their helmets like so many evil bells. Henri
clawed himself as deep as he could into the largely illusory shelter of his scooped-
out hollow, pressing his face against the earth until it hurt and trying to draw his
feet inside his body, while around him his mates burrowed like moles in an attempt
to escape the terrible deluge. The air became foul with choking fumes, and the
shrieks of wounded men mingled with the coughing and gasping of those more
fortunate. The unbearable din increased as 210mm. shells crashed down, sending
up great fountains of flame and dirt, and officers and soldiers scrabbled frantically
to release comrades buried alive under heaps of earth and rubble. Bodies blundered
over Henri's legs as he strove to breathe, his ears aching as the shock waves churned
the pressure of the air around his scanty refuge. He felt quite certain that this was
the end, for no creatures of flesh and blood could live through such a ghastly onslaught. Yet hour after hour the storm went on, and he continued to live, and
soon he lost all sense of passing time; his mind retreated into some inner sanctuary,
and his body endured. When the horror suddenly ceased and he slowly became
aware of the deafening silence, the regiment had endured its punishment for eleven
hours.

The Captain tried the telephone, but it was hopeless; the lines had been cut in a hundred places, and already the field-grey masses could be seen moving quickly in the wake of their barrage. He called for rockets, and although minds were confused and reactions painful, a series of red flares arched into the air in an urgent prayer for help.

The leading ranks of Germans were now approaching the French line at a run, and as Henri dazedly cleared the dirt and mud from the chamber of his rifle he heard officers and NCOs bawling out words of encouragement, and the weary, battered 66th responded to the familiar orders, and prepared to defend themselves. As rifle and machine gun muzzles were individually levelled at the approaching menace the first salvoes whined over the head of the defenders in response to the rocket signals, raising a wall of flame and smoke just behind the foremost assault troops. The order 'Bayonets!' was shouted down the line of positions; Henri's trembling fingers slipped on the smooth steel hilt as he clicked the wicked twenty-inch needle with its cruciform blade into place. Tired eyes squinted through back and front sights, magazine covers were flicked open,[9] and the men of Camard, freed from their passive fear, poured volley after volley into the faces of brave enemies who had escaped the vengeance of the French artillery. The Lebel bolts slammed back and forward, thirty-round strips flashed through the breeches of the machine guns,[10] and bombing squads hurled their grenades into the groups which struggled to climb over their own heaped dead and wounded. Only a few of the attackers got close enough to die on the licking blade of *Rosalie*.

Henri, in an exhausted trance, realised that there was nothing more to shoot at, but before he could collect his wits whistle blasts sent him automatically scrambling forward in a wild charge, in pursuit of the broken, defeated men who seconds before had appeared as fearsome giants looming against the smoke of shell-fire. As he ran, stumbling over the broken ground with its terrible carpet, his tortured senses were aware of a clamour of small-arms from Hill 287, where the 32nd were beating off their second attack. Yards ahead of him he saw movement in a sprawled tangle of grey-clad corpses; a white face glared at him through a mask of blood, and a hand clawed at the loop in the handle of a stick grenade. He hesitated, realised that he could never get his bayonet into the German in time, and flung himself on his face. As a rending detonation tore at his ear-drums, drowning the gurgling cry of the man behind him, Private Gautier felt a crushing weight descend on his legs and back. He drifted into unconsciousness almost immediately.

T HE Sacred Way was still crammed with trucks, and as the ambulance came to a grinding halt the agonising jolt brought Henri briefly back to his senses. He was aware of very little except the terrible pain where his left leg should have been, and the sensation that his back was on fire. He tried to think, but as the forward motion was resumed he was rocked down once more into confused dreams of home, and persistent images of terror.

NOTES

With the exception of Henri Gautier and his family, all persons mentioned by name in this chapter are known to history.

1. *Jeune Armée*: the name applied to the reconstituted French Army after the Franco–Prussian War of 1870-71: literally, 'Young Army'.
2. *clairon*: bugle; the same word was used for the bugler himself.
3. *bleus*: raw recruits; the term was originally coined in the days when a tight stock was worn at the throat of the tunic, and refers to the complexion of recruits not yet accustomed to breathing with this grip on their windpipe.
4. *pot-au-feu*: a thick soup or thin stew made from meat, bones and vegetables added progressively to a stock-pot kept simmering for days.
5. The basic pay of one *sou* was equal to an English ½d. of 1914. It was supplemented by a 'loan' from the government, to pay for needles, thread, and so forth. The 1914 English values of the various grades of pay in the French ranks were: Private, ½d.; Corporal, 2¼d.; Sergeant, 7¼d.; Sergeant-Major, 10¼d.; and Adjutant (senior warrant officer), 2s. The British Army 'Tommy' of that time received 1s. per day and was thus, in superficial terms, twenty-four times better off than his French ally. Expressed in terms of 1971 "spending power", one 1914 *sou* was equivalent to 1½p. (sterling) or 4 cents (U.S.).
6. *Marie-Louise*: an inexperienced newcomer; an expression used at the St. Cyr military academy, and applied to officers only. It derives from the Napoleonic period; the Empress Josephine was held in great affection by the French troops, and they resented her being discarded in favour of Marie-Louise.
7. *Bataillon d'Afrique*: popularly known as the *"Bat-d'Af"*, this labour organisation was normally based in Algeria, and was the military alternative to civilian prison for criminals sentenced to moderate terms—two or three years—if they so opted. It moved to France early in the First World War and widened its scope to include military offenders.
8. *fanion*: a pennon bearing the insignia of a French military unit. It was the French practice for each company to be identified by a *fanion*, and in the infantry these were carried into action flying from the fixed bayonet of a junior NCO designated as the *porte-fanion*.
9. The Lebel, like many other bolt-action rifles of the first half of the 20th Century, was fitted with a magazine cut-off. Normal practice was to fill the magazine, push the cover into place, and load and fire a succession of single shots placed in the breech; for rapid fire, the cover would be flicked off and the bolt worked to feed rounds up from the magazine.
10. The standard automatic weapon of the French infantry was the Mod. 1913/14 Hotchkiss heavy machine-gun. The light machine-gun, fired from the shoulder, appeared in 1916 but was not in universal use until late in that year.

SELECT BIBLIOGRAPHY

Album de l'Armée Française, various annual issues, from 1906.

General Colin, *La Côte 304 et le Mort-Homme*, Paris, 1934.

Cyril Falls, *The First World War*, London, 1960.

Gervais-Courtellemont, *Les Champs de Bataille de la Marne*, Paris, 1915.

Paul Heuzé, *La Voie Sacrée*, Paris, 1919.

L'Illustration, various issues, January 1916–January 1918.

M. Macdonald, *Under the French Flag*, London, 1917.

Michelin Guides to the Battle Fields, 1914–1918: Verdun, Clermont-Ferrand, 1919.

Henri P. Pétain, *La Bataille de Verdun*, Paris, 1929.

John Terraine, *The Great War 1914–1918—A Pictorial History*, London, 1965.

Richard Thoumin, *The First World War* (English translation, 1963, from *La Grande Guerre* by René Juilliard, Paris, 1960).

14: Jürgen Stempel

IN the high summer the bare plains of the Kuban and Kalmuk steppes are ruled by the merciless sun. The searing heat beats down from a sky impossibly huge, impossibly blue, and at noon the temperature can reach 130° Fahrenheit. Every step sends the fine grey-brown dust of the desiccated topsoil smoking into the air. Tanks and trucks and marching infantry drag huge, ragged banners behind them in the sky, visible for twenty miles. The dust has the texture of flour; it sifts into every pore and delicate crevice of a man's body, rasping and caking his eyes, choking his windpipe, and forming a sweaty, abrasive paste which chafes armpits and crutch, and rubs shoulders bloody-raw under the weight of pack-straps.

In August 1942 the divisions of Army Group 'A' of the German *Wehrmacht* were driving southwards over these harsh prairies, with their enemy melting before them; they saw more camels and gazelles than Russians, and they knew that the war was nearly over. Certain of victory, they were more concerned with getting off that gridiron of a plain and up into the hills of the Caucasus. Every morning they stared at the mocking gleam in the southern sky, where the eternal snows on Elbruz and Kazbeck hung like clouds, apparently no nearer than they had been the day before, sixty kilometres back. Water was precious on these steppes, and the men of *XL. Panzer Korps* carried huge cisterns on their trucks, and charted their advance from water-hole to water-hole like their comrades in the *Afrika Korps*. If a rearguard from one of Timoshenko's ragged divisions managed to cling to the dry banks of a *balka* for a few hours, and bar the way to the next watering point, then another score of the horses which drooped in the shafts of the wagons and limbers would die.[1]

When the steppe gave way at last to the slopes of the Caucasus massif, the young men of von Schweppenburg's Corps had their reward. Cool woods stretched up from the banks of the thousand streams which rushed down the ribs of the ancient mountains. Dusty grass gave way to mile upon mile of wheat and millet, and sunflowers as tall as a man. The orchards of the tiny wooden villages were heavy with peaches and apricots, apples and pears, mirabels and white cherries. There were huge tomatoes, and so many eggs a man could eat a dozen a day, and the children held out bunches of grapes on sticks as the sunburned battalions slogged past. Vast herds of pigs brought a gleam to the eye of harassed quartermasters, and fiercely-horned sheep were hustled out of the path of the half-tracks by shaggy-capped men in loose blouses and soft leather boots, men who grinned at the soldiers and traded silver-worked daggers and fiery *arak* for a handful of cartridges. The people of this timeless country, Moslem and Orthodox Christian alike, regarded the Germans as no more foreign than the Red Army, and welcomed them as they had not been welcomed since the first heady weeks in the Ukraine. Zagorodniy and his Cossacks rode in to offer their swords to the *Wehrmacht*, savagely happy at the chance to strike back at a system which had oppressed and tormented them for twenty years. Blond boys riding tanks laughed and whistled at the dark Georgian girls, bright as birds in red and yellow, and at Ossetians with straight Circassian features and deep grey eyes shaded by heavy, tawny hair. If a man had to march from Poland to the Caspian, this was no bad route to take.

Ten-man German infantry squad, 1940. (Imperial War Museum)

Victory was in the air, for Ivan had few places left to run. In another 300 kilometres they would be out of Russia altogether, and what were 300 kilometres to an army which had fought its way from Voronezh to the Terek in a month? A few more weeks and the passes would be theirs; the squat grey tanks would rattle down the age-old conquerors' roads to the south, where the ruins of miniature castles had guarded the gates of Turkey and Persia for a thousand years. If they turned east to the Caspian they could seize the *Führer's* great prize, the oil-port of Baku. If they drove south and west, they could meet Rommel in Damascus!

But in the second week of August Timoshenko's armies stopped running. With the ridges and gorges of the Caucasus around them, rather than the empty plain where tanks could outflank them at will, the carefully husbanded infantry dug in, and the edges of the great penetration began to feel an unexpected constriction. In the western highlands the *Alpenjäger* from Austria and Bavaria struggled vainly to break through the stony passes. The screeching, worn-out tracks of the tanks carried the black-clad troopers of *13. Panzer Division* into the Maikop oilfields, to find the storage farms blazing. The Danes and Norwegians of the SS 'Viking' Division picked among the dynamited pumps and torn-up sidings of the depots.[2] In the central and eastern hills the most stoic infantry in the world still barred the way to the Georgian and Ossetian Military Highways. Just as before Moscow, nine months earlier, the last few miles would prove decisive.

It was fitting that the *Wehrmacht*, isolated at the tip of a 1,500-mile line of communication, should face the reckoning in the high valleys and echoing gorges of these ancient frontier marches, where warfare had been a way of life for two thousand years. Armies uncounted have contended the crossroads between Europe and Asia in this narrow neck between the Black and Caspian seas. It is a land of harsh bones under its fertile skin; while German and Russian died in the passes, men in high, secret villages still bartered for shirts of mail, and settled blood-feuds with two-handed swords. Here, within living memory, counterfeiters were punished by having molten metal poured down their throats, and women who killed their husbands, by burial alive to the neck. If one more army left its bones along the stony river beds, the Caucasus would not notice.

'*ACHTUNG, kameraden—der Spiess kommt! Alle Mann auf! Antreten!*' Beside the crowded road leading south from the outskirts of Mozdok to Ischerskaya on the Terek river, a section of dusty infantry from *2. Kompanie, I. Bataillon, Panzer Grenadier Regt. 394* are clambering to their feet at the order of their acting corporal, *Obergefreiter* Jürgen Stempel. It is the afternoon of 26th August 1942; the previous day the 394th and *Pz. Gr. Regt. 3*, the other mobile infantry unit of *3. Panzer Division*, captured the town in bitter street fighting supported by the divisional artillery and the PzKpfw III and IV tanks of *Panzer Regt. 6*, the division's main striking force.[3] Now General Breith's division moves on towards the Terek; and among the plank houses, fruit trees and trampled picket fences on the fringes of Mozdok, the men of *2. Kompanie, I/394* are waiting for their transport in the chaotic remains of a Russian postal clerk's vegetable garden.

Jürgen, who does not regard the appearance of the company sergeant-major as sufficient reason to stop eating an apple from a small hoard in his gas-mask canister, is a very ordinary-looking young man. He is of middle height and medium build, with middling blond hair, now shaggy and matted with dust. The only interesting thing about his sunburned face is a certain air of focus, of organisation, unusual in the blurred features of a twenty-one-year-old. Face and body alike carry no spare flesh, and he moves with the unselfconscious grace of the teenage athlete he used to be. There is something more, something perhaps only another soldier would recognise; the puppy-bounce of the boy who spent his evenings vaulting and springing with the other apprentices in a Hamburg *Sportverein* has given place to an entirely new set of reflexes in the fourteen months he has spent as a front-line infantryman in the world's most professional army. He moves in a muscle-saving slouch, but a sudden sound or voice jerks him to immediate and visible tension. In conversation his eyes are not steady, but slide away to search the middle distance. Though such an abstraction would probably be meaningless to his pedestrian mental processes, he has become rather a menacing young animal; the layer of social habit acquired slowly during childhood and adolescence has been sloughed off in a matter of months.

His thigh-length field grey tunic and rather baggy trousers are stained and discoloured. In the 80° heat he wears no undershirt under the wool-rayon tunic, and the sleeves are rolled to the elbow. Above the right breast pocket is an eagle badge woven in grey thread, and the collar, worn open, bears the traditional barred patches of the German soldier. The dark grey shoulder-straps are piped in the white of the infantry, and the double chevron of his rank is sewn to his left sleeve. Heavy leather marching-boots, thickly hob-nailed and with steel plates at toe and heel, reach almost to the knee.[4]

His canvas and leather M34 pack, with his blankets, spare clothing, cleaning kit and personal effects, is at this moment slung from a wire on the hull of the armoured half-track personnel carrier in which he usually rides. He wears only his assault harness, the bare necessities for twenty-four hours in action. Leather Y-straps are hooked to his wide leather belt at front and back, and a webbing frame clipped to D-rings behind the shoulders carries his rolled waterproof tent-quarter of camouflaged gaberdine, a cotton bag of tent-pegs, and his aluminium mess-tin. A pale canvas 'bread bag' is slung on the back of his belt, and currently contains his field grey sidecap, his shaving kit, a filthy towel, and an 'iron ration'; this last consists of nine ounces of army biscuit, seven ounces of cold meat and five of vegetables (both tinned), and small packets of coffee and salt. A small newspaper parcel thrust to the bottom of the bread bag contains some sugar, a piece of Mett-wurst sausage and three packets of *Gauloises* cigarettes—all purloined by a friend who is an officer's orderly. A felt-covered aluminium canteen with a mug strapped over the screw cap is hooked to the bread bag so that it hangs behind his right hip, and contains turnip-*arak* to its full capacity of just under a quart. On a webbing strap slung round his chest and over his shoulder is a fluted tin gas-mask canister, a jolting nuisance in combat but a useful container for unofficial comforts if one dumps the pointless gas-mask. On his left hip hangs a short entrenching spade reversed in a strap-work case, with his eight-inch Mauser bayonet of good Solingen steel tucked under the straps. A canvas pouch over his left ribs holds three magazines for his machine-pistol; he should have two pouches, but an improvident comrade 'borrowed' one and he has not yet received a replacement. Another canteen, containing warm, mineral-tasting water, hangs on the right of his belt. His helmet lies at his feet, among the applecores. On the march he usually hangs it from a convenient hook on his right Y-strap. To him it is just a helmet, but to the rest of the world its practical, rather sinister outline has become a symbol of menace during the past three years.

Beside the helmet at his feet lie the two basic tools of Jürgen's trade. The *Stielhandgranate 24*, a grey-painted metal cylinder on a short wooden handle, he picks up and tucks into its familiar place under his belt. The slim, elegant machine-pistol he slings from his right shoulder and rests on his hip. It is just over two feet long, with a skeleton butt folded forward under the body. At nine pounds it weighs almost as heavy as the Mauser K.98 rifle he lugged from Hamburg to the Izyum Bend, but unlike that elderly weapon, with its useless five-round magazine, the machine-pistol has his complete trust. The 9mm. Schmeisser MP.40, with a capacity of thirty-two rounds and a rate of fire of nine rounds per second, is probably the finest submachine-gun of this war and is used by men of foreign armies in preference to their own equipment.

In the pockets of his tunic and trousers Jürgen has a grubby handkerchief, a comb, a steel pocket-mirror, fourteen loose 9mm. cartridges, a green-painted egg-shaped smoke grenade with the stencilled legend *Nb. Hgr. 39*, two field dressings (these in a special pocket low in the right-hand lining of the tunic), a cheap imitation-leather wallet containing fifteen *Reichsmarks* and photographs of his parents and fiancée, a pin-up picture of a busty U.F.A. starlet named Gerhild Weber torn from a recent issue of '*Signal*', and a German-Russian phrasebook courtesy of *Verlag E. S. Mittler und Sohn, Berlin*. This boasts '3000 words for field use and everyday life'; it does not contain the word 'Sorry'.

Liberator's welcome from Russian peasants, soon to learn the realities of occupation. (Imp. War Mus.)

The dirt-surfaced road out of Mozdok is rapidly turning into a dust-bath under the tyres and tracks of more traffic than it usually bears in a month. Jürgen and his squad mooch over to peer at the noisy procession in search of their own vehicles, and are rewarded with a diversion. A horse-drawn field kitchen a hundred metres away somehow manages to tear a wheel off in one of the concrete-hard ruts, bringing the whole convoy to a halt. Opel and Mercedes trucks, Steyrs, Henschels, big Krupp ten-wheelers, fussy little VW *Kübelwagens*, huge artillery tractors, angular *Granit* ambulances, press-ganged Renaults and Fords and Russian GAZ trucks—all boil to a standstill in the dust, and a chorus of cursing and banging doors comes muffled through the shimmering air.

'*Beeil' dich, du langweiliger Dummkopf!*' '*Was gibst?*' '*Keinen dunst, aber . . .*' '*Ach, scher' dich zum Teufel, Scheisskerl!*' '*Anfänger!*' '*Halt' die Fresse, Schwachsinnige! Schnauze! Platz da!*'

Eventually a bouncing BMW motorcycle roars up the side of the convoy, and a pair of hard-faced *Feldgendarmerie* NCOs leap off and stride over to the lop-sided trailer, pushing up their goggles. The apoplectic teamster stutters into silence as the senior '*Kettenhund*' slowly unholsters and cocks his Walther automatic.[5] The horses are unhitched, and the policeman waves on the next vehicle in line, a massive caterpillar tractor towing one of the 10.5cm. howitzers of *Artillerie Regt. 75.* The trailer is swept out of the road in splintered ruin, and the convoy jerks forward again.

Through the dust Jürgen spots the *Hanomag* half-tracks of *2. Kompanie.* He grins as he sees that *Oberleutnant* Dürrholz has tucked his aerial-bedecked command carrier in behind the clattering bulk of a PzKpfw IV, and is happily jumping the queue in the wake of the grey monster, with the other company carriers tight on his tail. As the '*Stumpf*' draws level with the lounging grenadiers it rocks to a halt, and the company scramble forward to board their half-tracks while the black-uniformed tank officer grins at the furious drivers of vehicles stalled behind them.[6] The *Feldgendarmerie* sergeant runs back, but stops, muttering, at the sight of the officer's silver epaulettes and gold pips. The grenadiers clamber up through the angled doors in the backs of the carriers, and with a blatting of exhausts the tank

MG.34 team in action in a Russian sunflower field, 1941. The NCO carries an MP.40 and binoculars;
the gunner uses his 'No. 2' as a rest. The 'No. 2' carries a case for a spare barrel. (Imp. War Mus.)

lurches out into the stream again. Jürgen deduces from its faded black and white
turret number—*201*—that the grimy, goggled figure in the high steel cupola must
be Vopel, whose *2. Zug* seized the vital bridge at Novgorod Severskiy for the 394th
the summer before.

The squad sort themselves out on the padded benches, and Jürgen settles in the
seat beside the driver and draws himself a mug of water from the barrel welded to
the transmission tunnel, adding a large jolt of *arak* to the last couple of mouthfuls.
He glances back and nods approvingly as the big, red-haired machine-gunner slips
the squad's MG.34 into the swivel mounting on the canopy-bar.[7] He is *ein ganzer
Kerl*, that Swabian; a bit slow, but reliable. One of the casualties in Mozdok was
the machine-gun NCO, a yelping lance-corporal who was more trouble than he was
worth. The farm-boy and his 'number two' would get on fine without him. All the
same, the squad is down to six now, and Jürgen hopes the *Herr Oberleutnant* can
grab them some good replacements. The platoon went into the Manych Gorge at
full strength just three weeks ago—four ten-man squads and a mortar team, led by
an experienced *Feldwebel*.[8] Now they were down to twenty-six. He had over-
heard Dürrholz talking to Ziegler, the battalion adjutant, during a halt on the
drive from Baksan three days before, and they had been discussing assault-boats.
If Captain Baron von der Heyden-Rynsch thought his battalion was in shape for a
river crossing under fire, especially one of these damned rushing mountain rivers
full of hidden banks and eddies, then he had rocks in his aristocratic head.

Even old '*Dickarsch*' was gone now. It would be strange without him, never
saying much but always there, with his perpetual cigarette gummed to his lip, and
his uncanny talent for 'organising' Schnapps, or officers' rations, or even whores.

They had been working down an old-fashioned street of tall stone houses in the centre of Mozdok; 'Dickarsch' had followed the old routine—kick in the door from one side, toss in two grenades taped together, then follow them with everything blazing before the splinters stopped pinging off the walls. A wounded Ivan had got him from down beside the doorway with one of those long needle-bayonets like something left over by Frederick the Great. It had been a horrible wound, up under the ribs and into the guts at a sharp angle; Jürgen had kicked in the Ivan's face and put half a magazine into him, but it was too late for 'Dickarsch'. He was quiet until they pulled the bayonet out, then he started screaming like a gutted horse, and bled to death before the Sanitäter could reach them and carry him back to the Verwundetennest in the church. Not five minutes later they reached the edge of a big square, and the machine-gun Gefreiter had stood gawping at it like a Sunday tourist at the Bismarck Denkmal; an anti-tank slug had hit him in the chest.[9] The Swabian had been lying at his feet, and later Jürgen had seen him stolidly wiping mementoes of the NCO off his trousers like a farmer scraping off mud.

Jürgen unbuckles his belt and wriggles into a more comfortable position, fumbling for his cigarettes. Behind him the squad finish dividing the kit of the latest two casualties, pull out a greasy pack of cards, and resume their interminable Skat tournament on a stretched blanket.[10]

JÜRGEN was born in Hamburg in August 1921, the second son of Paul Stempel, railwayman, and his wife Elisabeth. His wholly unremarkable childhood was spent in a fair-sized, over-furnished flat at Augustenburgerstrasse 23, near the Alsen Platz. Home to him would always mean that flat, and the fragmentary memories of childhood: sitting on the balcony on summer evenings, playing in the sandpits behind the block with his brother Heinrich, warming his hands on the big tiled stove after helping his father in the allotments on a winter afternoon, the smell of diced pork and swedes cooking for supper. When he was thirteen he joined the Hitler Youth with all his contemporaries. He loved the uniform, the camps, the marvellous daggers, the music—everything, in fact, except the political lectures, which bored him to distraction. The leader of his Schar explained the significance of the black and white 'Nord: Hamburg' badges on their shirts, a mark of proud distinction for the ancient free city. To a thirteen-year-old, to be given a uniform and a dagger and a big drum, and to be told that one is, by birthright, a member of an élite body, is heady stuff indeed. Jürgen did well in the organisation, mainly because of his obvious and growing prowess as a gymnast.

When he left Volksschule at Easter in 1936 he joined his father at the Altona Hauptbahnhof as a railway apprentice. He felt no great enthusiasm for the job, and went about in a semi-daze after he had mastered his simple duties. His spare time was filled with organised recreation. He enjoyed the hikes to the Sachsenwald, and listened to stern lectures on Germany's destiny at the Bismarck mausoleum in Friedrichsruh. He attended summer camp on the Baltic, swimming, and sailing, and joining in rolling choruses of the Horst Wessel-Lied round the campfire.[11] His absorption in Hitler Youth facilities faded when he was seventeen; strolling around the Hamburger Dom with a group of friends, he was introduced to a lively blonde girl named Ilse Muller, and promptly fell in love with all the agonising intensity proper to a strictly brought up boy with no knowledge or experience of the opposite sex.[12] He pursued her doggedly at the dancing-class which they attended, but it was not until a Sunday swimming trip to Blankenese that he began to make real progress. Jürgen, muscled and graceful in the sunny shallows of the Elbe, was vastly more impressive than Jürgen, tongue-tied on a dance-floor. Soon he was squiring Ilse round the more respectable haunts of Hamburg's young people; it was a relationship of enormous innocence, yet it made Jürgen think about himself in a new light. He decided that he wanted to join the Army.

They spent the summer of 1938 like most couples of their age—window-shopping along the Jungfernstieg, taking water-bus trips on the Alster, gorging on cream cakes at Hagenbeck's Tierpark, holding hands and gazing at the view from the tower of the St. Michaelis Kirche; and always Jürgen's mind turned to his future. He was determined to leave the soot and grease of the Altona Hauptbahnhof to seek glory and excitement in the *Wehrmacht*. He pictured himself marching home from war—no particular war, just any war—with his chest covered with medals. What would Ilse say then? He proceeded to imagine what Ilse would say, and do, and very pleasant it was, too.

His ambitions were understandable. To the ill-informed romanticism of youth had been added, by patient indoctrination, an aggressive and chauvinistic nationalism. He had grown up in a society in which a man's virility was measured in a military context, a society in which soldiers shouldered civilians off the pavement. Wireless and newspapers fed his illusions, and nothing in his father's attitudes gave the lie to the pervading mood. Paul Stempel was a dull, decent working man whose views on Communism had been shaped by an incident in his youth when he had got caught up in a street-battle over the river in Harburg.[13] It was in 1920, when the bare rumour of a steady job was worth a day's travelling at least. Hiding in a doorway, he had watched appalled as a gang of Communists had carefully kicked to death the much-decorated and crippled fighter pilot, Rudolf Berthold. Though an ex-soldier himself—he had seen little action, spending most of his service at his regiment's depot in Hamburg—Stempel had not been involved in the political passions of the day; he had a wife and a baby to feed, and regarded both Communist and *Freikorps* movements as a waste of time. Yet he had a simple respect for human dignity, and what the Reds left in that reeking Harburg gutter had been an affront to dignity. When the government which had given him steady work and a roof over his head told him that all his troubles had been the work of the International Bolshevist Conspiracy, why should he not believe them? When they told him that the Jews were in league with the Reds, he forgot the half-dozen decent Jews he had known, and remembered only the one pawnbroker who had sneered at him when he was desperate to feed his family. When they told him that the Poles were ill-treating the German minority in Danzig, and that Germany must be strong to protect herself, why then should he feel anything but pride when his son announced that he wanted to help guard them all from 'that sort of thing'? Paul Stempel was simply an unsophisticated, unimaginative human being, and no match for the machine which had taken power in Germany in 1933.

Jürgen told his family of his decision in February 1939, on the evening of the day when he saw his *Führer* in person. Hitler visited Hamburg to launch the mighty *Bismarck* from the slips of the Blohm & Voss yards, and the Hilter Youth paraded at the station. Carried away by a day of blood-red banners, of marching feet, of pulsing waves of '*Heil!*' crashing in his ears, Jürgen could contain himself no longer. It was a tactful time to pick, and his father agreed that when he had done his *Arbeitsdienst* and reached his nineteenth birthday, he could volunteer.[14] Among Jürgen's more persuasive arguments was the revelation that if he signed on for twelve years and retired as an NCO, he would get a cash grant to buy farming land.[15]

The boy's year in the *R.A.D.* was spent in roadwork and dyke-mending on the coast, and lasted from Easter 1939 to Easter 1940. It was punctuated by the news of Germany's lightning victories in Poland, and his return almost coincided with the holocaust in the West. The photographs and newsreels of tanks and dive-bombers slashing deep into enemy territory, and streams of demoralised prisoners trudging past the cameras under the guns of grinning troopers, sent the young Jürgen nearly mad with impatience lest his chance for glory disappear in final victory before he could play his part. His father still insisted that nineteen was young enough; Heinrich, called up at twenty-one, was away in the Navy, and the middle-aged couple found the flat on the Augustenburgerstrasse rather lonely. But in the autumn of 1940 Jürgen finally made his farewells to his parents and the misty-eyed Ilse, and walked to the Viktoria Kaserne near the Holstenstrasse station. He passed a searching physical, he put his hand on the Book and swore loyalty unto death to the *Führer*,[16] and became that despised thing, a *Hammel*.[17]

The basic training of a German soldier was carried out by an *Ersatz Bataillon*, based at the depot of each field formation and feeding trained replacements to the parent unit as required. In his sixteen weeks with the battalion Jürgen passed by stages through the *Stammkompanie*, the *Ausbildungskompanie* and the *Marsch-kompanie*—reception, training and transfer pool companies respectively. The priorities of training were combat techniques, shooting, lectures, drill and sport. Jürgen's experience in the para-military Hitler Youth and *R.A.D.* had prepared him for the realities of barrack life, and he was a healthy and athletic youth in an environment partly based on the glorification of physical fitness. He thrived, and learned fast. Although one or two of the instructors were in the habit of knocking the lessons home with their fists, the worst excesses of the Prussian system had been replaced by an insistence on individual initiative and responsibility. The days when a recruit who forgot to button his tunic had buttons sewn directly to the skin of his stomach were long past. Jürgen was taught that second only to his duty to the *Führer* was his duty to his comrades. In all things, and especially in combat, the golden rule was that it was better to do something wrong but decisive than to wait for orders which might never come. The philosophy of unremitting attack extended even to technical terminology—anti-tank guns were for 'attacking tanks' rather than for 'defence against tanks'.

In the later stages of training Jürgen took part in battle exercises with live ammunition, learning the techniques of the mobile infantryman in close support of tanks. During his training his unit, the Harburg 69th Motorised Infantry Regiment, was reorganised as the 394th, to form with the 3rd the infantry brigade of the 3rd Panzer Division—the famous 'Bear Division', heroes of Warsaw and the Albert Canal. Jürgen was taught that the mixed force of tanks and lorried infantry complemented one another; the tanks burst through the enemy infantry and machine-guns, and the infantry de-trucked and moved up to deal with any anti-tank weapons encountered by the armour. This basic technique of *blitzkrieg*, combined with air superiority and close support, and strong mobile artillery operating close up with the spearhead, had smashed the armies of Poland in three weeks and those of France, Holland, Belgium and Britain in ten.

Jürgen proved to be a good shot with the K.98 rifle, the MG.34 Spandau belt-fed machine-gun, the 9mm. machine-pistol and the Luger automatic.[18] He learnt to handle the 81mm. mortar, the stick-grenade and the bayonet. As he acquired a working familiarity with the tools of his trade, he picked up the knowledge necessary for survival in the jungle of military life. He learnt the slang—a corporal was a 'Kapo', the senior warrant officer was a 'Spiess', an officer haranguing an awkward squad was 'handing out cigars'. He found out that the Spiess could be recognised not only by the two silver stripes around his cuff, but also by the fact that his second tunic button was permanently unfastened, to permit a quick draw with the 'crime book' in his inside pocket. He learnt that on the rare occasions when he encountered an officer, he must address this exalted being in the third person—'If the Herr Hauptmann permits . . .'. He found out—and the lesson was hammered home by seven days 'Ausgehverbot'—that if one wanted to pass the NCO on the gate when 'walking out' it was not enough to be wearing an immaculate uniform. One's pockets must also contain ten Reichsmarks, a comb, a clean and pressed handkerchief, and one's paybook.

In due course, proud and confident, Jürgen marched off to the station and began the long train journey to his regiment's staging area somewhere in the General-Gouvernement—a dismal region in the east, once known as the Kingdom of Poland.

EARLY on the morning of 22nd June 1941 Army Group Centre, Field Marshal Feodor von Bock commanding, crossed the Bug river in the Brest-Litovsk sector and thrust eastwards 'to save European civilisation'. The greatest confrontation of armies in the history of the world had begun; three million men in Wehrmacht grey, Panzer black and Luftwaffe blue surged forward, side by side with men from Finland and Rumania. One of von Bock's spearhead formations was the Second Armoured Group led by Heinz Guderian, tank general supreme. One of the corps under Guderian's command was XXIV Motorised Army Corps, General Baron Geyr von Schweppenburg commanding. In this Corps were one motorised, one horsed cavalry and two tank divisions, the 3rd and 4th. In the 3rd, Lieutenant-General Model's 'Bear Division', was the 394th Motorised Infantry Regiment. In one of the trucks of 2. Kompanie, I/394, rode Private Jürgen Stempel; he was rather white, and swallowed a lot, and as his truck rumbled over the bridge at Koden he leaned far out over the racks of jerry-cans and vomited his quarter-bottle of Schnapps (courtesy of the Führer) on to the startled bull-frogs in the reeds below. He smoked his thirty free cigarettes before night fell.

The German columns raced into Russia, knocking their vehicles to pieces on the appalling roads but pressing always eastwards. The Red Army, its command structure paralysed by the terrible purges of the 1930s, its men half-trained, its weapons outclassed, was routed. Great masses of men and equipment were encircled and engulfed and left far behind the roaring tanks. The Soviet Air Force virtually died in the first two days, and from then on the German troops had the comforting silhouettes of the Stukas and Messerschmitts almost constantly in sight. The Soviet defences lost all cohesion, and in the panic and chaos which

reigned everywhere the bewildered troops who found themselves under crushing attack by German columns were as likely to be lost and disoriented reinforcements as deliberately positioned rearguards.

Jürgen's mental picture of his first taste of action had been clear cut, limned in strong, heroic colours, and he was ill-prepared for the series of indecisive experiences which actually overtook him. When was one 'in action'? When a few shells from a Russian 7.6cm. 'Crash-Boom' field gun landed fifty metres from the road? When he saw brown-uniformed figures scurrying through distant trees? When he heard the buzz of almost spent bullets above his head? Time and again he and his comrades crouched in some ditch or cornfield, listening to the flat, tearing detonation of mortar bombs and the 'ripping canvas' sound of the Spandaus up ahead, only to be herded back to the trucks and told that the tanks or the dive-bombers had taken care of the obstruction by themselves.

The tank armies looped and swerved and fanned across the plains, cutting the routed Ivans into great, helpless pockets and leaving them to be dealt with by the mass of infantry following at a slower pace. By early July, 3rd Panzer was across the Berezina and heading for the Dniepr, leaving 250,000 Russians trapped in the Bialystok-Minsk pocket. The division was checked at Rogachev by human waves of Ivans, as Timoshenko traded lives for the time to build a cohesive line. After sharp fighting Guderian side-stepped to Stary Bykhov and forced his way across the Dniepr at this obscure and badly guarded crossing point. Another fourteen Soviet divisions were entombed when Smolensk fell on 16th July; the campaign was twenty-five days old, and 3rd Panzer was 440 miles into Russian territory, with only half that distance left between them and Moscow. On the 19th they took Yelnya, and held against desperate counter-attacks from the south-east. It was here that Jürgen first killed at close range. He crouched in a ditch on the edge of a nameless hovel-village, parched and choked by the dusty heat, working his rifle-bolt until his fingers bled and the breech was hot to the touch. The tattered herds of Ivans, staggering with vodka, goaded on by commissars and N.K.V.D. machine-gun teams. came screaming across the trampled corn with linked arms. Many had no rifles. They kept up a nerve-racking howl of '*Urra! Urra! Urra!*' as they came, and fell in great broken swathes under the lash of the machine-guns, the *flak*-guns, and the swooping fighters. After the first shock of seeing a real, live human being collapse in his sights, Jürgen fired and loaded and fired again mechanically; the fluttering brown dolls ceased to have any meaning. At dusk the breeze carried a terrible sound to the fox-holes of 2. *Kompanie*—a low, hopeless moaning and wailing from the tormented harvest in the cornfield. That day, and in the days that followed, Jürgen learnt several things not covered by the instructors at the Viktoria Kaserne.

He learnt that an Ivan was still deadly dangerous after suffering wounds so hideous that they would have killed a Westerner with shock. He learnt that a three-day battlefield under an 80° sun has a stench of such gagging vileness that there are no words to describe it. He learnt that the hecatomb in the Yelnya corn had been composed of men who had been in uniform for less than a week, and that many of them had never even handled a gun when they died. He learnt that the death-song he had heard in the dusk was extremely rare—that Ivan lived and died in an eery silence, apparently indifferent to mutilation. He saw, in the endless rivers of prisoners plodding westwards over the steppe, men with arms blown off at the shoulder, men with faces burned away, men holding their entrails in place

Landser *in action; and* right, *the face of the enemy—a column of T-34/76 tanks.* (*Imp. War Mus.*)

with their hands—and they made no sound. They must indeed be *Untermensch*, sub-human. He and his comrades felt a frustrated resentment at the stubborn heroism of these wasted, stupidly abandoned thousands. How could they still be willing to die in defence of the holy earth of Mother Russia, they who had been so cruelly oppressed by a cynical dictatorship for twenty years?

At Rodnya he learnt that while it was wisest to keep running when caught by mortar-fire, one should dive for cover at the terrifying elephant-bellow of the *katyusha* rocket-mortar, which sliced men in pieces at a range which rendered a normal mortar-bomb almost harmless. From supply drivers he learnt that swordsmen on shaggy ponies could turn careless German bivouacs far behind the lines into butcher-shops in a matter of moments; and that the vast regions to the west of the main fighting were haunted by thousands of leaderless Russian soldiers and civilian partisans, ever on the watch for a chance to strike at German traffic, and skilled in the infliction of unimaginable tortures on captured invaders. From worried tank crews he learnt that while the PzKpfw IIIs and IVs could rip open and incinerate most of the angular, old-fashioned Soviet tanks without difficulty, there were rumours of new and formidable types coming into service with the Russian brigades.

Jürgen's metamorphosis from staring *Hammel* to hardened *Landser*[19] was as gradual and undramatic as his introduction to combat had been. As the weeks passed the sight and stink of roasted, burst human bodies became almost a commonplace. He learned to identify and assess the significance of the different sounds of battle. He absorbed the lessons of terrain and movement, light and weather; he no longer leapt from his blankets every time a jumpy guard loosed a burst of Spandau fire at shadows in the night. He began to keep his Schnapps down, and to enjoy it; and he found that he was smoking forty cigarettes a day whenever opportunity offered. He learned that it was wisest to keep his eyes inside the truck when they passed through the area of operation of an *Einsatzgruppe* of SD men, and that if there was anything worth looting in a Russian cottage, it was usually buried in front of the stove.[20]

In August 3rd Panzer turned south and made an epic forced march to link up with another column at Lokhvista, entombing the cretinous Budenny and his million men around Kiev. With the southern threat removed the *Führer* set his legions once more on the road to Moscow; but as his generals had warned, the surgery in the Ukraine had cost precious weeks. The *Wehrmacht* was still winning, more than half the Red Army had been slaughtered or sent staggering west under guard—but on 7th October the first soft snowflakes fell. They melted at once, but the autumn rains became more persistent and turned the roads to glue. The Briansk pocket became a graveyard for Yeremenko's 663,000 men and 1,200 armoured vehicles; but each day 3rd Panzer, churning north across country, moved a little slower.

The forest tracks turned to mires, and six times a day Jürgen stumbled wearily from his lorry and took his place in the screen of infantry in the woods while cursing pioneers laid roadbeds of tree-trunks for the bogged tanks. The Ivans became bolder, and more numerous; often they would slip through the infantry and rake the vehicles with automatic fire before vanishing like Indians into the endless forests. More frequently now the sinister cowled silhouettes of the new T-34 tanks would loom out of the fog and hack into the convoys with their heavy cannon. Every hour they held the crawling *Wehrmacht* meant another anti-tank ditch dug before Moscow, another workers' battalion armed, another tank off the production line and on its way to the front almost before the rivets had cooled. And every hour brought Russia's ancient ally nearer.

The first frosts of November were, incredibly, welcomed—they gave the frustrated tank crews hard going for once, and for a few days progress speeded up. Third Panzer was fighting at Tula, the armaments centre a hundred miles south of Moscow. The proud *Grossdeutschland* Division broke on the stubborn maze of rubble, and two days later 3rd Panzer were driven back over their corpses. Only a tiny neck of ground in the north prevented Tula's complete encirclement, but the *Wehrmacht* never broke it; for by now, winter was upon them.

The ice-wind screeched down from Siberia, bringing with it the worst winter for 140 years, and the German advance shuddered to a halt along a 600-mile front. The horror of the weeks which followed was beyond the conception of European soldiers, and sheer paralysing shock played as great a part in their misery as the conditions themselves. The temperature dropped to ten, twenty, *fifty* degrees below zero Centigrade; blizzards blinded men and machine alike, and the cold tore the heart out of the thousand-and-one sophisticated devices on which a modern army depends. Without a functioning supply and transport system they starved, or ran out of ammunition. The wounded could not be evacuated, and died; the fuel could not be brought up for the tanks, and they were abandoned; the *Luftwaffe* could not get into the air, and the army lost its greatest trump card. In some sectors German regiments broke and ran in the face of the sudden Soviet counter-offensive, and dull-eyed men clogged the few open roads, intent only on escape. Some units even shot their officers.

The 394th did not shoot their officers, and did not run. They died in hundreds from frostbite, exposure, disease, starvation and wounds, but somehow they held together and made a fighting retreat under conditions of such numbing horror that

men went insane from sheer cold. Without proper clothing, they muffled themselves in blankets and sacks and strange creations of canvas and straw, and fought the cold by drinking themselves stupid on Schnapps whenever they could. When the cold split the engine-blocks of their trucks, they took to their feet and shuffled through the waist-deep snow. When the very oil in their rifle-bolts froze solid, they fought with grenades and bayonets. Zhukov's Siberians, the last great reserve from the Far Eastern Front, harried them like wolves; the retreat turned into a series of bitter defensive battles for the huddles of log huts which meant life or death when night fell. The Siberians slipped round them on skis, infiltrated them in white camouflage suits, outflanked them, cut them off, butchered them. Warmly dressed in quilted outfits and huge boots, born and raised to the rigours of the northern winter, they bore little resemblance to the bewildered cattle of Minsk and Yelnya.

Jürgen survived, thanks to his sturdy constitution, a great deal of luck, and a burning determination to live out the winter. He won a race with two other men to the warm corpse of a Siberian in the woods south of Tula, and fought his comrades off while he fumbled with bloody fingers for the quilted *fufaika* and felt boots. The next day the men he had outrun were stiff and blue under their thin blankets, and Jürgen was alive. When his company was cut off by a force of Ivans, he kicked his way on to the very last half-track in the regiment; he was one of forty-two men who clung to it as it swerved and skated off down the icy road to safety, and one of the eighteen whom Sergeant Schröder counted on their feet when it caught up with the division two days later. When Jürgen's weird collection of garments, not removed for three weeks, visibly seethed with vermin, he resisted the temptation to strip off and hunt them with a cigarette-end. He stank like a midden, but survived. Once they came upon a dead horse, and, after axe and saw had turned on the blackened, granite-hard carcass, dismembered it with grenades and par-cooked it over a fire of ammunition baskets and *Esbit* capsules.[21] Next day the entire company was racked with dysentery, which persisted for a fortnight. Jürgen closed his mind to the shaming wretchedness of living amid his own waste, and thus was not one of the men who bucked and screamed in the fouled snow as they died of congelation of the gut—an occupational hazard of performing one's functions in the open at a temperature of forty below. The 394th left more than half its total strength along the road to the Izyum Bend, a black trail of stiff-limbed corpses in fluttering rags; at one point Jürgen's battalion could muster less than sixty men fit for any sort of action, commanded by a Second-Lieutenant with ancient eyes in a gaunt child's face; but when the snow turned to mud, and the first warmth of spring made them blink and stretch among the birch-trees, Jürgen was still alive.

He emerged from that icy northern hell with acting corporal's stripes, a new Schmeisser, and a twist of red, white and black ribbon in his button hole. Some of the holders of the Winter 1941–42 Medal called it The Order of the Frozen Meat, but Jürgen did not laugh. His other military trinkets—the silver Infantry Assault Badge, the black Wound Badge for stopping a grenade splinter in the leg at Nepokrytaya (in truth, it had hardly penetrated his paper-wadded trousers)—he stowed in his pack; but his Winter Ribbon he wore from that day on.

When the *Wehrmacht* had finally sealed off and cauterised the wounds torn in its front by the Russian offensive, it performed a miracle of recovery and regeneration —always the greatest strength of the armies of the Third Reich. New men, new guns, new vehicles flowed to the front line, and the army shook itself and prepared to go back on the offensive. The reverses of the Winter had taken a toll among the gentlemen in red-striped breeches, and from now on the *Führer* would take a more direct hand in planning. (Jürgen's platoon sergeant, thwarted by a thin-lipped *Schmalspurhengst* in a complicated ration swindle, was heard to remark that these days even generals had arses, and sometimes got them kicked.[22]) The *Führer* turned his eyes south, to the oilfields of the Caucasus. He planned a vast encirclement on the Don, and a bold drive to the south-east. The operations in the Crimea, to guard the right flank of this thrust, were completed without mishap on 3rd July, when von Manstein's sappers silenced the last great steel and concrete fort of Sevastopol; but on the left flank, at Voronezh, things did not go as planned. The city held out for longer than expected, giving time for Timoshenko to pull his other forces back towards—what was its name? Ah, yes . . . Stalingrad.

In the second week of July the picture clarified. Part of the huge forces at Hitler's disposal would push on due east, until the obviously beaten and broken Soviets could be brought to battle and decisively destroyed. The other armies would strike southwards and eastwards, to Rostov, and on across the steppe to the blue Caspian. In the southern prong Geyr von Schweppenburg's *XL. Panzer Korps* advanced over the summer plains, and despite a sharp check at Millerovo it seemed as if Ivan had had enough at long last. In his brand new half-track lounged Jürgen Stempel, whose digestion was untroubled this time. He became absorbed in a long argument with a friend about the chances of smuggling a Ukrainian prostitute into one of the company's supply trucks, and continued to wrangle about it in the intervals between several short and victorious battles. They crossed the Don on 20th July. Three days later, while the SS 'Viking' Division and Soviet N.K.V.D. units fought a ghastly house-to-house battle in the barricaded streets of Rostov, Jürgen's company crossed the Sal at Orlovka. A daring assault-boat attack across the reservoirs of the Manych Gorge, and 3rd Panzer was advancing over the soil of Asia. Ahead lay mile upon mile of dusty grass, and the road to Pregatnoye, Voroshilovsk, Pyatigorsk, the Baksan Valley—and Mozdok.

So Jürgen Stempel rode towards the Terek on an August afternoon, in a half-track with too many empty seats. At dawn on 30th August he scrambled into a frail assault-boat and survived the hail of fire from well-sited Russian positions along the eastern bank of the swirling brown river. He and a few score of his comrades clung to their fox-holes on the far bank for five days, in open terrain and without heavy weapons. Captain Baron von der Heyden-Rynsch and the adjutant, Ziegler, were shredded by a shell while still on the German bank; *Oberleutnant* Dürrholz was ripped out of his boat by a splinter, and posted missing, believed killed. The young regimental commander, Major Günther Pape, crossed on the first afternoon and organised the thin perimeter, striding about within sight of the guns of Mundar-Yurt with his Knight's Cross flashing in the sun. There were other crossings, eventually; but Jürgen's fox-hole on the far side of the Terek was to mark the deepest German penetration into Russian territory. There were never enough replacements, enough shells, enough tanks and planes to break that final Soviet line; far to the north in the Volga bend whole divisions were soaking into the rubble of Stalingrad for the sake of one shattered factory, or three blocks of a wharf-side street. Mere territory meant nothing—every kilometre Jürgen had captured simply gave him a longer journey home. Statistically, his chances of ever seeing the Augustenburgerstrasse again were very poor.[23]

Because he was a magnificent infantryman he fought almost as well during the long retreat that was to come as he had done in attack—and in attack he had few equals in the world. He was strong, brave, and trained to a high degree of skill and familiarity with his weapons. He was confident of final victory even when the immediate prospects seemed hopeless. He had a healthy urge to survive which prevented him taking unnecessary risks with the lives of his squad, and he recognised and accepted his responsibilities—except in circumstances of such peculiar terror that any man in the world would be inclined to look after his own skin. He did not follow orders blindly, and gave his officers respect and obedience only after a careful scrutiny of their behaviour in action. If he trusted them, he was capable of responding with enormous courage and dash. The structure of his army placed effective automatic weapons, mortars and light artillery at the disposal of small units low on the chain of command, allowing great flexibility and initiative in the attack by isolated companies and platoons, and encouraging a self-sufficient attitude. There were fewer company officers than in other Western armies, and Jürgen and his comrades were quite confident in the ability of the experienced NCOs who were their immediate commanders; this had an automatic stabilising effect in the face of battlefield setbacks, and the men were unlikely to lose their momentum in the absence of silver shoulder-straps.

Jürgen's natural patriotism, and an admirable regard for the concept of duty, were perverted by the society in which he grew up into an exaggerated pride in physical and military prowess, and an over-romantic concern with his nation's 'Destiny'. In pursuit of the victory which he had been convinced was his birth-right he was capable of a remarkable degree of callousness, both active and passive, towards his brave and tenacious enemy. He was neither inclined nor mentally equipped to question the system which directed him, and his mind worked in hierarchical patterns. He was a creature of contradictions. If he had one genuine-ly disturbing trait, it was his complete inability to identify emotionally with any person or cause outside his own restricted pattern of loyalties and relationships. He lost little sleep over the medieval treatment of Russian prisoners, accepting the empty rationalisation that since Ivan had not signed the Geneva Convention he was not entitled to the slightest consideration.[24] At the same time Jürgen felt a sincere indignation when he encountered the frequent reciprocal atrocities in-flicted by Russians on German prisoners. A few soothing words about the necessity of rooting out the 'partisan bandits' were enough to quiet his conscience when he came across instances of sickening brutality towards Russian civilians. Yet in the midst of butchery unrivalled in recorded history, he could be reduced to a mood of heavy sentimentality by a letter from his girl or a sugary ballad warbled by Lale Andersen over some forces' radio programme.

From a coldly practical military point of view, Jürgen was probably the perfect soldier; but any broader based judgement must conclude that he was, quite simply, *too* good.

NOTES

The Stempel family and Ilse Muller are fictitious; all other named persons lived and died as described here.

1. *balka:* a dried-up watercourse. The German forces in Russia were heavily dependent on horsed transport; every military necessity had to be brought over such vast distances that transport space was at a premium, and the troops were forbidden parcels from home. This led to a lively black market with Hungarian and Rumanian troops who were not restricted in this way.
2. *SS Pz. Gren. Div. 'Wiking'*, later 5. *SS Pz. Div. 'Wiking'*: formed from German, Dutch and Scandinavian cadres late in 1940, this was the first major foreign *Waffen-SS* unit. It operated only on the Russian Front, where it earned a high fighting reputation.
3. The basic establishment of a *Panzer Division* comprised a tank regiment of two battalions, in practice mustering some 100 tanks; two infantry regiments, lorried or mounted in personnel carriers; an artillery regiment equipped with some seventy 7·5cm, 10·5cm, and 150mm howitzers and 8·8cm *flak* guns; and divisional units of reconnaissance, anti-tank and anti-aircraft troops. Total strength was about 14,000 men.
4. The boots, fitted one size too large and worn over socks and wrapped woollen squares, almost guaranteed frostbite in cold weather.
5. '*Kettenhund*': literally, 'chain-dog': this translation fails to convey the loathing behind the phrase. Field Police personnel had wide powers and not infrequently used their firearms.
6. '*Stumpf*': 'Stumpy': a reference to the short 7·5cm cannon mounted by early marks of the PzKpfw IV tank.
7. The 7·92mm MG.34/41 light machine-gun was the standard infantry automatic weapon until replaced later in the war by the MG.42 of similar calibre. These excellent belt-fed guns had rates of fire of 1,000 and 1,200 rounds per minute respectively —double the rate of comparable British, French, Russian and Italian weapons.
8. A three-man machine-gun team and seven riflemen and submachine-gunners made up the normal infantry section. Four sections and an eight-man 81mm mortar team made up the platoon, usually led by a sergeant. A company consisted of three platoons, with a seven-man, three-weapon anti-tank rifle squad and a head-quarters section; it was normally led by a *Leutnant* or *Oberleutnant*. Three rifle companies, a heavy weapons company with twelve heavy machine-guns and six mortars, a signals platoon and an HQ team made up the battalion, with a total establishment of twenty-five officers and 813 men.
9. *Sanitäter*: medical orderly. *Verwundetennest*: forward aid post. *Bismarck Denkmal*: large statue of the Iron Chancellor, overlooking Hamburg harbour.
10. *Skat*: infinitely the most popular card game among German soldiers, as obsessive as poker and pontoon among U.S. and British troops.
11. The 'Horst Wessel Song', broadcast with wearisome monotony by government radio stations, was the marching song of the Nazi *Sturmabteilungen* or Storm-troopers, written by the Party's gutter-poet of that name. The first verse may be translated: 'Raise the banner high, form the strong ranks/The storm-troopers march, with powerful tread/Our comrades shot down by the Red Front and the reactionaries/March in our ranks in spirit.' The other verses are of similar literary quality, but the tune is fairly rousing.
12. *Hamburger Dom*: a large annual fair, held on the open area of the Heiligengeistfeld.
13. The years immediately following the end of the First World War saw bitter fighting between rival factions of ex-servicemen who enrolled in the Communist party and the right-wing *Freikorps* units.
14. The *Reichsarbeitsdienst* (*R.A.D.*) was a uniformed labour corps run on para-military lines.
15. The pay structure of the *Wehrmacht* was extremely complex. A regular soldier signed on for four-and-a-half or twelve years, receiving an enlistment bonus of 100 or 300 RM respectively. His peacetime pay (*Friedensbesoldung*) was made up of base pay and quarters allowance, and was

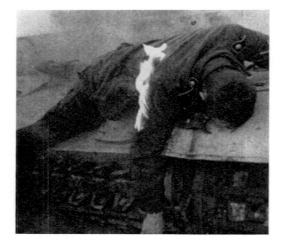

taxed. An additional *Wehrsold*, or combat pay, was awarded tax free, monthly in advance. As a regular *Obergefreiter* Jürgen received about 110 RM a month, plus 1 RM daily as a 'front line allowance'; a proportion could be paid direct to dependents through the civilian administration. This approximates to a 1971 'spending power' of £25·70 sterling.

16. Every German serviceman swore a personal oath of obedience to Adolf Hitler upon enlistment: 'I swear by God this holy oath, that I will render unconditional obedience to the *Führer* of Germany and of her people, Adolf Hitler, the supreme commander of the armed forces, and that as a brave soldier I will be prepared to lay down my life in pursuance of this oath at any time.'

17. *Hammel*: literally, a castrated ram; this word was applied to raw recruits, possibly in the belief that they were 'all bleat and no balls.'

18. The gunner of a machine-gun team was issued with an automatic pistol in place of a rifle.

19. *Landser*: virtually untranslatable, this term is the exact equivalent of the British 'Tommy' and the American 'G.I. Joe'.

20. *Einsatzgruppe*: 'Action Group': the euphemism for mass murder squads which operated behind the Russian Front, under the control of the Reich Central Security Office in Berlin and largely manned by personnel of the SS Security Service—the *Sicherheitsdienst* or SD. The majority of the victims were Russian Jews, but other categories, such as local Party officials and administrators, were also considered fitting candidates for the mass graves. Estimates of the total numbers killed by these groups vary, but a figure of one million is thought to be reasonably accurate.

21. *Esbit* capsules: cakes of hexamethylene tetramine fuel for the efficient German trench cooker.

22. *Schmalspurhengst*: 'narrow gauge stallion': slang term applied to administrative officers in reference to their narrow epaulettes. The full humour of the phrase is entirely lost in translation.

23. This raises the question of leave. The German soldier in Russia was entitled to no leave during his first year at the front; thereafter there was an annual entitlement of three weeks, exclusive of travel, if local conditions permitted. Rest camps for sick and wounded were established behind the lines in Russia.

24. Official German figures for deaths of Russian prisoners in German camps—military personnel captured under arms—total 1,981,000. A further 1,308,000 deaths are recorded under the headings 'Exterminations', 'Not accounted for', and 'Deaths and disappearance in transit.' The failure of Soviet Russia to repatriate large numbers of German prisoners at the end of the war becomes more understandable when these figures are taken into account.

SELECT BIBLIOGRAPHY

Thomas Armstrong, *A Ring Has No End*, Cassell, London, 1959.

J. A. Barlow and R. E. W. Johnson, *Small Arms Manual*, John Murray, London, 1944.

Paul Carel, *Hitler's War on Russia*, Harrap, London, 1964.

Alan Clark, *Barbarossa*, Hutchinson, London, 1965.

J. Coggins, *The Fighting Man*, Doubleday, New York, 1966.

John Laffin, *Jackboot*, Cassell, London, 1965.

Signal, various bi-monthly issues, 1941–43.

United States Army *Handbook of the German Armed Forces*, 1944.

The author also wishes to express his gratitude to Bella Buckley, Ingeborg Magor and Franz Durst for their generous assistance and access to unpublished material.

15: Albert Arthur Fisher

PART of the ceiling seemed to have collapsed when a tank shell had ploughed through the bedroom above, and the young lieutenant had to kick aside piles of plaster, bricks and smashed laths before he could force the splintered door open a foot or so. He squeezed through the gap, his camouflaged uniform and equipment straps snagging on jagged ends of timber, and picked his way over the littered floor to the raw hole in the opposite wall—once, he assumed, the parlour window. Evening was falling, a blustery late September evening, and squalls of chill drizzle gusted into the room on a wind which carried the acrid reek of smoke and the strange, unforgettable smell of crumbled bricks and plaster. The room faced eastwards and despite huge rents in the fabric of the little house the light was dimming. The sound of artillery fire from the south, beyond the river, was clearly audible; although the majority of the British shells were falling nearer the banks of the Rhine, occasional explosions from the streets round about shook the weakened structure, bringing drifts of dust down from the shell of the upper storey. *Untersturmführer* Wennecke glanced up at the ragged edge of the ceiling where a bed hung precariously in the gloom. His sergeant grunted as he bulled his way through the choked doorway, apparently unworried by the wreckage above his head; but then the *Scharführer* had been in Normandy, and probably preferred to have anything but the open sky above him, however threatening. Wennecke glanced round the shambles of the once-immaculate Dutch parlour, and realised—with a small start which he hoped his sergeant did not notice—that there was a corpse huddled in the corner behind the door. He edged round the scarred table in the middle of the room, and looked closer.

The Englishman lay in an awkward heap, his feet tangled in the remains of a wooden chair. His bare head was twisted, one cheek pressed against the filthy, gouged floorboards. Wennecke had only seen his first dead man the week before, and privately he was appalled by the contrast between these lumps of human wreckage and the graceful, heroic dead of the cinema screen. At the Bad Tolz Leadership School they had not told him how dirty a corpse looked, how ungainly, and forlorn, and . . . *undignified*. He forced himself to stand over the Englishman in a suitable pose—hands on hips, lips pursed in manly appreciation of his fallen foe. Out of the corner of his eye he saw that the effort had been wasted. The *Scharführer*, supremely uninterested in the young officer's antics, was rooting around in the rubble under the table. Wennecke looked down again.

The loose smock of camouflage cloth was torn and soiled, and dark-edged rents in the chest and stomach showed where the machine-gun bullets had entered. The paratrooper had been a tall young man, rather skinny and adenoidal-looking, with lank dark hair. His face was already waxy under the stubble and caked grime of three days of gruelling house to house fighting, and the half-open eyes, white slits in dark and puffy sockets, disturbed Wennecke. The Englishman's jaw hung slack, exposing dirty teeth and a pale, gummy mouth. One thin white forearm with a sparse growth of wispy black hairs protruded from a rolled-back sleeve; there was a shell-dressing bound round it, rusty with blood. The tail of the smock,

which could be brought forward between the legs and fastened in front to protect
the groin, had come loose, and trailed between the legs of the man's thick khaki
serge trousers. Wennecke thought it looked ridiculous. The soldier's belt,
pouches, shoulder harness and anklets were made of grubby yellowish canvas
webbing, the brass buckles darkened to prevent reflections. Under the matted
hair Wennecke noticed a crumpled maroon beret with a silver winged badge. He
bent to retrieve it—a Red Devil's beret would make a fine souvenir.[1] As he dragged
it free the cold face rolled against his palm in a horrible travesty of a caress, and
at the same moment he became distastefully aware that the man had fouled himself at the moment of death. He jerked the beret free with a curse and stumbled
back, feeling a burst of anger against the tatty bundle at his feet: how dare the
swine die so squalidly? He flushed under the sardonic glance of his sergeant, who
was relaxing against the wall under the window and expertly stripping and examining a more practical piece of booty—a Bren light machine-gun, apparently in
working order despite the bullet-chipped butt and the film of plaster dust which
clung to the breech assembly.[2]

Wennecke joined him, slapping the beret against his thigh to knock off the dust.
Outside, in the torn and rubble-strewn streets of Oosterbeek, a group of prisoners
were being herded past by a section of middle-aged reservists in *Wehrmacht* uniform. They were a ruinous looking crowd, thought Wennecke, unconsciously
straightening his carefully pressed camouflage tunic, with its dramatic epaulettes
and eagle arm-badge. (Wennecke was a vain young man, and secretly modelled
himself on the style affected by General Heinz Harmel, the handsome commander
of the '*Frundsberg*' Division,[3] whose tanks and guns were at this moment fighting
off the Allied advance a few miles south along 'Hell's Highway'.) There seemed to
be a lot of wounded among this particular batch, their tattered bandages and
stained pads of lint emphasising their scruffiness. The smocks flapped loosely
around their legs; some were bare-headed, some wore pot-shaped helmets covered
with netting and rags, a few still retained their red berets. A cameraman from an
SS-Kriegsberichter company was skipping along beside them like a happy terrier,

*Paratroopers from 1st Airborne Division dug in near the Hartenstein Hotel. (Photo: Imperial War
Museum)*

and Wennecke saw a beefy guard, his camouflaged poncho belted at the waist like a medieval surcoat, throwing a chest and grinning at the camera.

'God in Heaven, what a dirty crowd of gangsters they look, eh, *Scharf*?' Wennecke remarked, aware that his soldierly image required some hasty repairs. Under the rim of his cloth-covered helmet the sergeant gave him a look of mild contempt.

'Has the *Herr Untersturmführer* noticed their feet?' he asked.

'Feet? What about their feet?'

'They are marching in step . . . They have been fighting for nine days, with little sleep, less food, and most of their ammunition falling into our laps. We cut the water off days ago. They had a few stupid little pop-guns, no armour, and very little air-cover. They have been fighting off King Tigers with grenades and the odd *Panzerfaust*.[4] It is said that we have killed or captured three out of every four who landed. Yet the *Herr Untersturmführer* will observe that they are marching in step, their backs are straight, and their heads are up?' The sergeant paused to work his jaws and spat on the littered floor, trying to clear the dust from his throat. 'Someone told me that when we finished them off down at the bridge, two of them came out of a cellar at us with knives. They were both wounded, and the only way to stop them was to shoot them again . . . I was at Kiev with the *Leibstandarte* last year, and I fought the English Guard Division on the Vire in the summer, and I can assure the *Herr Untersturmführer* that these *Fallschirmjäger* do not resemble gangsters.'[5]

Before Wennecke could frame a suitably stern homily on the dangers of defeatist talk, the sergeant had turned away. Since Falaise, he had found it hard to summon up much fear of little men with shiny new shoulder-straps. He wandered over to the grimy corpse in the corner and jerked the identity tag from the Englishman's throat, examining it with idle curiosity as he walked to the door. *1536130 Fisher A.A., C of E*. Well, *Herr* Fisher A.A., you won't be needing your gun any more, or your pretty hat . . .

WHEN war broke out in September 1939 Bert Fisher was seventeen, and working in a market garden a few miles from his home in West Bridgford, south of Nottingham. He was a withdrawn, rather awkward boy, and the solitary work suited him. His home had not been a happy place during the years of his childhood and adolescence; his Dad had been out of work a lot during the Depression, and his Mum had not taken it well. She was a querulous woman, convinced that she had married beneath her, and her unflagging tongue had driven Bert senior, naturally taciturn, into almost total silence. Young Bert was an only child— Mrs. Fisher often regaled her female neighbours with accounts of the hard delivery —and he had entered his teens a silent, defensive, gangling lad.

He earned the usual boy's wage of eighteen shillings a week. It was adequate. In a rare flash of rebellion his father had insisted that the lad keep ten bob for himself; and after ten or twelve hours' work in the fresh air, six days a week, Bert had little taste for social life beyond the occasional pint with his younger workmates of a Saturday night. Girls terrified him. On the one occasion when two mates had persuaded him to accompany them to the Nottingham *Palais de Danse* he had overdone the Dutch courage to such an extent that while self-consciously steering a giggling factory girl round the floor to the strains of '*Deep Purple*' he had been suddenly overcome, and had brought up his all. Humiliated by the girl's scathing comments, he had fled; from then on he firmly sublimated his vague hunger for the opposite sex, and yearned silently for Rita Hayworth from the front stalls of the local Astoria.

The news of the war was exciting, but anti-climactic. Ten British divisions were in France, but by the end of the year not a man had been killed. The R.A.F. were flying over Germany loaded with leaflets. The blackout was inconvenient and depressing, food rationing was introduced, the newspapers shrank, the park railings were torched free and carted off for the hungry rolling mills of the war industries—but the threatened clash of giants simply didn't happen. Bert found it hard to reconcile posters which screamed in scarlet '*Freedom is in peril—defend it with all your might!*' with a ration of one egg per person per week, and earnest entreaties from official sources that he limit the depth of his bath-water to four inches.

On the evening of 9th May 1940 Bert and a friend were in the public bar of a Nottingham pub studying the *Evening Standard*. 'Premier's Resignation Now Likely' said the main headline; and the second front-page lead announced that conscription had been extended and all men between the ages of nineteen and thirty-six inclusive were now liable. Bert's mate was nineteen, and announced to the assembled company that the bloody government must be daft as a brush. What was the bloody point of calling him up, he'd like to know, just to go and sit on his arse in France listening to George bloody Formby bashing his bloody ukelele?[6] The following dawn the *Luftwaffe* bombed most of the airfields in eastern France to rubble, and the *Panzer* generals threw away the rule book and began their dash through the Ardennes.

Throughout the rest of 1940 and most of 1941 Bert continued to work at the market garden, now earning the man's rate of £2-10-0; two of the older men had been called up. The threat of invasion seemed rather remote, so far from the south coast; oh, he knew it might happen all right, but it just seemed unthinkable that Jerries could actually land in England. But there was no denying that it made life interesting. He joined the Local Defence Volunteers—partly to get away from his mother's endless complaints about rationing, and the impossibility of getting soap and toilet paper and elastic and knitting wool . . . Bert's Dad seemed to find some new charge of life in the air. Wireless assurances that he was needed, that he had a part to play in a great national crisis touched some chord deep within him, not quite snuffed out by his wife's tongue. He became a fire-watcher, and later a Special Constable, and exacted a subtle revenge on his wife by his martinet insistence that she keep buckets of sand around the house, and tape up the windows, and keep the bath filled overnight.

For the first time father and son began to be friends. They had the occasional pint together when they were off duty, and once the older man even forgot himself to the extent of getting boozily flirtatious with two Land Girls outside the local. Bert was frankly astonished by the line of Great War medal ribbons on his father's tunic. They would sit by the wireless together, grinning as the cool BBC accents announced the numbers of enemy 'planes shot down each day: laughing together at Jack Warner reading 'letters from me bruvver Sid' on '*Garrison Theatre*': humming in tune with Vera Lynn. Bert senior was a life-long Labour man, of

The face of mechanised war—dead horses on a French road, and a dead English tank commander on "Hell's Highway". (Photo: Imperial War Museum)

course, but that didn't matter when Churchill spoke; he was speaking for them all, and they sat straighter in their chairs and nodded stern agreement with the booming, lisping phrases which rolled out into their home. They were spared the worst of the night bombing; all the great manufacturing cities suffered repeatedly during the winter of 1940–41, but they were relatively safe at West Bridgford—except for a few straying Heinkels which unloaded their cargoes close enough to lift tiles from the Fishers' roof. As a Special Constable Bert senior had a couple of narrow escapes, but they were spared the horrors which visited the cities themselves, taking the lives of 23,000 English civilians before the end of 1940.

By the time the long-anticipated buff envelope summoned Bert for his medical in late 1941, the pattern of a long, hard war had become set. He found himself in a shuffling group of self-conscious, half-naked boys being prodded and peered at by a bored, fiftyish R.A.M.C. lieutenant. He was passed fit, and a matter of weeks later shook hands with his proud-eyed father, kissed his mother, and set off clutching the rail warrant which would take him to the Primary Training Centre of the Sherwood Foresters.[7]

The Lincoln depot was an old brick-built barracks now surrounded by sprawling Nissen huts and temporary structures. In bewilderingly short order Bert found himself sitting on the edge of a hard iron bed, staring around helplessly at the drab green walls and lockers, the bare light bulbs, the black-leaded stove, and the meaningless mountain of serge, raw canvas webbing, leather and metal with which he had been presented. His ears ached from a merciless haircut; he was now 1536130 Private Fisher A.A., bastion of democracy for two bob a day and all found.

He loathed every minute of the first month at the P.T.C. Because of his scrawny height he had always worn clothes awkwardly, and he looked like a scarecrow in the ill-fitting battledress. The coarse, hairy serge was as stiff as wood, the boots were like iron, and all the straps and buckles were a mystery to him. With the unsightly side-cap a shapeless bag on his head, a four-inch gap between blouse and trousers, his anklets upside-down, his broken and roughly knotted laces trailing, and his conspicuous height, he attracted more than his fair share of attention from the instructors. These permanent depot staff had no time for subtlety; there was a war on, and they had a strictly limited period to turn civilians into something like soldiers—if only 'hostilities only' soldiers. There was no regimental feeling at this level, just 'bullshit'—the brutal, traditional, and effective army method of breaking a man down to his components and building him up again in the pattern most useful to the army. The staff-sergeants handled this process without interference from the officers, who wisely let them get on with it; apart from 'Foxy' Crowder, their company commander, and the distant, spindly figure of 'Anklets Web' Sullivan-Tailyour, the C.O., Bert hardly saw an officer during the first month.[8]

The tricks of improving one's turn-out came hard, and Bert went through hell before he mastered the art of smoothing the toe-caps with a hot spoon, and brushing the muddy blanco on to his webbing in just the right way to give a smooth, caked finish. The drill square became an asphalt Calvary, stalked by instructors who glared under the near-vertical peaks of their caps and howled at him in the weird mock-genteel accents of the British drill sergeant.

'Ho my GAWD! H'I ain't nevah SEEN nuthink laike you lot! 'Ow am I h'ever goin' to turn this SHOWAH into SOLJAHS! . . . Squa-a-a-d SHUN! H'as'y' WERE! Sufferin' CHRAIST 'ow many taimes do you need TELLIN'. . . . THAT man there, yes YOU, you long streak o' piss, GET them h'elbows IN!' On and on, in a terrible sing-song rhythm, the voice rising to a falsetto screech . . . 'Lef'ri'-lef'ri'lef'ri . . . Squa-a-a-d . . . HALT! Orda-a-a-h . . . HIPE! down two three across two three CUTAWAY! Well that was bloody 'ORRIBLE Fishah, so the 'ole squad will now do it again for YOUR benefit . . .' Sweat pouring down the back, arms and legs shaking with fatigue, the rough serge rasping the neck raw above the collarless flannel shirt, rigid and impotent while the contorted face bellowed and writhed inches from his own . . . 'Y'know what h'Im goin' to do, Fishah? H'Im goin' to CLAIMB up your front by the button'oles, FORCE your nostrils open with me pace-stick, CRAWL up into your pointy little 'ead, AND KICK SOME MUCKIN' SENSE INTO IT!' And when it was over for another day they would collapse on their beds for a full half-hour before finding the strength to take off their equipment. The food was adequate but drably institutional—soggy boiled spuds, greasy, evil-looking bully beef, grey, unidentifiable mush of root vegetables, doughy puddings. In the evenings there was nothing but the N.A.A.F.I.—tepid beer and torn copies of *Reveille* or *Blighty*.

Bert had eagerly looked forward to his first forty-eight-hour pass at the end of the month, but when it came he didn't really enjoy it. His parents couldn't understand his new life, even his Dad had forgotten, and he was almost glad when he climbed into the train to return. In the next six weeks he progressed to basic infantry training—hours of square-bashing still, but now alternated with lectures, aptitude tests, assault courses, weapon training. It was the latter which first stirred a faint flicker of interest. The .303 Lee-Enfield was simple and sturdy, no mystery after his evenings carrying a Home Guard P-14;[9] but it was the Bren light machine-gun which caught his attention. Blunt, functional yet somehow attractive, dully gleaming, easy to strip, comfortable to fire, uncannily accurate—he began a slow, passionate love affair with the Bren. His excellent score on the Bren range gave him new confidence, which spread to other things. He began to smarten up, take a pride in avoiding the eagle eyes of the sergeants; he pressed his uniform under his mattress each night, acquired a private cache of little brushes

A British infantry squad approaches the banks of the Rhine in 1944. (Imperial War Museum photo)

and soft rags and polishes, made weighted chains to hold down the pull-downs of his trousers. He was healthy, and getting stronger all the time, and his fitness only needed direction. The assault course stopped being a purgatory, and became almost fun. By the spring of 1942, when his intake were posted to the 16th. Bn. Sherwood Foresters at Great Yarmouth, he was beginning to be a soldier.

The year he spent at Yarmouth frankly bored him. They were billeted in a pre-war holiday camp, two men to each unheated wooden hut. His bunk-mate was a leathery little Scouse[10] called Jacko, a veteran of the regiment's blooding in North Africa. Jacko had found something elusive and fulfilling in the desert, a perspective he had never dreamed existed. The foggy Broads and beaches were a poor substitute for the luminous skies of Cyrenaica; the Co-op Cafe in Yarmouth provoked longing reminiscences of the joys of rolling into the 'Melody' in Cairo, back-pay burning a hole in your pocket, the first cold beer in three months waiting on the bar and all the little Greek bints eyeing you up. The atmosphere in a fighting battalion was a revelation after the depot, but Bert was impatient to get into the war, and didn't find the exercises in the Stanford Battle Area absorbing. There were few diversions; Yarmouth was crawling with matelots,[11] English and Norwegian, and the hot competition for the few available girls caused some memorable fights.

It was Jacko who suggested that they volunteer for Airborne Forces.[12] Their mates said they were barmy, and told macabre tales of hideous accidents during parachute training, but the idea appealed to Bert. The prospect of doubling his pay was worth serious thought, and he had been a soldier long enough to discount most of the horror stories.[13] Though he would never have admitted it, the idea of a red beret and a line to shoot to the girls had a strong appeal for him, rather insecure, as he was, in his own masculinity. They put in their applications in the spring of 1943, and heard nothing for months. Apparently their applications made their way steadily 'through channels' collecting the necessary initials and rubber stamps, for in September they were told to report for a selection course.

The course was the most gruelling experience of Bert's life. Every physical ordeal he had ever heard of was included, and to a fiercer degree. He burst his lungs going over obstacle runs with his pack full of bricks, ran for mile upon mile in full kit, crawled and climbed and swung and balanced, answered searching quizzes, was tested with every weapon and piece of equipment in the book, was

medically and psychologically scrutinised—and, somehow, passed. In the autumn
both Jacko and he went through the main parachute school at Ringway outside
Manchester. They jumped from the roofs of hangars in harness attached to fan-
checked spools, they pulled their stomach muscles learning how to roll on landing,
they were lectured and tested and tested again on the handling of the parachute
pack and ancillary equipment; finally they made four mouth-drying jumps from the
eery silence of a gondola swaying beneath a tethered barrage balloon, and another
four from an old Whitley bomber. They were finally in. They put up their pale-
blue parachute wings, and reported, cocky in their red berets, to the 10th Parachute
Battalion 'somewhere in England'. Now they would really have a chance to take
a crack at Jerry.

They were wrong. It would be another ten months before Bert heard a shot fired
in anger—nearly three years after he had been called up.

A T three o'clock on the afternoon of Monday 18th September 1944, the thirty-four
C-47 transports which had carried the 10th Parachute Battalion from Folking-
ham in Norfolk approached the sandy drop-zones among the pinewoods eight miles
north-west of the towns of Arnhem and Oosterbeek on the north bank of the Neder
Rhine. They had been delayed by bad weather. The first indications that their
briefing might not have been one hundred per cent correct came with the unexpectedly heavy German anti-aircraft fire which chopped down several of the
laden transports in cartwheels of flame. The battle of Arnhem was already a day
old, and was already going wrong. Bert's battalion had been briefed to take up
defensive positions on the high ground north of the towns, to block German
counter-attacks. By now the vital Arnhem bridge, the town, the drop-zones and
the high ground should have been secured. Within forty-eight hours the Sher-
mans of the Guards Armoured Division should be at the bridge, after driving
through weak resistance up the Eindhoven–Grave–Nijmegen corridor secured by
the American parachute attacks.

Bert would never know exactly what went wrong. He would encounter the
deadly results of overconfident planning, faulty intelligence appreciation, and
plain bad luck—but he would never know why. The 1st Parachute Brigade,
dropped the day before, was still bogged down between Oosterbeek and Arnhem,
and would never succeed in fighting its way into the latter town in any strength.
The bridge, or one end of it, had been reached by only a single battalion—2nd
Para—and a handful of 'odds and sods'; they would hold it until they were anni-
hilated, but no help would ever come, neither from the main body of the division
nor from the tanks of 30 Corps, struggling painfully up 'Hell's Highway' from
Eindhoven. The 'ear and stomach battalions' of medical rejects which they had
been briefed to encounter would turn out to be components of two crack SS *Panzer*
Divisions. The radios connecting 1st Airborne Division with the outside world,
and the divisional command structure with its own units, would give endless
trouble. Some of the pitifully few anti-tank guns would never reach the men who
needed them; the jeeps would go astray, leaving the paratroopers on foot. The
supplies would be dropped into the Germans' hands. The R.A.F. would inex-
plicably fail to provide fighter cover. The relief force would take not two, but
nine days to arrive. The eight miles between drop-zones and target would prove

(Left) In the early stages of the Arnhem fighting a German general drove into a Bren-gun road block at a Dutch crossroads. (Right) The paratrooper in the foreground has a PIAT anti-tank projector

fatally long. Some of this Bert would puzzle out, but his view of the battle would be limited to his own experience.[14]

The red light went on: five minutes to go. 'Prepare to jump', and the sixteen men shuffled out of their bucket seats and into line down the fuselage. They were grotesquely burdened, weighed down by the big parachute back-packs, the musette bags of ammunition and rations and radios and weapons hitched to their legs, the Sten guns[15] thrust under the chest-straps, the vital static-line strops tethering them to the overhead wire. Bert's stomach was fluttering, not at the thought of the jump itself nor of the coming battle, but with a private fear. The Bren was lagged in a bulky green felt valise, attached to his right side by loops of strap around leg and neck. When he was out he would have to pull a quick-release and lower the valise on a twenty foot rope, so that it struck the ground first. During the training for one of the seemingly endless series of operations for which 1st Airborne had been briefed since months before D-Day—operations which had always been cancelled, leaving the men keyed-up and frustrated—Bert had seen a man killed when he couldn't free his Bren in time. The impact of landing with a heavy, rigid gun still strapped to his body had killed him instantly, his neck broken and his legs shattered. Bert had a horror of being unable to release the gun in the air.

In front of him Jacko, his jaws moving in the confinement of helmet straps and chin-pad as he chewed his everlasting stick of gum, turned and gave him an encouraging grin. *Oh, Jesus, don't let the bloody Bren hang up on me* . . . Green light —the line shuffling quickly back towards the door, Jacko gone in a blur, an instant's view of brown and green checkers 250-odd feet below, the dispatcher's slap on his shoulder, and out—out and down in the battering slip-stream, the LMG valise clasped tight in his arms, eyes shut. The big X-type canopy of pale silk cracked open, and he glanced swiftly up to see that it had deployed fully, then concentrated on the Bren. There was no time to mess about when you jumped as low as this. The release worked like a dream, and he paid out the yellow rope as fast as he could. Even so, the bundle had hardly reached the limit of the rope when the ground started to rush up at his feet. He gripped the lift webs above his shoulders, checked his legs—slightly bent—his feet—tight together—dropped his head on his chest, and then he was down and rolling. It was his eighteenth jump, but as he sat up, killed the canopy and began to strip off his harness he still felt that funny surge of animal pleasure, almost of lust.

Jacko seemed to smell something wrong the first night. They had moved off the DZ under scattered fire from the fringe of some woods, and now, about four miles to the south-east, Captain Queripel had passed the word to dig in. Bert thought his mate was coming the old soldier, bellyaching on about something being cocked up if the DZ wasn't completely secure after a day and a night. Personally he was quite happy. He was in enemy territory, he was warm and dry—well, fairly dry— he hadn't been aware of being in danger at all since they landed, and he had a passion for the concentrated oatmeal block in his forty-eight-hour pack.[16] He chewed away cheerfully, then curled up in his end of the slit trench and slept, lulled by the mutter of guns to the south and the monotonous voice of a radio operator somewhere nearby endlessly repeating a netting call into his 38-set, and apparently getting no reply.[17]

On the Tuesday morning they moved off through patchy woodland, heading south-east along both sides of a railway embankment. Bert's optimism did not last long. They were fired on from cover almost every yard of the way, it seemed to him. The trees of the thick copses, the undergrowth, the ditches, the few brightly painted wooden houses standing in their open gardens, all seemed to shelter nests of determined defenders. Men fell, and continued to fall. The dirty fountains of mortar explosions began to blossom along the tracks and across the open patches, and then heavier stuff started coming in. Soon Bert was panting and soaked with sweat, as he and Jacko scrambled crouching through the woods, occasionally throwing themselves down on the pine-needles and giving flanking fire at half-seen figures between the tree-trunks, covering for the squad who advanced in little rushes from cover to cover—but slower and slower as the morning wore on. In a short lull they could hear the sound of battle raging to the south—mortars, heavy automatic, the pecking of Brens, the thud of heavy shells. Someone was catching a packet down there . . .

By noon, crouched in a ditch beside a track through thin woodland, Bert and Jacko were peering through the trees at a high ridge in front of them; from behind the pines they could hear the sound of tracks, and the shells that were crashing into the undergrowth around them seemed to Jacko's experienced ear to betray the presence of heavy self-propelled guns up ahead. There was a dead Jerry in the ditch with them; they had killed him as he crossed the track half an hour before. He was in his twenties, big and well-muscled, and his ears and stomach seemed in excellent shape. Under his camouflaged jacket he wore a tunic bearing a black lapel patch with two silver lightning-flashes. Jacko pursed his lips, and said nothing.

Early that afternoon the word came up that they were to disengage and move back. Jacko was incredulous. 'They don't bloody think a bunch of 'ard bastards like these are gonna just let us get up an' swan off, do they?' He was right. The battered 4th Parachute Brigade[18] was harried every step of the way south and west, as they fought to join up with the rest of the division. The Germans who had blocked their path now followed on their heels. There were infiltrating units between them and the division, and more hastily-gathered German reinforcements to the west of them. In the battle around the Wolfheze station, the only crossing-point for the precious transport and anti-tank guns north of the embankment, the paratroopers fell in scores. In the withdrawal that afternoon, over 1,000 yards of open ground under the sights of the German automatic weapons and mortars, they were closely followed by tanks, SPs and mobile *flak*. They panted from cover to cover, the squads leapfrogging each other, the covering parties short of ammunition, and the slaughter never stopped. Bert saw Captain Queripel, bleeding from three wounds, lead a desperate counter-attack with a handful of men; then the corporal screamed at Bert to get moving again, and he never saw the captain again.[19]

In the woods the battalion, inevitably, got split up. On and on they stumbled, harried by snipers in the trees, running into machine-gun nests, diving for cover and losing contact in the shadows under the trees. Once Bert saw smocked figures walk out into an open ride, and heard them shout down the leafy corridor, 'Come out, Tommy, OK Tommy, come on . . .' Three of his mates, grinning with relief at this evidence that somebody, somewhere, seemed to know what was happening, stood up and walked out waving. The SS-men dived into the undergrowth and the concealed Spandaus cut down the paratroopers in their tracks. They were not the last to die thinking Germans were Poles from Sosabowski's Brigade. Bert and Jacko slogged on with their dwindling platoon, into a dark night and a wet, miserable dawn.

On the afternoon of Wednesday 20th September the remains of the 10th Parachute Battalion, led by their dying colonel, marched into the divisional perimeter around Oosterbeek.[20] They had jumped 600 strong; now there were just 250 of them. Hours later the Brigadier, 'Shan' Hackett, emerged from the woods with seventy-odd stragglers from the three battalions of his command. He had personally led the bayonet charge which enabled them to break through the German chain around the woods.

Bert and Jacko, staggering with exhaustion, were shown where to dig in among the trees east of the HQ at the Hartenstein Hotel. They fell into an aching sleep, to the constant lullaby of guns from the south-east. The bridge was still holding out.

O N the morning of Friday 22nd Bert was slumped in a chair in the ruined parlour of a small house on the eastern edge of Oosterbeek. He had not slept for a long time, but he couldn't remember just how long. The effects of two benzedrine tablets were wearing off. The Bren was on a table in front of him, pulled well back from the window, and the spare barrel case was at his feet; Jacko had not returned from a 'scrounge' for ammunition the day before. The whole perimeter was being raked with mortar and shell-fire, the water had been cut off, and there was no food. There was no sign of 30 Corps, and no word of their progress. German snipers had infiltrated all along the line, and the gardens behind the houses were death-traps.

Two hours before a German SP had come grinding cautiously down the road outside, and Bert had summoned a grin at the sight of a PIAT bomb wobbling through the air from the next house and hitting it square on the engine-decking. The fuel had exploded, and the squat yellow vehicle had burned with a terrifying, furnace-like violence. Its blackened bulk now blocked off the road to the right, which was a bloody good thing because that had been the last round they had for the PIAT. In fact they were all short of ammunition, all four of them in the house. There were two other 10th Para blokes out back in the kitchen, and some straggler, who had been scooped in by the officer, up in the attic. He said his name was McNeil, but he had a bloody funny accent. Anyway, he seemed an efficient and steady sort of bloke, and he had a couple of gammon bombs with him, so he was a welcome addition.[21] The officer—Bert didn't know him, he thought he was from 156th Para—was organising all the houses in this row, braving the snipers in a series of short visits to keep each post up to the mark.

Despite the effects of the benzedrine Bert found that his chin kept sinking on to the butt of the Bren, and his eyelids would close involuntarily every few moments. He strained to concentrate on the buildings across the road and the gaps between them through which the enemy must come. His hunger was a detached thing; indeed, he was conscious of few sharp sensations, except for his anger at the faceless men who had condemned the Division. Somewhere up among the brass-hats some useless, dozey, victory-happy bastard had made a right cock-up of the whole thing . . . Now the Div was on the chopping-block, and when it was all over They would get some more gongs, while he and his mates pushed up—tulips?

It may have been an hour later, it may have been two, when McNeil poked his head round the door and told him to relax for ten minutes. With such a pitifully thin perimeter they were all 'on stag' the whole time, but the officer was trying to give them each a short break in turn. Bert shifted the chair round, and after a moment's hesitation brought out his last cigarette. His hands were shaking, and he used up four matches before, with the ponderous concentration of a drunkard, he managed to light the crumpled tube. The deep, slow drags made his head spin; it was his first smoke for twenty-four hours, and on top of hunger and drugs it made him as light-headed as the boy he had once been, hiding behind the school lavatories with a furtive Woodbine. He had just stubbed out the last sodden half-inch when McNeil's Sten opened up in the loop-holed attic.

Clumsy with haste, Bert scrambled behind the Bren and jerked back the cocking handle, just as a knot of Germans burst out from behind the house opposite and made a crouching dash for the road. He fired too quickly, and as his second, corrected burst chopped down the last two tiger-suited[22] figures he saw the first three reach the cover of the wrecked SP. Covering fire was coming from the darkened windows opposite, and he could hear bullets smashing into the tiles above. He cuddled his cheek against the butt and shifting his aim to place searching two-second bursts through the windows across the street: how the Christ had they got in, weren't the blokes up the street supposed to be covering the back gardens? Mortar bombs were falling close behind his house and the ones on either side, and in a momentary lull he thought he could even hear the hollow *tonk* of a round leaving the tube; Jerry must have dug them in right behind the houses opposite, and was firing almost vertically to cut off the paratroopers' avenue of retreat. A new sound could be heard above the cacophony of mortars and small-arms—a squeaking rumble of tracks, coming from somewhere in front and to the left. The top of a young elm in one of the gardens behind the German-held houses suddenly jerked and swayed as a huge steel bulk shouldered its trunk.

Bert came to the end of a magazine, fumbled the stubby tin horn off the top of the gun, and groped for another in the tinkling layer of brass cartridge cases which now littered the table. Out of the corner of his eye he saw movement only yards away, and looked up in time to see three mottled figures hurl themselves out of sight to his right; the SS soldiers who had reached the refuge of the brewed-up SP were now pressed against the wall of the next house along, safe from British fire. As they disappeared Bert saw that one had a pair of dirty-white bags slung on his ribs, like angular water-wings, and almost before he had realised what was happening there came a flurry of grenade explosions and a shriek of agony from the house on his right. It was all happening too quickly, he couldn't concentrate, where was the sodding magazine, why had McNeil stopped firing? He found the fresh magazine at last, and slammed it into place as a huge buff turtle-shape ground into view around the left-hand side of the house facing him, barging contemptuously through the corner of the building, bricks and tiles rattling off its massive hull as a gun the size of a telegraph pole swung ponderously towards Bert's hiding place. He kept his finger tight round the trigger, sobbing with frustration as the bullets splashed uselessly off the turret in silvery streaks. He was not aware that the tank's co-axial machine-gun was firing until the window frame shivered and leapt, and something hit him in the chest with bewildering force. He was hurled backwards by the impact, crashing down over the back of the chair as if he had been hit by some montrous fist. There was no pain, just incredulity, and a great tingling weight, and a feeling of spreading warmth and looseness as if something was flowing and moving within him. He died almost immediately.

A study in exhaustion: a British paratrooper supports a wounded comrade. (Photo: Imperial War Museum)

WHEN the survivors of the 10th Parachute Battalion mustered on the south bank of the Rhine on 26th September they numbered thirty-six men, of whom none were officers. Out of more than 2,000 men who had landed with 4th Parachute Brigade, nine officers and 260 NCOs and privates regained the British lines. Of 8,905 airborne soldiers and 1,100 glider pilots who had landed around Oosterbeek, a total of 2,163 escaped death or capture.

NOTES

Of the named persons in this chapter, Fisher and his family, Jacko, and Wennecke are fictitious.

1. The nickname 'Red Devils' was first applied to the British airborne troops by the Germans during the campaign in Tunisia in early 1943, and has been used ever since.
2. The Bren LMG was of .303 (rifle)

calibre, weighed 23 lbs. and was 3 ft 9½ ins. long. Feed was by a spring-loaded 30-round box magazine above the breech, and the rate of fire was between 450 and 550 rounds per minute. It was effective up to 2,000 yards and un-usually accurate up to 1,000. The Bren, one of the most reliable weapons ever carried by the British Army, was the standard infantry light machine-gun from the mid-1930s to the mid-1960s.

3. The two main combat units committed by the Germans at Arnhem were *9.SS Panzer Division 'Hohenstaufen'* and *10.SS Panzer Division 'Frundsberg'*. Both units had suffered heavy losses in Normandy in June 1944, and only ele-ments were available for combat in September. They were reinforced by 'scratch' units of army reservists, marines, renegade Dutch police troops, and some independent armoured forma-tions; among the latter 503 Heavy Tank Detachment, with 'King Tiger' vehicles was prominent. Survivors of the battle mention an extraordinarily wide range of quality between the best troops they encountered—who were formidable—and the worst—who were pathetic.

4. The *Panzerfaust* was the German equivalent of the bazooka; this is the term a German soldier would use to describe the P.I.A.T. (Projector In-fantry Anti-Tank) used by the airborne troops.

5. The incident of the two young para-troopers with knives is mentioned by several sources, British and German. *Fallschirmjäger*: paratroopers. The opinion of the bearing and fighting qualities of the airborne troops voiced by the sergeant is taken from the sur-viving German 'post-mortem' report on the battle, prepared by an SS officer named Sepp Krafft.

6. The comedian George Formby travelled to France to entertain the troops of the British Expeditionary Force during the 'Phoney War'.

7. The Sherwood Foresters (now the Worcestershire and Sherwood Foresters Regt.) trace their ancestry back through several amalgamations and changes of title to the 45th Foot, raised in 1751. The 16th Bn., based at Great Yarmouth in the mid-war years, was redesignated the 1st Bn. in January 1943; the original 1st Bn. 'went into the bag' at Tobruk in June 1942, after suffering heavy casualties in a series of campaigns in the Middle East.

8. 'Foxy' Crowder was an ex-R.S.M. Lt.Col. Sullivan-Tailyour got his far-fetched nickname from his extremely slender physique; the troops maintained that his legs were so thin that he had to have special anklets made, as the issue garments would merely revolve around his ankles without gripping.

9. The American .303 Pattern '14 bolt-action rifle was one of several obsoles-cent weapons gladly accepted by the Local Defence Volunteers (later the Home Guard) which was notoriously short of effective small arms.

10. Scouse: Liverpudlian.

11. Matelots: sailors.

12. British Airborne Forces were born in 1941 when, at the direct instigation of Churchill, Lt.Col. Eric Down raised the first battalion of paratroopers, quickly followed by two others. Raids had been made in France and Italy during 1942, and the brigade was committed in Tunisia, Sicily and Italy in 1943, dis-tinguishing itself in all three cam-paigns. By D-Day two divisions—1st and 6th—were in being, each comprising parachute and air-landing (glider-borne) infantry formations. Volun-teers from other branches served for three years.

13. Two shillings a day parachute pay was added 'across the board' to the daily rates of all non-commissioned ranks. In 1944 these were: Private, 2s.; Lance-Corporal, 3s. 3d.; Corporal, 4s.; Lance-Sergeant, 5s. 3d.; Sergeant, 6s. A very rough guide to the purchasing power of these amounts is the contemporary price 20 cigarettes—11½d., against today's price of at least 3s. 6d. (18p.).

14. The detailed history of the contro-versial battle of Arnhem has no place in this chapter; the brief summary of difficulties faced by the airborne troops must suffice. Interested readers will find the whole story admirably examined in the works quoted below.

15. The 9mm. Sten submachine-gun was introduced into the British forces during the mid-war years as an answer to the German MP.40; it was designed to take captured ammunition, a feature useful to the European partisan groups to whom it was air-dropped in large numbers. A simple and extremely cheap weapon fed by a 32-round box magazine, the Sten's lightness and shortness (6 lb. 6 oz. and 30 ins.) made it an ideal weapon for para-troopers. It was, however, unreliable in some particulars. This writer has seen a loaded Sten, with the safety catch engaged, fire off a complete magazine after being dropped to the ground. Its 'ersatz' characteristics gave rise to the nickname 'Spam-gun'.

16. The forty-eight-hour emergency ration pack, small enough to be carried in a battledress knee-pocket, comprised highly concentrated foods such as com-pressed oatmeal, dehydrated meat, beef extract cubes, glucose and dried milk tablets, chocolate, sweet biscuits, and blocks of tea, sugar and milk combined. Most of the 1st Airborne Division had to make one pack last nine days, as re-supply was minimal.

17. 38-set: short range wireless set for inter-unit communication. This could be carried by one man, fitted with a headset and throat microphones.

18. 4th Parachute Brigade comprised 10th, 11th and 156th Parachute Battalions.
19. Capt. Lionel Queripel was awarded a posthumous Victoria Cross for his gallantry in this action, during which he lost his lfe.
20. Lt.Col. K. B. I. Smyth, O.B.E. died in the dressing station that night.
21. Gammon bomb: more properly, 'Grenade, Hand, 82 Mk.1'. This was a charge of plastic explosive in a stockingette bag fitted with the fuse from a bakelite grenade. Detonator and striker were separated by a weak spring, blocked by a loose fitting safety pin. A length of tape with a lead weight on the end was fixed to the pin. When the bomb was thrown the tape was unwound by the pull of the weight, the pin came free, and the bomb exploded on impact. It was an all-purpose weapon used with some success against armoured vehicles.

    'McNeil': 21 Independent Parachute Company, the Arnhem 'pathfinder' force, included several German Jews who took false names, almost invariably of Celtic origin.
22. The Waffen-SS camouflage clothing was known from as early as 1940 as Tiger-jacke—'tiger jacket'.

While the paratroopers smashed their homes to make strongpoints, the Dutch civilians made them tea. (Photo: Imperial War Museum)

SELECT BIBLIOGRAPHY

(Two of the works cited below* are novels; they are, however, based on personal experience, and are of great interest in the context of Arnhem and other campaigns in North-West Europe 1944–45.)

Alex Bowlby, *The Recollections of Rifleman Bowlby*, Leo Cooper, London, 1969.

Anthony Farrar-Hockley, *Airborne Carpet—Operation Market Garden*, Macdonald, London, 1970.

David Holbrook, *Flesh Wounds**, Methuen, London, 1966.

Maj. Gen. R. E. Urquhart, *Arnhem*, Cassell, London, 1958.

'Zeno', *The Cauldron**, Macmillan, London, 1966.

The author would also like to express his gratitude to the staff of the Parachute Regiment Museum, Browning Barracks, Aldershot, particularly Private T. Ralph; to Kenneth Homer, and to Major Michael Hoskins.

INDEX

of actual persons, places, and units (from Corps level down) mentioned in text.